QuickBooks® for A
Guide to Setting up your Law Practice
From Trust Accounts to Billing

Cristie Will

First Printing, 2015

ISBN-13:1515176851
ISBN-10:**9781515176855**

WillWrite Productions Inc.
www.cbwill.com
www.soswill.com

Trademark Acknowledgments
QuickBooks® and QuickBooks Pro® are registered trademarks of Intuit, Inc. All the software
images include in this book are from QuickBooks Premier®.

Disclaimer
This book/guide was written using QuickBooks Premier 2014 and 2015. This is to help you get started
using QuickBooks. Be sure to check with your CPA to make sure your accounts are correct.
Be sure to check and verify with your State Bar Association on the practices in this book. Some States are
really strict on how to handle Items that concern Trust Accounts along with Retainers as well. My book
shows you how to set up and run them, but it doesn't say how each State will accept them.

Introduction

This book was written to help Attorney's with Their Accounting. After working for several Attorneys and seeing them using different programs for different accounting Tasks, I realized there is a better way to stream line their accounting.

I recommend QuickBooks® Premier from the get go. It has more space, but more importantly the Premier edition has special billing solutions such as charging different clients different rates.

QuickBooks® offers a vast amount of ways attorneys can use in their Practice. You can use QuickBooks® to track your time for billing your clients and for payroll purposes as well. The Customer/Client can track conflicts of interest. Write checks, reconcile all bank accounts, checking, Trust, Savings, Payroll and Credit Cards. The Payroll Processing is very easy to use in-house tracking time billable and non-billable time. Payroll can do anything an outside service can do including Direct Deposit, pay and file taxes as well. You can sign up for various options with Payroll. Another great feature for attorneys is the class tracking option. You can track your income and expenses from different departments, different locations and other ways to fit your needs.

Reports are a great tool with QuickBooks® as well. You can run a vast amount, customize them to your needs and memorize them to use every time.

Every Attorney must maintain a Trust Account no matter how often they need/use it. I give you the steps on how to setup your trust account to stay in compliance with your Bar Regulations. Be sure to check with your State Bar for the guidelines in your state.

Once you get up and running you will wonder how you ever went without having QuickBooks®.

If you want a Sample copy of My Attorney File that you can go in and change all the important legal information such as Your Company Information then email me at soswill@outlook.com. If you have an older version of QuickBooks I may not be able to supply the sample file, but feel free to check with me.

Table of Contents

Table of Contents

Table of Contents

Chapter 1
Getting Started

This chapter is a little bit of everything, such as installing QuickBooks, terms used, Setting up your company file, setting preferences and passwords along with backing up your data just to name a few.

Installing QuickBooks

Follow the directions on installing your QuickBooks software. One thing is or certain before opening the box make sure your computer system has all the requirements. This is important especially if your computer system is a little older and you just purchased a new QuickBooks Software Program. QuickBooks has multi user versions available for you if more than one user and computer will be used in your Practice.

Before Setting Your Company File and Using QuickBooks

You need to have your Federal and State Account numbers. Have your Bank accounts with beginning balances. The beginning balance needs to be the balance that you want to start from. If this is the month of July and if you want the beginning of the year then you will need to start with the Bank Statements showing the beginning balance as of January 1. The same thing for Credit Cards, you will need the beginning of the year Statements, or if you have a year end March 31 and want to start April 1, then that would be the Statements you need. Here's a quick run-down what you need:

- All your Law Practice Information like address, phone numbers your Fed and State ID's
- Federal Account Numbers
- State Account Numbers
- All Banking Account Numbers (Main Checking, Trust, Petty Cash, Savings, Payroll just to name a few)
- Clients/Customers/Receivables that you are doing business with or even ones you want entered.
- Vendors/Payables/Bill Pay that you owe and do business with
- Services/Products you offer such as the legal services and you may sell other products.

Main QuickBooks Terms

You may already be familiar with these terms and that's one step closer for those that know the terms. Here is a summary of what the main terms are and meaning.

Chart of Accounts

This is the heart of your Practice basically. It tracks all money coming in and going out. These are the accounts you set up to enter everything into the appropriate category. You can use a preset chart of accounts, use your own set of chart of accounts or a combination of both. An example of an account would be say you bought postage to send out client invoices and anything else you mail out, the money for the postage would go into the postage expense account. You can break it down of course and bill out to particular clients or departments, it's your choice how you want and need to track it.

Item List

The item list is what your Law Practice sells and resells in your business. Most of what you will list is your legal services, but some may sell products, so in this case you would have services and products. To invoice out any of your charges it should be set up on your item list. Example let's say an account you use to charge a client is called Legal Fees then that would be an Item.

Class

Class helps you categorize your income and expenses for your Law Practice. A great example is if you have more than one attorney in your practice you can specify a different class to each one to track how much each attorney clients they bring in and how much they spend. If you have more than one location you can set up a class per location. These are just two examples you can use class tracking for.

Customer/Client

The Customers are your clients that you bill for your services rendered.

Vendors

Vendors are your suppliers and anyone you do business with that you pay for their products and/or services. One example would be if you are leasing your office space you would write a check for Rent or the phone company or office supply place just to name a few.

Jobs/Cases/Matters

Jobs/Cases/Matters are basically your Clients that hired you. By using the Jobs feature you can group all your Clients' cases/Matters with the Client. They will be separate of course but with the Client. You would set up the Client then set up each case for this Client as a separate job.

This is a quick run-down as to what are the main terms. We will do the Company File Set up next and then as you progress through the book you will learn all the steps to set up Clients, Cases, and Vendors etc.

Ok let's get started!

Creating Your Company File

You can have lots of companies within QuickBooks, so it's a good idea to make your own sample company to follow along in this book to get the hang of everything. After getting the hang of it all go back and make your company file, however if you feel comfortable enough make your company file from the get go.

1. Click on the File button from the top Main Menu Bar.
2. Select and Click on New Company.
3. Next you will see the following screen and then click Detailed Start.
4. You will be asked about your company, so have your information ready to enter.

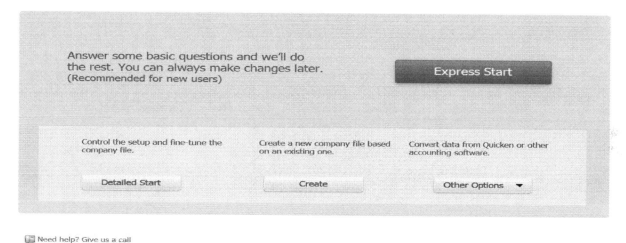

Need help? Give us a call

1. You will be asked to enter your Company Information, see below in the screen.
2. Once you fill in your information click the next button.

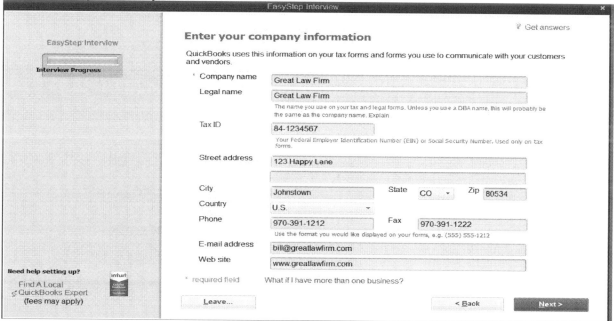

1. The next screen will ask you to pick your Industry.
2. Scroll down and select Legal Services, then Click Next.

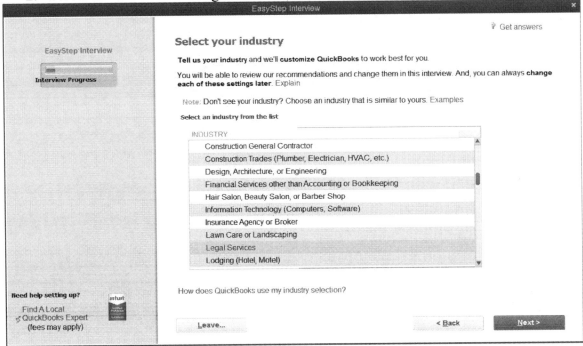

1. This next screen it asks you to select how your company is organized.
2. Make your selection then click next.

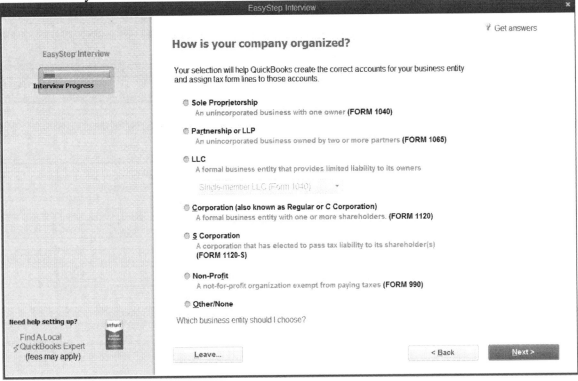

1. The next screen ask you to select the first month of your physical year. If you don't know then ask someone or if you can ask your CPA. Some company's year-end is say March, so their first month would be April 1.
2. When selection is made click next.

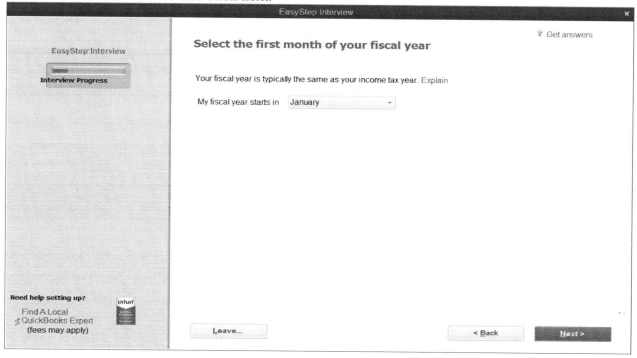

1. This Screen ask you to set up your administrator password which is optional, but I recommend setting a password. Be sure to put a memorable password and write it down and put away for safe keeping.
2. When you are finished click next.

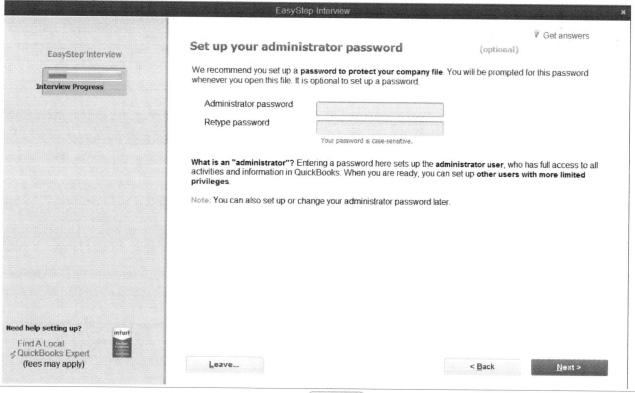

1. The next screen says create your Company File. It asks Where you want to Create it and I would create it where you can find it say either the desktop or your documents.
2. Make a company folder on your Desktop or your documents or you can leave as is and save to the folder that says Company Folder. When you make your selection click the next button.

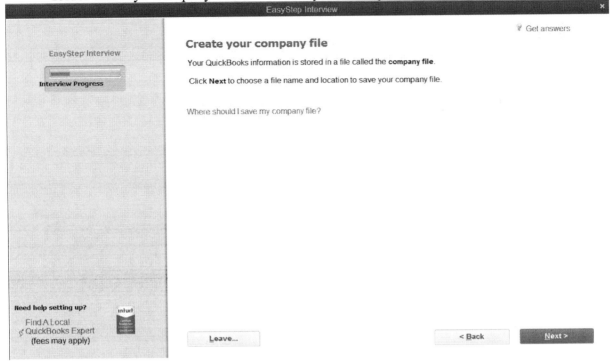

1. The next screen says customizing QuickBooks for your Business and click next.

1. This Screen ask you to choose What you Sell, so click on if you sell both or just services then click next.

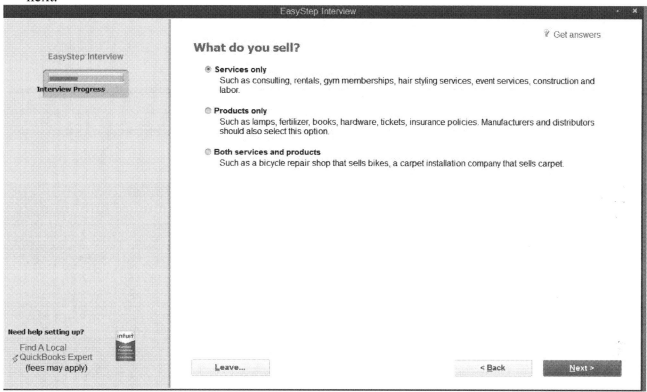

1. The next screen ask, Do you charge sales tax? Unless less you sell some kind of product then leave as is and click next.

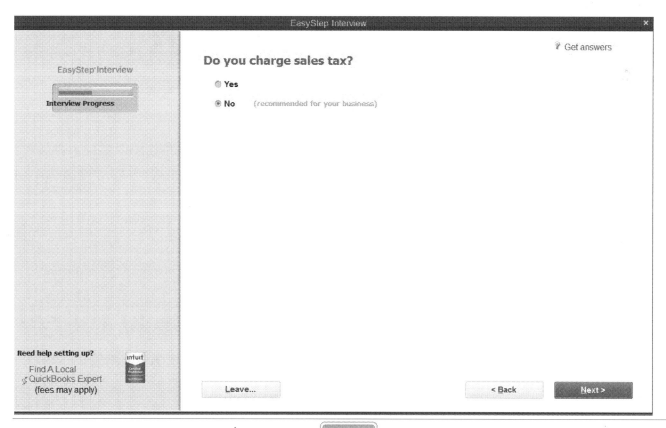

1.   The next scree asks, Do you want to create estimates in QuickBooks? Recommending no, but if you have a client or a reason to give quotes you might or you may just want to type up a quick quote. If you don't know then choose no. Click next.

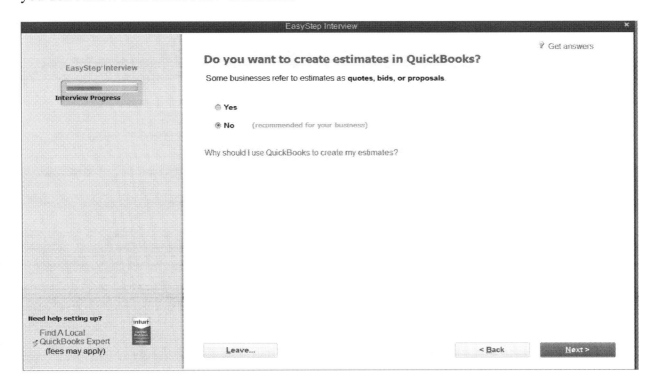

1.   Next screen says Using Statements in QuickBooks.
2.   Use the recommended setting and click Next.

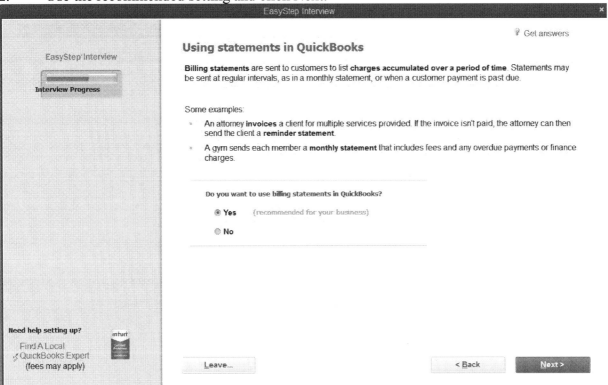

1.	The next screen says using invoices in QuickBooks. Depending on your choice. I have had clients use invoices and clients that don't. They both have their pros and cons. If you choose invoices it keeps each month nicely separated, but then you send statements too. If you choose statements the charges are directly on the statement and you can do just statements by date only, so it's your choosing. If you don't know then go by the recommended and leave as No and click next.

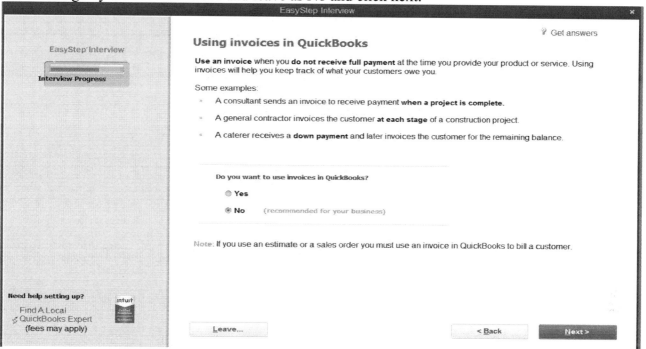

1.	The next screen says Managing Bills you owe, leave as is and click next.

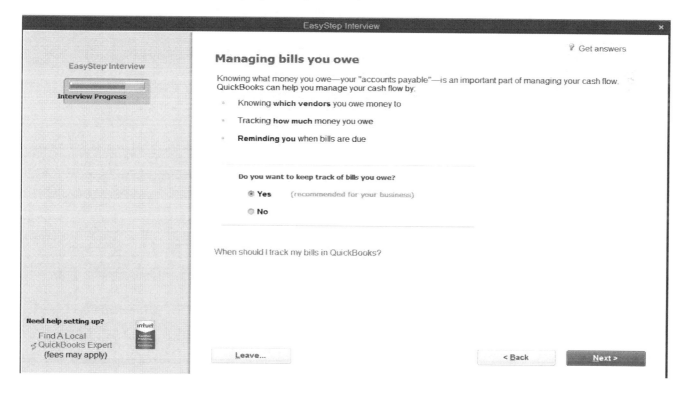

1.   Your next screen says Tracking time in QuickBooks. Leave as the recommendation and click next.

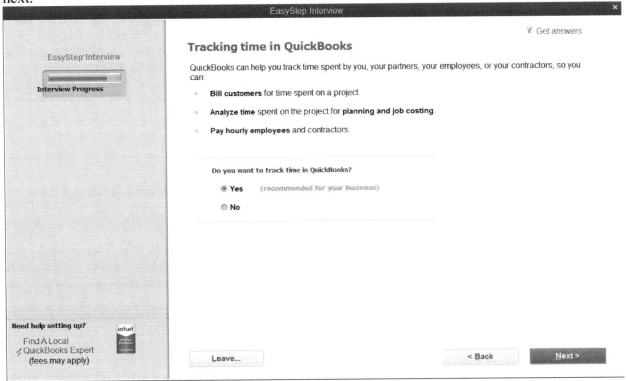

1.   The next screens says Do you have employees? This one is depending on if you want to run payroll through QuickBooks. It also asks is you have 1099 contractors. You would click 1099 Contractors if you pay say an expert witness that is not an employee. Make your choices then click next.

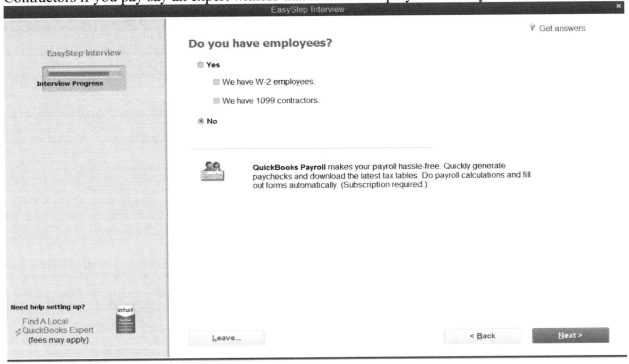

1.　　The next screen says using accounts in QuickBooks is stating we'll help you set up your Chart of Accounts, so click next.

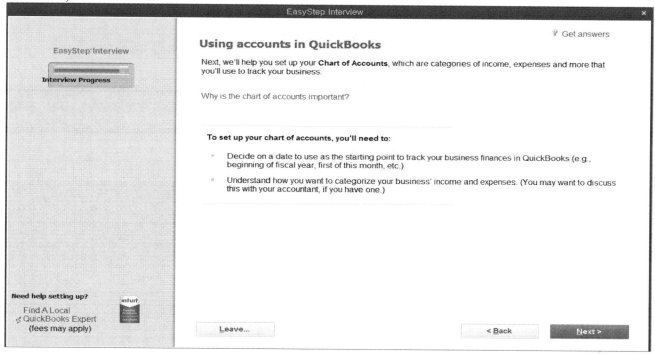

1.　　This next screen says Select a date to start tracking your finances. You would choose when your year end is, so it depends on that date it also depends on if you want to just start the day you set up your Company file. When you decide click next.

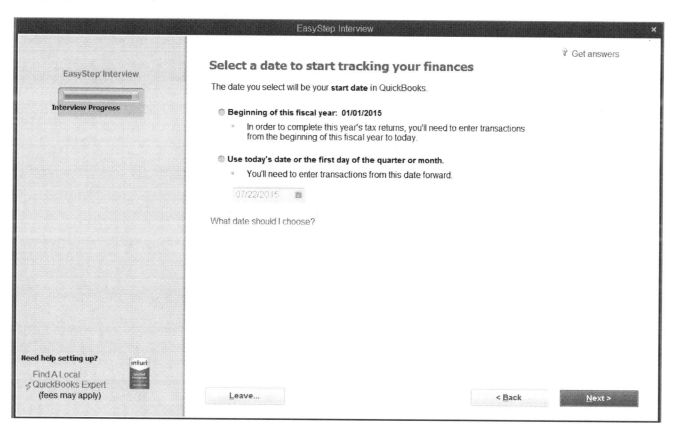

1.   This next screen is setting up your actual chart of accounts. QuickBooks has selected them For you. I have found more often than not I add on more. Go through and check on any additional Accounts you use or think you may use. If you choose an account you never use you can delete it later. When you are done with selections click next.

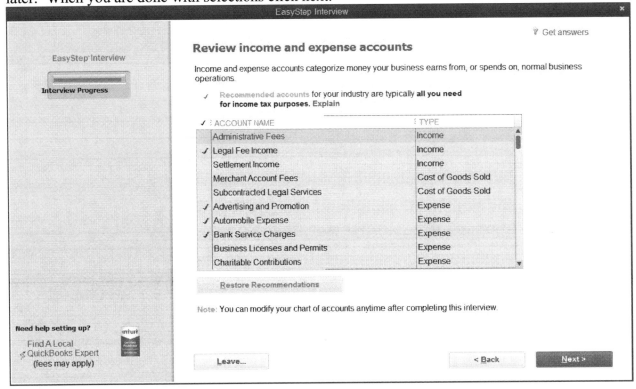

1.   The Next screen says Congratulations. Click on go to Setup. Next you will enter Clients/Customers, Vendors, and Employees. You can always click on start working and do this later. I do find if you have your stuff handy it will make things easier and smoother just to enter it now.

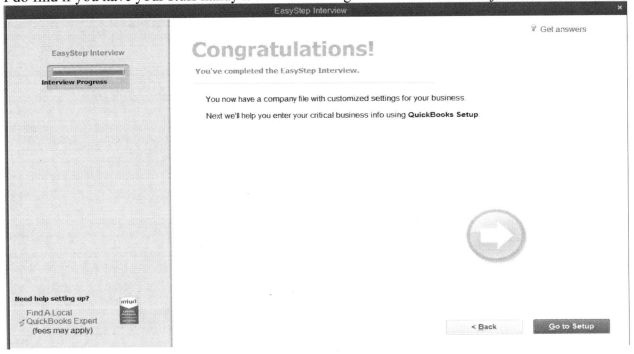

1.   Here's the next screen, so click on add the people you do business with or you can add more To the products/services, add more bank accounts or Start Working. For this book we will be adding Everything, so click add.

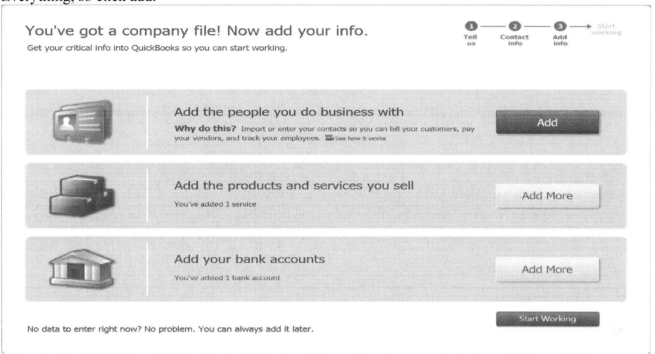

1.   It says add the people you do business with. You can import from outlook, yahoo, Gmail, paste from Excel or enter manually. This this is a sample file I am going to enter manually, then click continue.

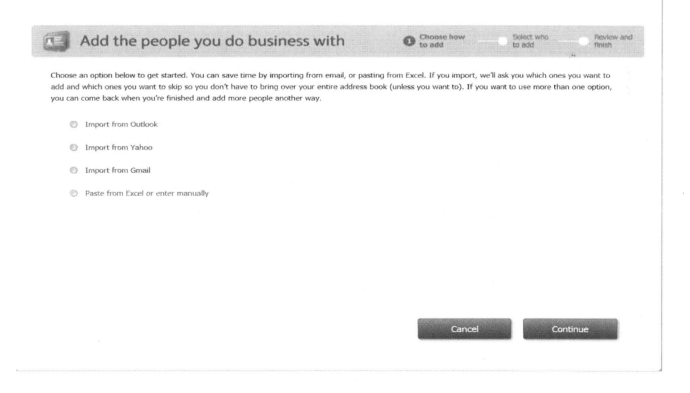

1.　　This is what your next screen looks like with added, customers/clients, vendors and employees. Click Continue then click continue again then Click on add more products and Services.

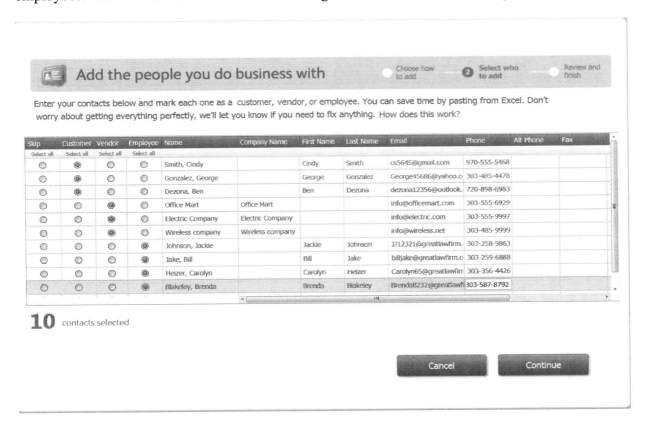

1. Click continue. Click Add more products and services.

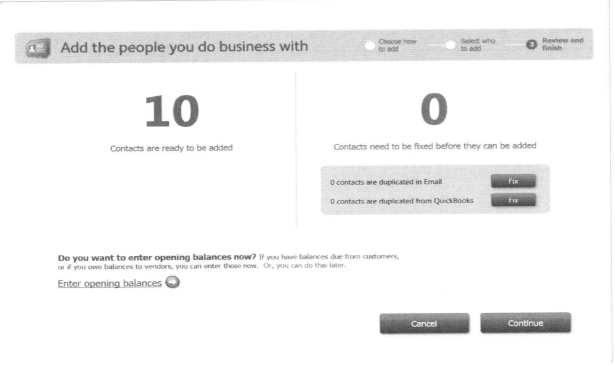

1.   The next screen says add the products and services you sell. For this exercise I am going with service. Click Continue for the next screen.

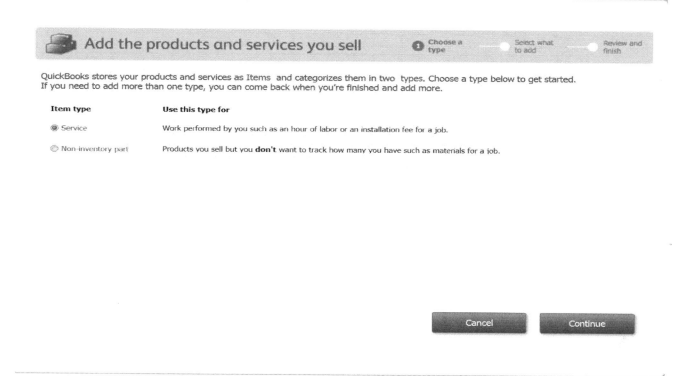

1.   Add services here and click continue.

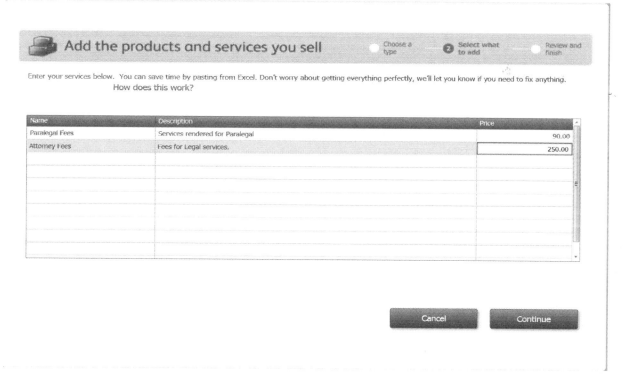

1. Click continue.

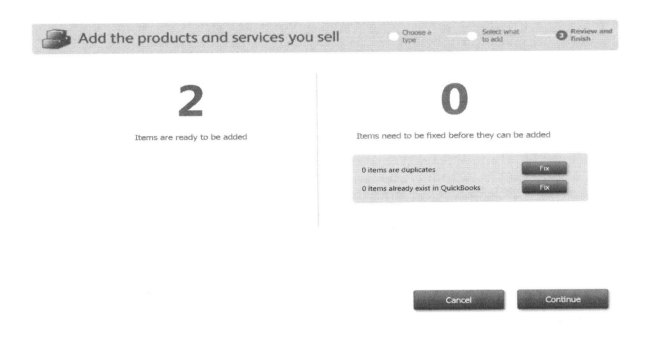

1. Click add more Bank Accounts.

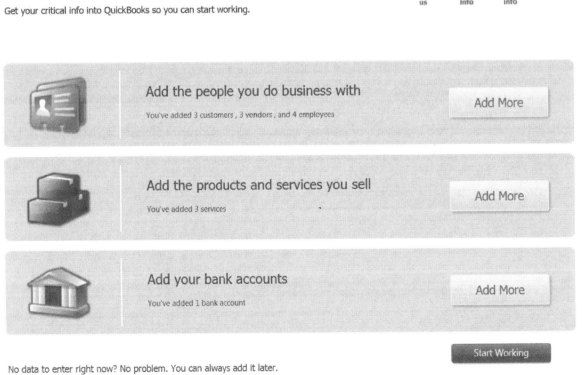

1.   Click Continue.

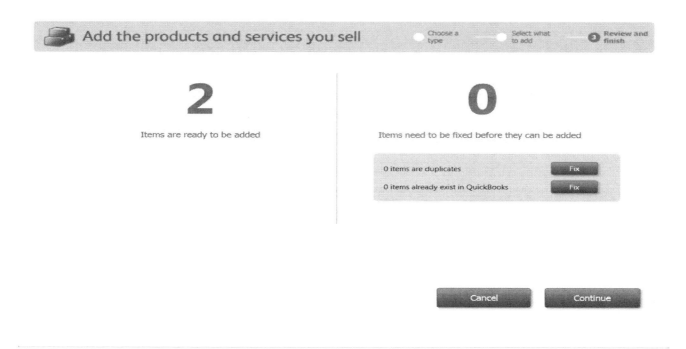

1.   Add bank Accounts then click continue.

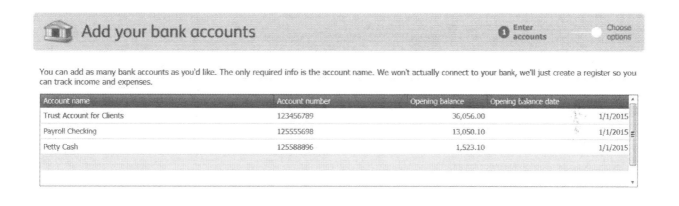

The next account asks if you want to order checks and I clicked no thanks. Click Continue and this takes you to start working.

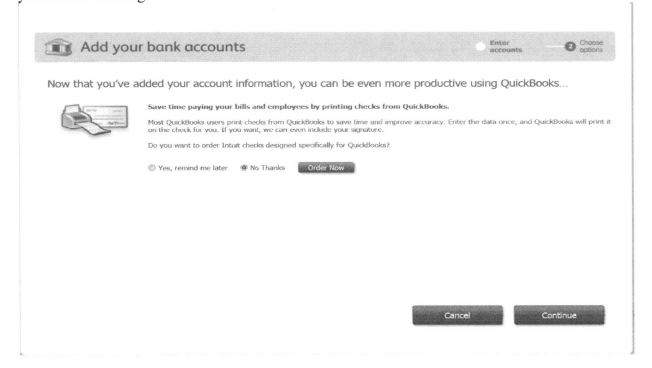

1. This is the next screen that pops up on top of your QuickBooks home page. For this exercise just exit out by clicking the X in the top right hand corner of this popup. Ready to work now.

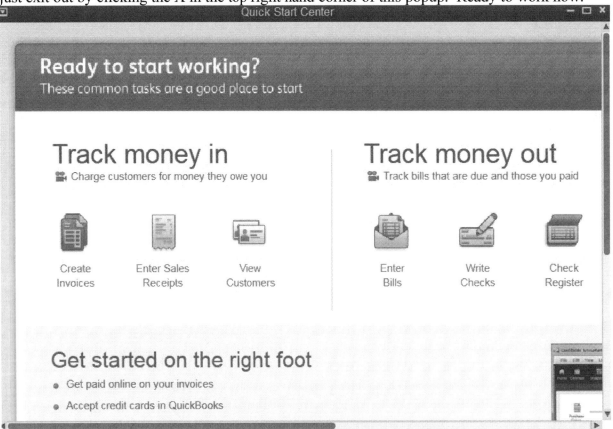

Getting Around in QuickBooks

QuickBooks has a vast array of features and a number of ways to use and navigate through the system.

There are three main ways to navigate through the QuickBooks system.

- The top Main Menu Bar
- I Icon Bar (for 2012 and earlier versions)
- The Home Page
- 2013 was change and the Icon Bar now shows up on the left, also known as the My Shortcuts.

See The Different Screen shots below.

This is Icon Bar 2012 and older versions

This is Home Page/Screen for 2012 and Older Versions

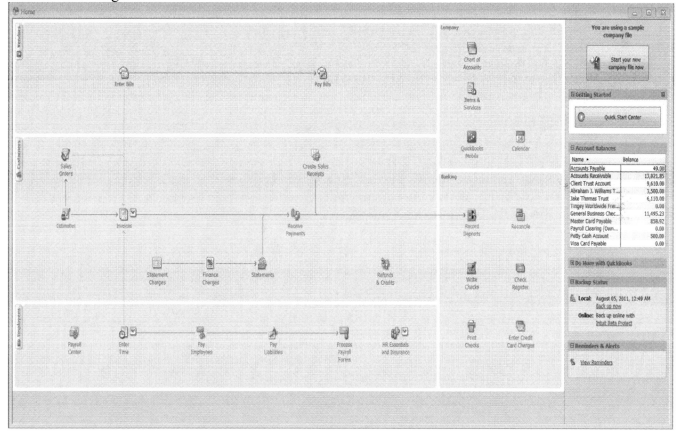

This is top Main Menu Bar, Home page and My Shortcuts (Icon Bar) in versions 2013, 2014 and 2015

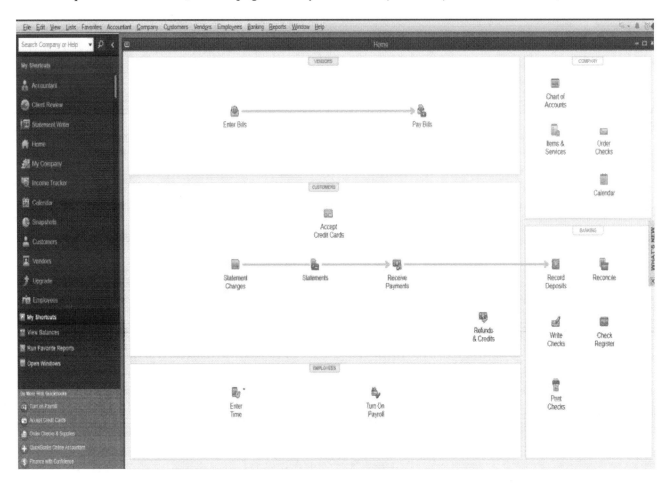

In the 2013 and newer versions you can customize the My Shortcuts (Icon Bar). You can remove/delete things you know you will not use and add things you will use. To customize the Shortcuts menu scroll all the way down to the bottom of the shortcuts menu and click on Customize Shortcuts and the Customize Icon Bar window pops up. You can even change the names if you want.

See next page with changes.

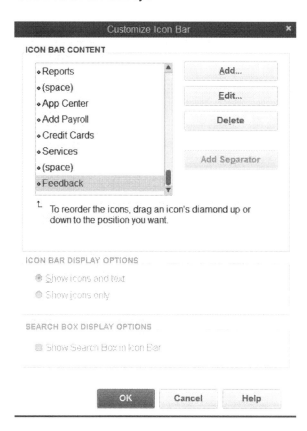

See the next screen shot where I changed the customer shortcut icon to client.

As you can see from this screenshot I changed the Customer name to Clients since this is for A Law Practice. However you cannot change the tab on the home page or Main Menu Bar.

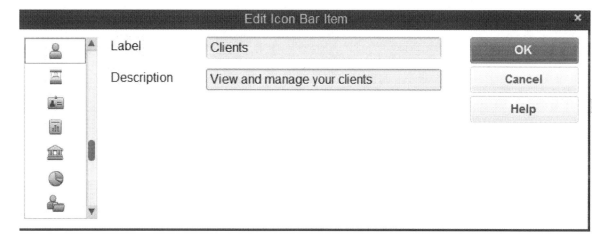

Setting Preferences

This is the next step after completing your company file to do. This is setting things to your personal style, such as having the decimal point automatically in place, this is not a standard setup. I like this option, but other don't, so it's your choice.

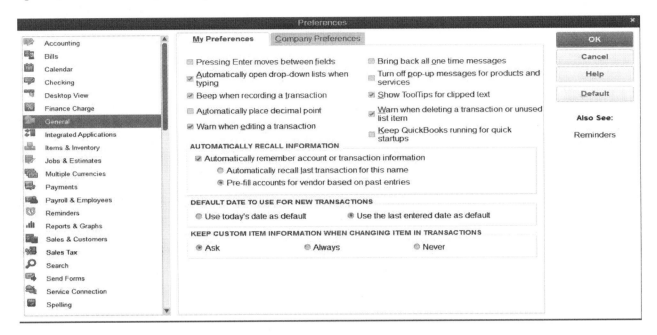

1. Click on File at the top Main Menu Bar, select Preferences then click on the General Tab.
2. Finish the General options by going through all of Company Preferences and My Preferences.
3. Click on My Preferences. These are default settings. Make any necessary changes then click ok.

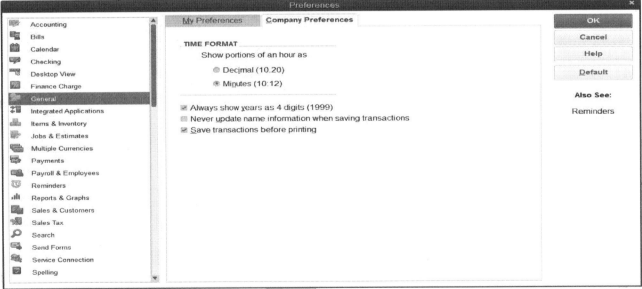

Most attorney's use the Decimal. You may want to test this out first.

Decimal: When you choose this format, QuickBooks will interpret time entries as decimal fractions. For example, when you enter 4:w0, QuickBooks changes your entry to 3.5 (three and 1/2 hours).

Minutes: When you choose this format, QuickBooks interprets time entries as hours and minutes. For example, when you enter 4.5, QuickBooks changes your entry to 3:30 (3 hours and 30 minutes).

This screen is as you can see the Preferences for accounting options.

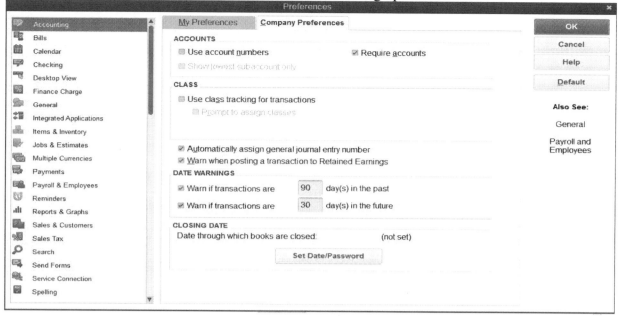

1. If you are going to use account number for your chart of accounts this is where you select that option.
2. If you are going to use class tracking this is where you choose this option.
3. I would set a Date Password. This is so that the books for the previous year you closed out and gave to your CPA. You don't want this being changed accidentally. Sometimes changes may need to be fixed such as an address for an employee. By having a password required it will help stop accidental mistakes. When done click ok.

1. This screen is for Bills Preferences. This is default settings. If you want any credits to be applied automatically then check automatically use credits if not you can apply the credits when you want manually.
2. If you take advantage of paying bills on the dates some vendors offer credits then you would choose automatically use discounts and set up an account for discounts. Click ok.

The next tab is to set up your calendar for dates as to your Practice needs.

1. As you can see this is for upcoming & Past Due Settings. The weekly view is 5/7 days working or 7/7 working or a 5 days fixed.
2. When done click ok.

This tab is to set up defaults in your checking. This is an important one if you use more than one checking account. This is under My Preferences.

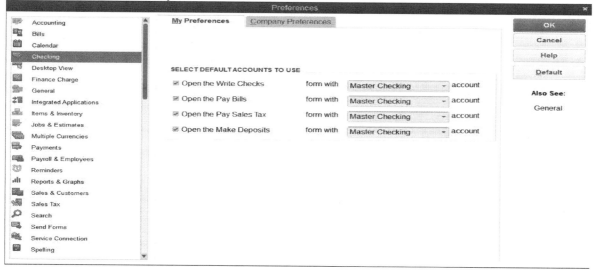

1. The default setting for the Select Default Accounts to use are blank. I went in and added Master Checking to all the accounts.
   - You can leave blank and remember to add the checking each time
   - You can assign a checking account as I did, but change when using a different account such as your Trust account or if using Payroll and you have separate checking you would change to that Checking.

This screen below is still the Checking tab, but it's Company Preferences.

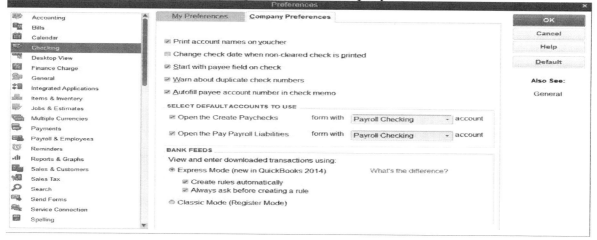

2. Here is options for you to make for your own choices. I clicked on Print account names on voucher, Start with payee field on Check and so on.
3. I add the Payroll Checking in the drop down lists for create paychecks (if you use payroll).
4. Bank Feeds as you can see it offers a new express mode for 2014 and newer or the classic mode.
5. When done click ok.

The Desktop view is below with for My Preferences. As you can see you can change the colors of your desktop view along with other choices to your liking.

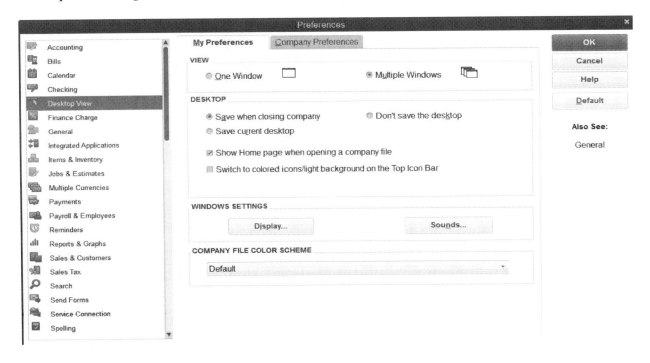

This screen is still Desktop View, but Company Preferences. As you can see some choices you can choose that were not setup in the building of your company file.

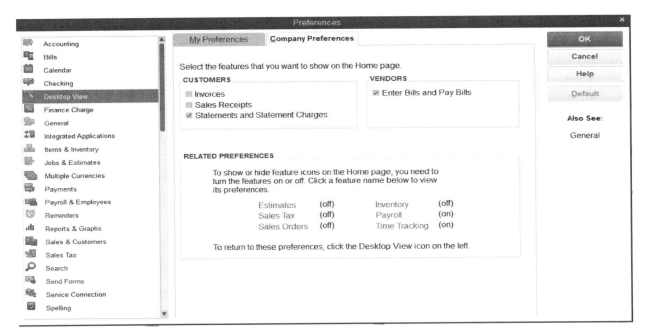

1. You would click on Invoices if you decided you wanted to use that feature or the Sales Receipts.
2. When done Click ok.

This next screen is the Finance Charge Preference. There's nothing under the My Preferences, so you would go to Company Preferences.

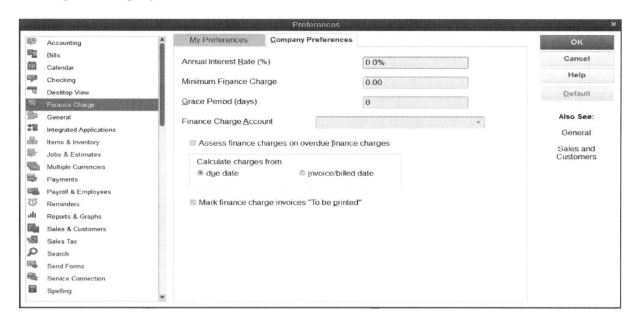

1. This is where you would set up finance charges for past due accounts.
2. If you allow any grace period days then enter the value for that.
3. you will need to enter the finance charge account in the drop down menu
4. Make your choice on the calculate charges from due date or the invoice date.
5. When done Click ok.

Since I went over the General Tab as the first one I will move to the Integrated Applications. The General tab for whatever reason is the one that comes up when you first click on Preferences.

1. The integrated applications has nothing under my preferences. Company Preferences is where you can bring in like a third party application such as The Square Credit Card Processing plus other programs.

I am not going to go over the Items & Inventory tab since most likely it will not pertain to a Law Practice, but if it does then you would go in and make those necessary changes.

I am not going to go over the Jobs & Estimates since most likely you will not be using this feature, but it's there if you are going to use this feature now or at any time, just change those preferences.

The following tab is multiple currencies.

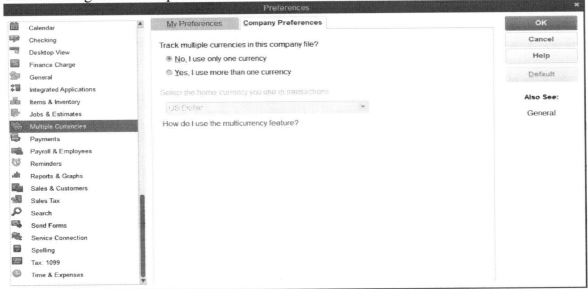

2. Click on yes, I use more than one currency if this is the case.
3. Click on the drop down list and choose the other currencies you use.
4. Click ok when done.

This next tab is Payments Preferences. There are no choices under My Preferences. The Company Preferences are as the screen below. The settings in this screen shot are the default settings.

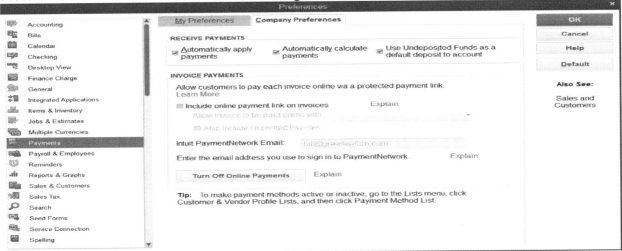

1. There are other options for Invoice Payments as you can see. If you choose this option just follow the instructions as to how to set up for your particular needs.
2. Intuit has a Payment/Network you can choose from to make your vendor payments.

This next Preference Tab is the Payroll & Employees. There are no options under My Preferences, so you will go to Company Preferences for your options.

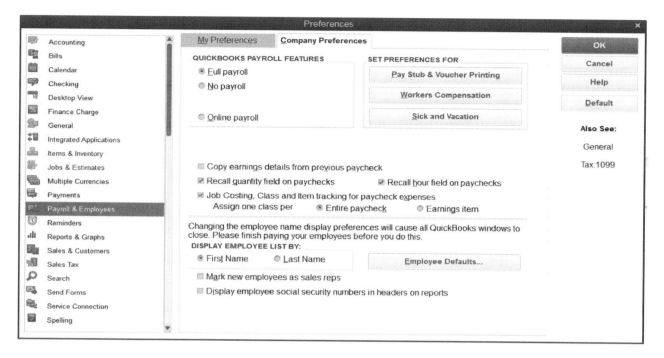

1. Click on your choice for payroll features, Full Payroll, No Payroll or Online Payroll.
2. Finish choosing your options and when done click ok.

The Next Screen is Reminders. Under My Preferences you have one option and that is either leave uncheck or check Show Reminders List when opening a Company file. Click on the tab for Company Preferences to choose your options below.

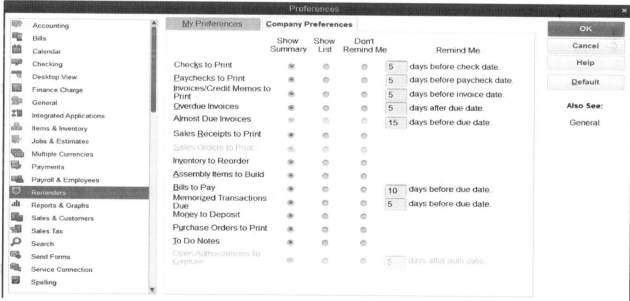

This screen is self-explanatory. Click on and fill in the values as to your needs.

Reports & Graphs is the next Preference Tab. The following screen is My Preference choices.

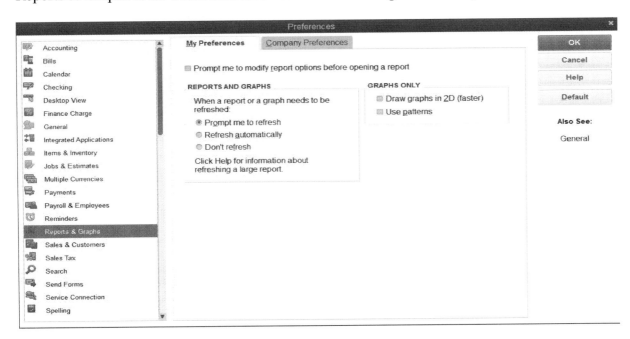

QuickBooks lets you choose between two methods of accounting for your reports. You can choose either Cash based accounting. Cash based is used when a practice records income and expenses when they receive the money. For example, you might invoice a customer for a service or product, but if you choose the cash method this will not be included on the Income Statement until the client actually pays you.

The other method is Accrual based accounting. Accrual based accounting is used when a practice records their income or expenses when they are incurred. For example, if you invoice a client for a product or service it will show up on the Income Statement for that date, even if the client has not paid the invoice.

Here's the Company Preferences for Reports & Graphs. Choose the options you prefer and click ok.

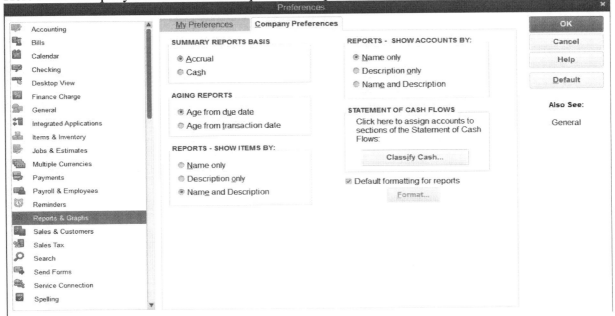

Sales & Customers Preference Tab. This first screen shot is My Preferences. This is a matter of your needs, so choose your best options and click on Company Preferences.

This is the Sales & Customers default settings for Company Preferences. Enable Prices Levels is selected and this is what you want if you are charging different clients different rates. Click ok.

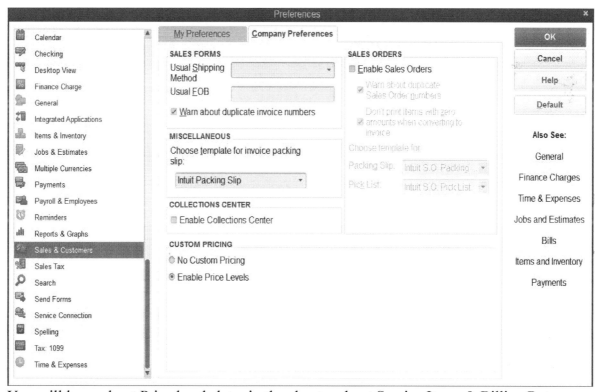

You will learn about Price levels later in the chapter about Service Items & Billing Rates.

Sales Tax is the Next Preference Tab and I will skip that since most likely you do not need sales tax options.

Search Tab is the next Preference Tab. I would leave the default settings as shown below.

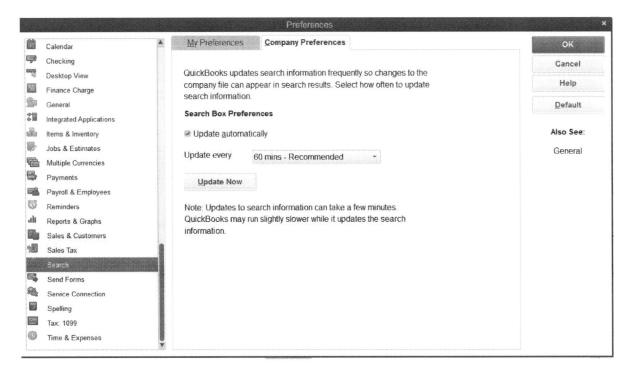

Send Forms is the next Preference Tab. This is My Preferences in the Send Forms tab. May your choices as to your needs. When finished click on Company Preferences.

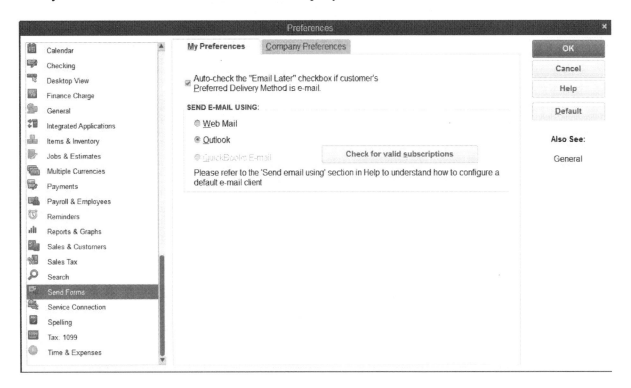

This is Company Preferences for Send Forms. This is where you would add Statement Templates if you email customers their statements, or any other forms on the show drop down list.

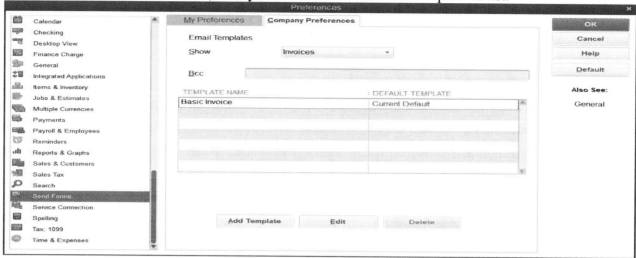

1. Click on your choices and when done click ok.

The next Tab is Service Connection. Check out the options, but I would leave them as default settings. The Service Connection is when you connect to Intuit/QuickBooks for updates and things like that.

The next Preference Tab in order is Spelling and I leave this in the default settings. Check this tab settings out just in case you want to make changes.

The next Preference Tab in order is Tax: 1099 and this is for if you pay outside sources other than employees such as say paralegal work, witness or another attorney etc. Click on this tab and make any necessary changes.

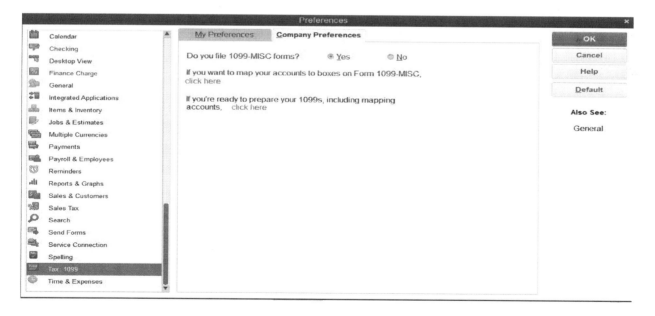

If you do use this Tax: 1099. You can see is mentions mapping your accounts. Click Here. After click here then follow instructions.

The last tab is Time & Expenses. This is an important tab for a Law Practice. There are no options under My Preferences. Click on Company Preferences to make your necessary choices.

1. QuickBooks Time Tracking allows you or your employees time spent to be tracked for different cases. You can choose this option to create a paycheck from the time data and have the option to bill your clients for this time spent on their case. Click on yes for under Do you track time? If you are not going to track time you may want to turn this feature off. You can always go back and change it if you change your mind.

2. Click on Create invoices from a list of time and expenses if you are using the Premier or Professional services version of QuickBooks and you decide to use the invoice way of billing your clients. You can still use statements as well as the invoicing.

Setting Up Users and Passwords

QuickBooks gives you the option of setting up users and passwords and of course it nots mandatory, but is highly recommended to secure your data. If you have someone that helps with the billing and payments. You would set this person up as a user with a password that can only see the accounts receivable information that pertains to their job.

How to setup Users and Passwords:
1. Click on Company from the top Main Menu Bar.
2. Click on Setup Users and Passwords.
3. Click Setup Users. A box will popup asking for the Administrator password (if you set up this password when setting up your Company File).

This User List screen will appear next. This lists all of the users that are currently setup in your company. The Admin is set up by default, but you have to setup the password either in the company setup phase or now. If you did not set up the Admin password yet then click on Edit User to set your password. Enter the password and enter it again in the confirm password box. Select challenge questions, and enter the answer. When you are done, click on next.

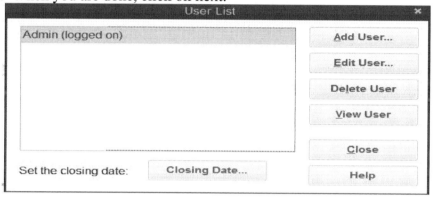

Setting up new User
1. Click on Add User

2. Enter under name and password
3. I didn't click on add this user to my QuickBooks License. You would click this on if you bought a QuickBooks license for say 5 users. (If you have two users that are part time and use the same station you don't have to list them as two users because they won't be using the same computer at the same time. Click Next.

This next screen asks all areas of QuickBooks, Selected Areas or External Accountant. Jackie is an employee in Purchases & Accounts Payable, so I am not giving her full access.

1. Click on your choice.
2. Click Next.

The screens will automatically be set to No Access, so if you don't need to give someone access just click next.

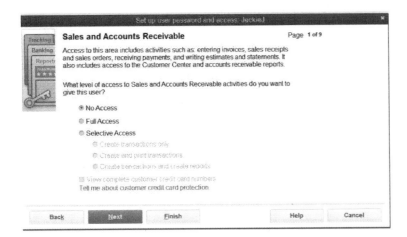

Jackie is in charge of Purchases and Accounts Payable, so I gave her full access. Click next after your selection.

I gave Jackie Selective Access to Checking and Credit Cards since she needs to print checks and entering credit card charges. Make your selections then click next.

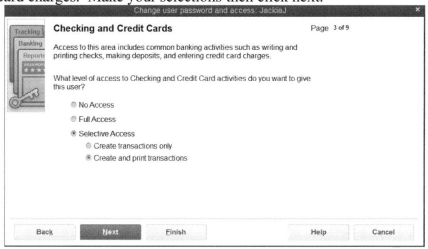

I gave Jackie no access on Time Tracking since she is not in this department. Make your selections then click next.

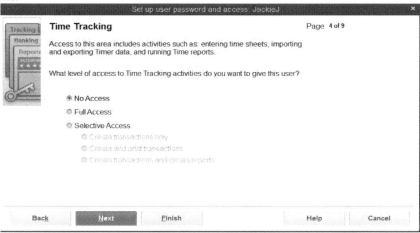

Jackie is not in the Payroll and Employees department, so I gave her no access. Make your selections then click next.

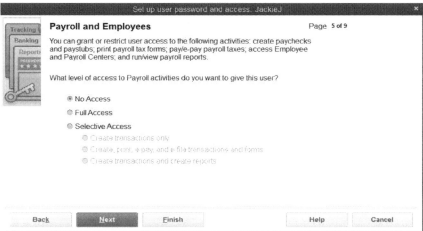

Jackie doesn't need access to Sensitive Accounting, so I left it as no access. Make your selections and click next.

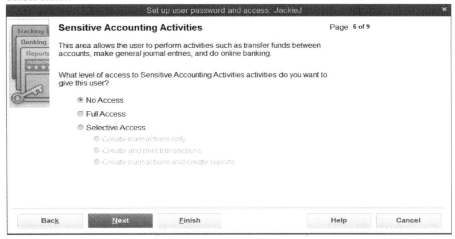

Jackie doesn't need access to Sensitive Financial Reporting, so I kept this area as no access. Make your selections and click next.

I gave Jackie access to change or delete transactions in her department that she has access to, but not able to change or delete transactions that were recorded before the closing date. These are the default settings for this screen. Make your selections and click next.

Below is the summary screen for Jackie's access. These settings can be changed anytime. Click Finish when done.

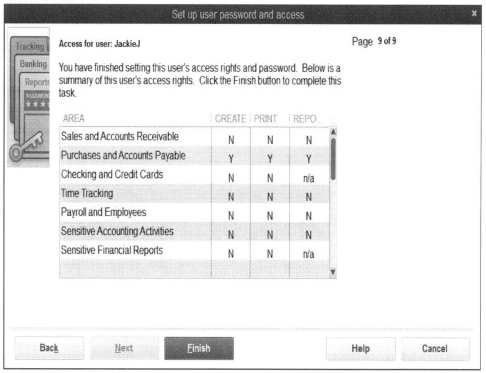

Click Close if you are finished adding, editing or deleting users. If not click add, edit, delete or view user.

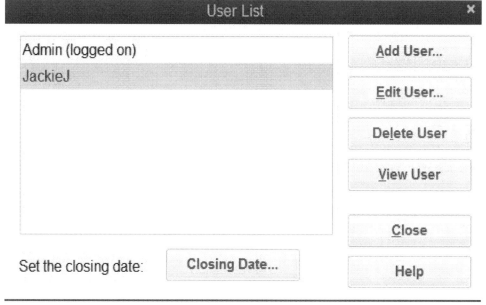

Backing up Your Company File

I can't begin to tell you how important it is to back up your Company File. I have and countless others have lost data due to not backing up regularly. Set a schedule at least weekly and if you have a larger company with a lot of transactions then daily is what I recommend.

To Make a Company File Backup
1. Click file from the top Main Menu Bar.
2. Select Backup Company.
3. Select Create Local Backup and Click Next. If you are saving to your computer a screen will pop up asking if you want to change locations click option to save to location you chose.

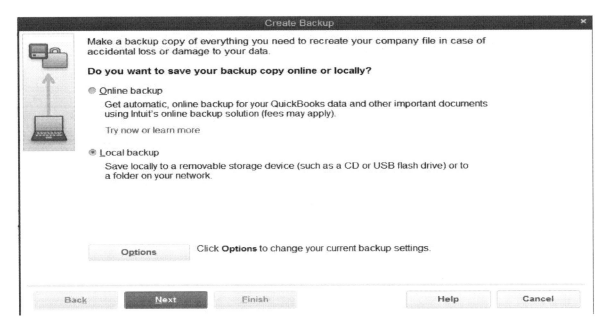

1. Click on Browse to choose where you want to save your backup. Be sure to save to a thumb drive that you can lock up in a safe place.
2. Click Ok. When backup is finished click ok.

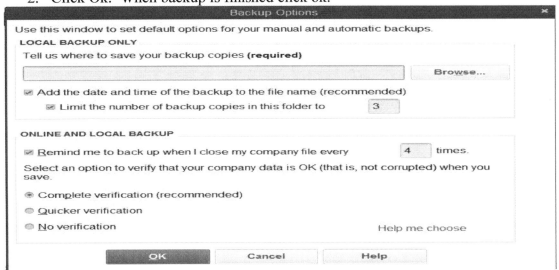

Schedule Backups

QuickBooks gives you the option of scheduling backups. This is great so you do not forget.

Setup Scheduled Backups.

1. Click on save it now and schedule future backups or select only schedule future backups.
2. Click Next.

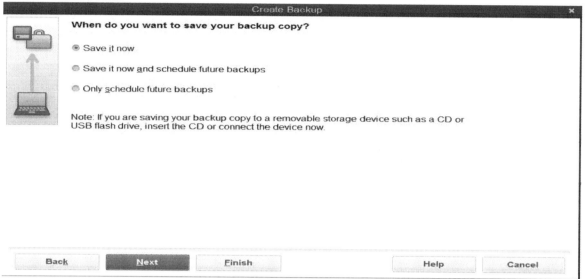

1. Click on save backup copy automatically when I close my Company file every 3 times or choose Back Up on a Schedule. I chose Backup on a schedule because you have more control over times and if you need to restore and reenter transactions you will know exactly or real close where to start to reconstruct.
2. Choose Backup on a Schedule and Click New.

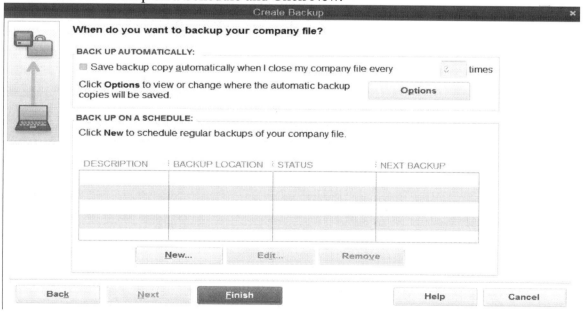

1. Enter your company information, Name/Description and Location
2. Set number of backup Copies to keep or can leave unchecked.
3. Select Time and days to backup
4. Click ok when done.

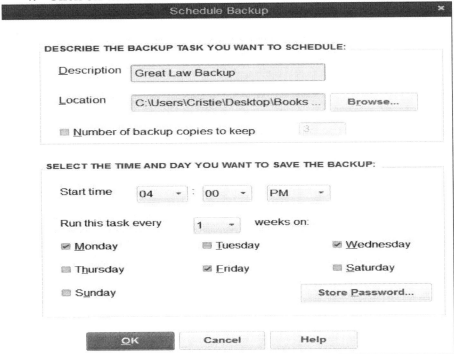

Here's the scheduled screen with backup scheduled. Click Finish. Remember you can edit these schedules anytime.

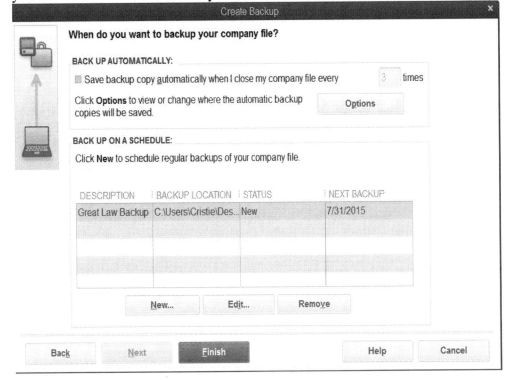

Restore a Company File

How to restore a Company File
1. Click file from the top Main Menu Bar
2. Select Backup Company
3. Select Restore Previous Local Backup and click on the last backup performed and click next
4. It will ask you to save your file, so be sure to save it or rename it where it will not overwrite another file.
5. Click Next.

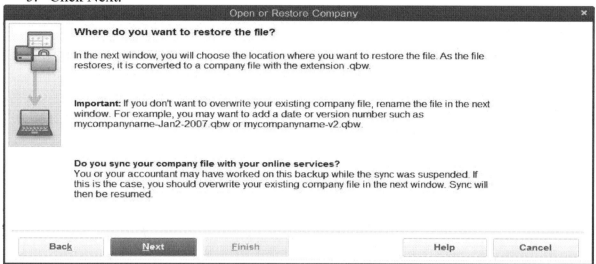

The following screen will come up. Type in a different place in the save in box or just give the file Name a different name, so it doesn't overwrite your current file and click save.

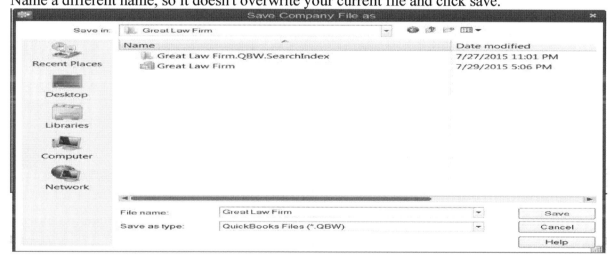

Once your backup has been restored this screen will pop up. Click ok.

Create Copy of Company Files

How to create a copy of your Company File for your Accountant or any other reason.

1. Click File at the top Main Menu.
2. Select Create Copy
3. Select Portable company file and Click Next.

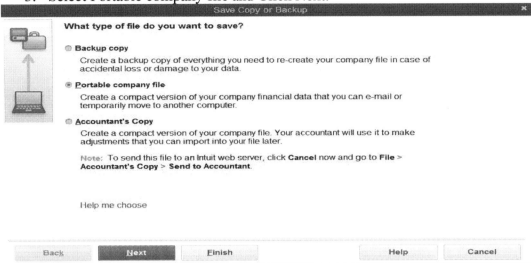

This screen pops up next and make sure you save it to the correct file and click save.

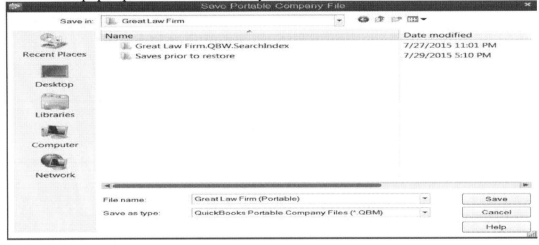

One the company file is saved this screen will pop up. Click ok.

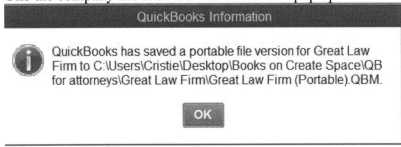

Chapter 2
Chart of Accounts

During the Getting Started phase of setting up your Company File, we set up your initial Chart of Accounts. This chapter will go into more depth about the Chart of Accounts.

Chart of accounts
> The chart of accounts is a complete list of your business' accounts and their balances

When you keep books for a company, you want to track:
> Where the income comes from
> Where you put it
> What the expenses are for
> And what you use to pay them

You track this flow of money through the chart of accounts

About assets, liabilities, and equity:

Assets
> Include what you have and what people owe you
> The money people owe you is called your accounts receivable, or A/R for short. QuickBooks uses an accounts receivable account to track the money owed you.
> The rest of your company's assets may include checking accounts, savings accounts, petty cash, fixed assets (such as equipment or trucks), inventory, and un-deposited funds

Liabilities
> What your company owes to other people
> The money you owe for unpaid bills is your accounts payable, or A/P for short. QuickBooks uses an accounts payable account to track the money you owe different people for bills.
> A liability can be a loan, an unpaid bill, or sales and payroll taxes you owe to the government.

Equity
> Equity is the difference between what you have and what you owe
> Equity = Assets – Liabilities

Cash versus accrual bookkeeping:

Cash basis
> Income is recorded when money (sales) is received and expenses when money (bills) are paid

Accrual basis
> Income is recorded when at the time of the sale and expenses when you receive the bill

Important: When you create reports in QuickBooks, you can switch between cash and accrual reports at any time, regardless of which bookkeeping method you have chosen for tax purposes.

Screen Shot of Chart of Accounts set up during Setup Company File.

NAME	⚡	TYPE	BALANCE TOTAL	ATTACH
◦ Master Checking		Bank	36,056.00	
◦ Payroll Checking		Bank	13,050.10	
◦ Petty Cash		Bank	1,523.09	
◦ 10900 · Client Trust Account		Bank	0.00	
◦ Inventory Asset		Other Current Asset	0.00	
◦ 12300 · Advanced Client Costs		Other Current Asset	0.00	
◦ 12310 · Court Costs		Other Current Asset	0.00	
◦ 12320 · Expert Witness Fees		Other Current Asset	0.00	
◦ 12330 · Filing Fees		Other Current Asset	0.00	
◦ 15000 · Furniture and Equipment		Fixed Asset	0.00	
◦ 17000 · Accumulated Depreciation		Fixed Asset	0.00	
◦ 18700 · Security Deposits Asset		Other Asset	0.00	
◦ 24000 · Payroll Liabilities		Other Current Liability	0.00	
◦ 30000 · Opening Balance Equity		Equity	50,629.19	
◦ 30100 · Capital Stock		Equity	0.00	
◦ 31400 · Shareholder Distributions		Equity	0.00	
◦ 32000 · Retained Earnings		Equity		
◦ Sales Income		Income		
◦ 45400 · Legal Fee Income		Income		
◦ 48800 · Settlement Income		Income		
◦ Cost of Goods Sold		Cost of Goods Sold		
◦ 51800 · Merchant Account Fees		Cost of Goods Sold		
◦ 53400 · Subcontracted Legal Services		Cost of Goods Sold		
◦ 60000 · Advertising and Promotion		Expense		
◦ 60200 · Automobile Expense		Expense		
◦ 60400 · Bank Service Charges		Expense		
◦ 61400 · Charitable Contributions		Expense		
◦ 61700 · Computer and Internet Expenses		Expense		
◦ 62000 · Continuing Education		Expense		
◦ 62400 · Depreciation Expense		Expense		
◦ 62500 · Dues and Subscriptions		Expense		
◦ 63300 · Insurance Expense		Expense		
◦ 63310 · General Liability Insurance		Expense		
◦ 63320 · Health Insurance		Expense		

| Account ▼ | Activities ▼ | Reports ▼ | Attach | ☐ Include inactive |

Measuring business profitability

The balance sheet
> A snapshot of your company on one date. It shows:
> - What you have (assets)
> - What people owe you (accounts receivable)
> - What your business owes (liabilities and accounts payable)
> - The net worth of your business (equity)

To run a Balance Sheet Report from the Chart of Accounts.

1. Click on the Reports button at the bottom of the open Chart of Accounts Screen.
2. Click on Report on all Accounts.
3. Select Balance Sheet
4. Click on Standard.
5. Press Esc button to exit report.

Great Law Firm
Balance Sheet
As of July 29, 2015

	Jul 29, 15
▼ASSETS	
▼ Current Assets	
▼ Checking/Savings	
Master Checking	▶ 36,056.00 ◀
Payroll Checking	13,050.10
Petty Cash	1,523.09
Total Checking/Savings	50,629.19
Total Current Assets	50,629.19
TOTAL ASSETS	50,629.19
▼ LIABILITIES & EQUITY	
▼ Equity	
30000 · Opening Balance Equity	50,629.19
Total Equity	50,629.19
TOTAL LIABILITIES & EQUITY	50,629.19

The profit and loss statement
A profit and loss statement or income statement shows income, expenses, and net profit or loss

To run a Profit and Loss Statement Report from the Chart of Accounts.

6. Click on the Reports button at the bottom of the open Chart of Accounts Screen.
7. Click on Report on all Accounts.
8. Select Profit and Loss
9. Click on Standard.
10. Press Esc button to exit report.

Great Law Firm
Profit & Loss
All Transactions

	Feb 5, 13
Ordinary Income/Expense	
Income	
Legal Fee Income	8,428.44
Total Income	8,428.44
Expense	
Advertising and Promotion	15.00
Automobile Expense	68.00
Client Cost	
Client Postage	0.03
Copies	0.02
Total Client Cost	0.05
Computer and Internet Expenses	486.00
Meals and Entertainment	43.00
Office Supplies	74.25
Postage and Delivery	37.50
Professional Fees	
Co-Couonsel	500.00
Total Professional Fees	500.00
Rent Expense	2,000.00
Telephone Expense	175.00
Total Expense	3,398.80
Net Ordinary Income	5,029.64
Net Income	5,029.64

Statement of cash flows
    Shows receipts and payments during a specific accounting period

To run a Statement of Cash Flows Report from the Chart of Accounts.

    11. Click on the Reports button at the bottom of the open Chart of Accounts Screen.
    12. Click on Report on all Accounts.
    13. Select Cash Flow
    14. Click on Statement of Cash Flows
    15. Press Esc button to exit report.

Great Law Firm
Statement of Cash Flows
All Transactions

	◇ Feb 5, 13 ◇
▼ OPERATING ACTIVITIES	
Net Income	▶ 7,541.25 ◀
▼ Adjustments to reconcile Net Income	
▼ to net cash provided by operations:	
Accounts Receivable	-2,511.75
Visa	290.50
Client trust Liability:Andrews, Emily	1,935.00
Client trust Liability:Baker, David	100.00
Client trust Liability:Firm Funds	100.00
Net cash provided by Operating Activities	7,455.00
▼ INVESTING ACTIVITIES	
Furniture and Equipment:Computers & Office Equipment	-698.00
Net cash provided by Investing Activities	-698.00
▼ FINANCING ACTIVITIES	
Opening Balance Equity	6,000.00
Shareholder Distributions:LB Distribution	-2,000.00
Shareholder Distributions:RB Distribution	-2,000.00
Net cash provided by Financing Activities	2,000.00
Net cash increase for period	8,757.00
Cash at end of period	8,757.00

You can run many more and different reports from the Reports menu. This is to show you what you can run from the Chart of Accounts and other accounts as well.

Adding new Accounts

How to add a new Account
1. Click on Company from top Main Menu Bar
2. Select Chart of Accounts
3. At the bottom of the page on the chart of accounts screen click on Accounts
4. Select New
5. Choose Bank
6. Click Continue

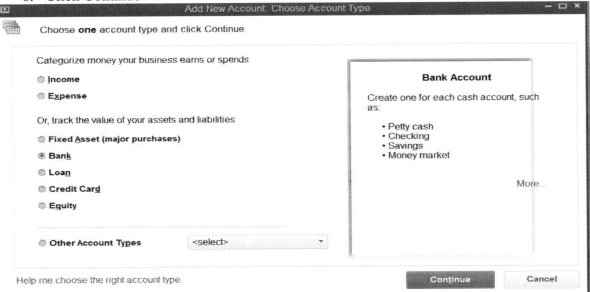

1. Enter the appropriate Information.
2. When finished Click Save & Close Button.

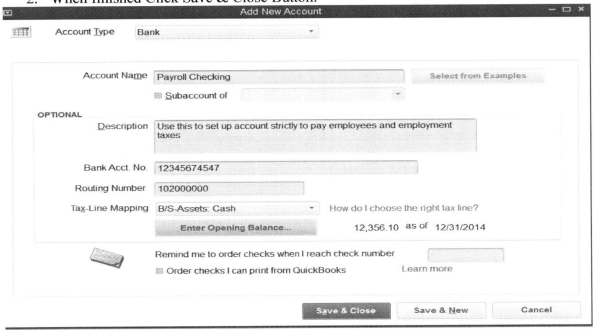

Editing Existing Accounts

How to Edit an Account

1. Click on Company from top Main Menu Bar
2. Select Chart of Accounts
3. Select Account you want to Edit by highlighting that account.
4. At the bottom of the page on the chart of accounts screen click on Accounts
5. Select Edit Account
6. Change the Name to Master Checking Account and update any other information
7. When finished Click Save & Close.

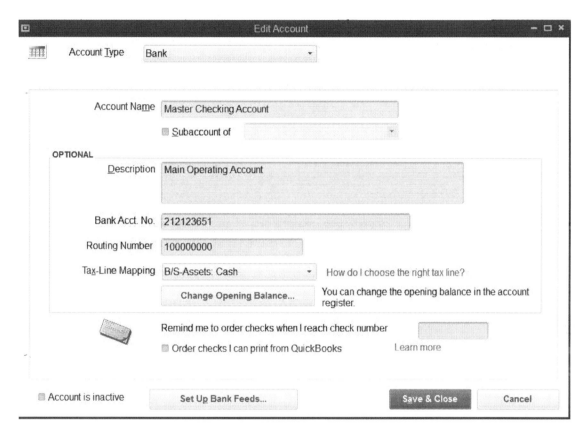

Note: If you did not set up your banking in the Setting up Company File stage then this would be the first thing you should do. Setup your banking.

Delete Existing Accounts

The first thing to keep in mind, you cannot delete an account that has any transaction history attached to it. If you have two of the same accounts with transactions in both accounts you can merge them into one and that will allow you to delete one of them. I will go over how to merge accounts on the next page.

How to delete an account with no transaction history

1. Click on Company from top Main Menu Bar
2. Select Chart of Accounts
3. Select Account you want to delete by highlighting that account.
4. At the bottom of the page on the chart of accounts screen click on Accounts
5. Select delete Account

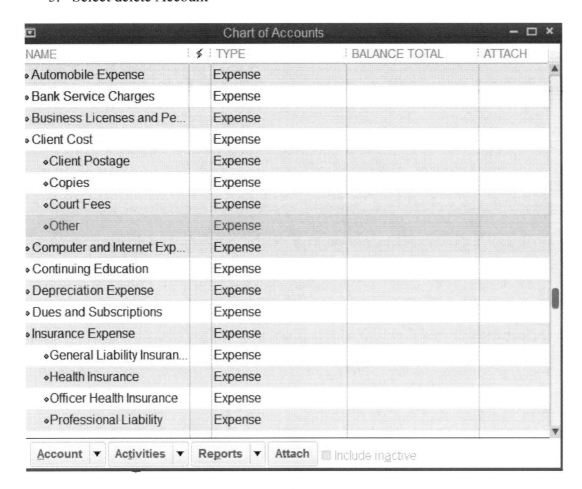

This screen will popup. Click the ok button and the account will be deleted.

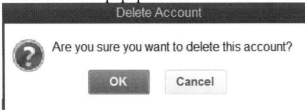

Merge Existing Accounts

QuickBooks allows you to merge accounts. It's really simple to do. The only trick is to name the account you want to merge by naming it the exact same name as the account you want to merge/combine.

A good example would be office supplies and office paper. See below.

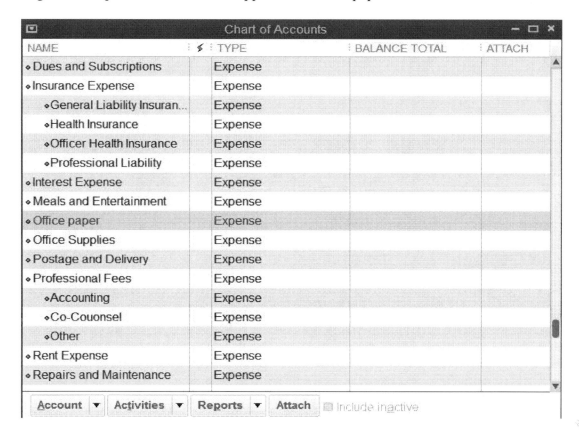

Click on Company from top Main Menu Bar
1. Select Chart of Accounts
2. Select Account you want to merge by highlighting that account.
3. At the bottom of the page on the chart of accounts screen click on Accounts
4. Select Edit Account
5. Rename the account, in this case I am renaming Office paper to Office Supplies.
6. Click Save & Close

This screen pops up and click Yes to merge and the two accounts become one.

Print Chart of Accounts List

To print the Chart of Accounts, click on the Accounts button at the bottom of the Chart of Accounts screen, and then select Print Listing. Click the Print Button to print the list. You can run this lists from the Reports menu that will give you more options if you need it.

This is the way the report looks printed from the Chart of Accounts menu.

	Chart of Accounts	7/29/2015 7:39 PM
Account	**Type**	**Income Tax Line**
Client Cost Account	Bank	B/S-Assets: Cash
Client Trust Account	Bank	<Unassigned>
Master Checking Account	Bank	B/S-Assets: Cash
Payroll Checking	Bank	B/S-Assets: Cash
Accounts Receivable	Accounts Receivable	B/S-Assets: Accts. Rec. and trade notes
Advanced Client Costs	Other Current Asset	B/S-Assets: Other current assets
Court Costs	Other Current Asset	B/S-Assets: Other current assets
Expert Witness Fees	Other Current Asset	B/S-Assets: Other current assets
Filing Fees	Other Current Asset	B/S-Assets: Other current assets
Undeposited Funds	Other Current Asset	<Unassigned>
Accumulated Depreciation	Fixed Asset	B/S-Assets: Buildings/oth. depr. assets
Furniture and Equipment	Fixed Asset	B/S-Assets: Buildings/oth. depr. assets
Computers & Office Equipment	Fixed Asset	B/S-Assets: Buildings/oth. depr. assets
Furniture	Fixed Asset	B/S-Assets: Buildings/oth. depr. assets
Security Deposits Asset	Other Asset	B/S-Assets: Other assets
Visa	Credit Card	B/S-Liabs/Eq.: Other current liabilities
Client trust Liability	Other Current Liability	B/S-Liabs/Eq.: Other current liabilities
Firm Funds	Other Current Liability	B/S-Liabs/Eq.: Other current liabilities
IOLTA Interest	Other Current Liability	B/S-Liabs/Eq.: Other current liabilities
Kehn, Dan	Other Current Liability	B/S-Liabs/Eq.: Other current liabilities
Rollins, Richard	Other Current Liability	B/S-Liabs/Eq.: Other current liabilities
Shelton, Lauren	Other Current Liability	B/S-Liabs/Eq.: Other current liabilities
Capital Stock	Equity	<Unassigned>
Opening Balance Equity	Equity	<Unassigned>
Retained Earnings	Equity	<Unassigned>
Shareholder Distributions	Equity	<Unassigned>
CK Distribution	Equity	<Unassigned>
DK Distribution	Equity	<Unassigned>
Legal Fee Income	Income	Income: Gross receipts or sales not on line 1a
Settlement Income	Income	Income: Gross receipts or sales not on line 1a
Advertising and Promotion	Expense	Deductions: Advertising
Automobile Expense	Expense	Other Deductions: Other deductions
Bank Service Charges	Expense	Other Deductions: Other deductions
Business Licenses and Permits	Expense	Deductions: Licenses
Client Cost	Expense	<Unassigned>
Client Postage	Expense	<Unassigned>
Copies	Expense	<Unassigned>
Court Fees	Expense	<Unassigned>
Computer and Internet Expenses	Expense	Other Deductions: Other deductions
Continuing Education	Expense	Other Deductions: Other deductions
Depreciation Expense	Expense	<Unassigned>
Dues and Subscriptions	Expense	Other Deductions: Other deductions
Insurance Expense	Expense	Other Deductions: Other deductions

Page 1

Chapter 3
Vendors

In this Chapter you will learn the different ways to handle bills, learn how to enter a bill, use the Pay Bills window, and learn how to enter a discount on a bill from a vendor plus much more.

Some business owners, especially if they own smaller, home-based businesses, pay their bills when they receive them. Most business owners, however, find it more convenient to pay bills less often. (They also like keeping the cash in the company for as long as possible.) If you don't plan on paying your bills right away, QuickBooks can help you keep track of what you owe and when you owe it.

The money you owe for unpaid bills is called *accounts payable*. QuickBooks uses the Accounts Payable account to track all the money you owe. Like any QuickBooks balance sheet account, the Accounts Payable account has a register where you can view all your bills at once.

1. **To see the Accounts Payable register:**
    From the Lists menu, choose **Chart of Accounts**.

2. Double-click **Accounts Payable** in the list to open the register.

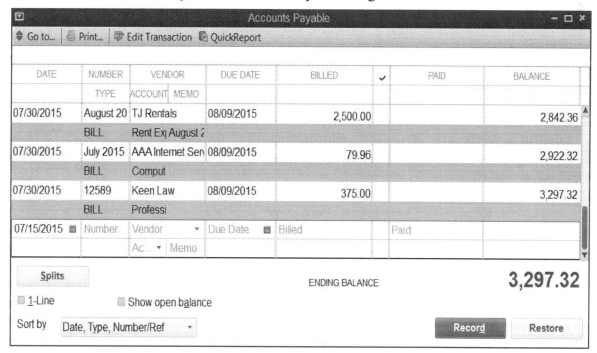

3.

The register keeps track of each bill you have entered, shows you the due date, and keeps a running balance of all the bills you owe. As a business owner, this helps you forecast your cash flow, and the QuickBooks reminder system helps you pay your bills on time.

4. Press **Esc** twice to close the two open windows.

Entering Bills

When you receive a bill from a vendor, you should enter it into QuickBooks as soon as you can. This keeps your cash flow forecast reports up to date and doesn't give you the chance to set aside a bill and forget about it.

To enter a bill:

1. From the Vendors menu, choose **Enter Bills**.

2. In the Vendor field, type **Willis Advertising**, and then press Tab.

3. When QuickBooks displays a message telling you that Willis Advertising is not on the Vendor list, click **Quick Add**.

4. In the Amount Due field, type **1500**.

5. Click in the Bill Due field.

6. Click in the Account column on the Expenses tab and type in category like office supplies.

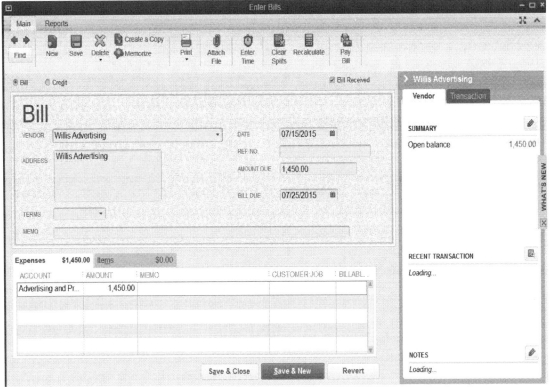

7. Press Tab to accept the account you chose.

8. Type **1450** to change the amount from 1,500 to 1,450.

9. Click in the Account column below the expense category you chose.

10. From the drop-down list, choose **advertising & Promotion**, and then press Tab.

11. Click **Save & Close** to record the bill.

Paying Bills

When you start QuickBooks or open a QuickBooks company file, a Reminders window appears that tells you whether you have transactions to complete, such as bills to pay or money to deposit.

When QuickBooks tells you that you have bills due, you can display the Pay Bills window and select the bills you want to pay.

To pay a bill:
1. From the Vendors menu, choose **Pay Bills**.

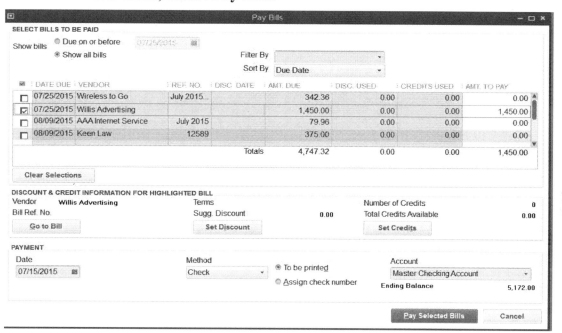

2. Select the "To be printed" option.

3. Select the Willis Advertising bill by clicking in the column to the left of the bill.

4. Click **Pay Selected Bills**.

5.
6. You could print the checks at this point, but for this exercise click **Done**.

Recording Your Bill Payments

When you pay a bill through the Pay Bills window, QuickBooks makes an entry in the accounts payable register, showing a decrease of $1,450 in the total payables. It also creates a check from your checking account to pay the bill.

To see the entry in the accounts payable register:

1. From the Company menu, choose **Chart of Accounts**.

2. In the chart of accounts, double-click the Accounts Payable account.

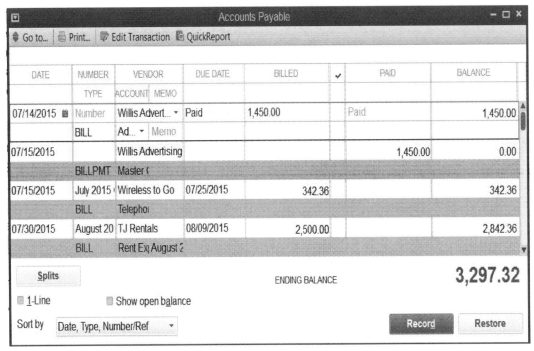

3.

4. Close the accounts payable register by pressing Esc. Button.

Recording Your Bill Payment

To see the entry:

1. In the chart of accounts, double-click **Checking**.

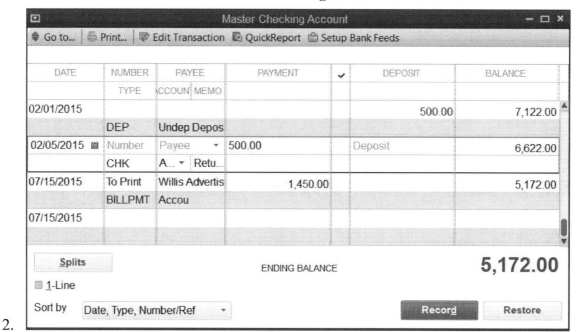

2.
3. Select the Willis Advertising transaction.

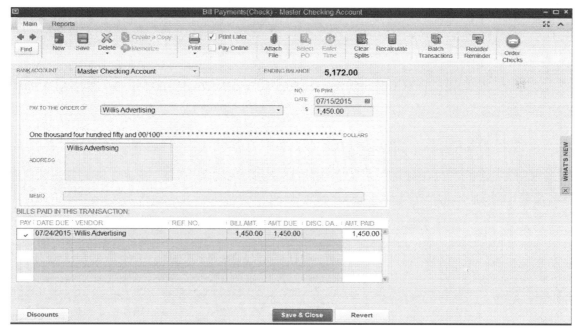

4.
5. On the toolbar, click **Edit Transaction**.
6. From the Window menu, choose **Close All** to close all the open QuickBooks windows.
7. Click **Home** in the navigation bar to open the Home page.

Setting up Discounts to apply to Vendors

If you take advantage of discounts for early payment offered by some vendors, you can record the discounts directly in the Pay Bills window. You can set up QuickBooks to track the discount amounts.

To apply a discount for early payment you have to make sure discounts are set up in Preferences.

1. Click on Edit then select Bills from the top Main Menu Bar.

2. Select **Due on or before**, and then type **1/08/2020** and press Tab.

3. Click to put a checkmark next automatically use discounts.

4. If you do not have discounts set up in Chart of Accounts, click on Default Discount Account and scroll to top and click on Add New.

5. Enter the value or select an option and click ok.

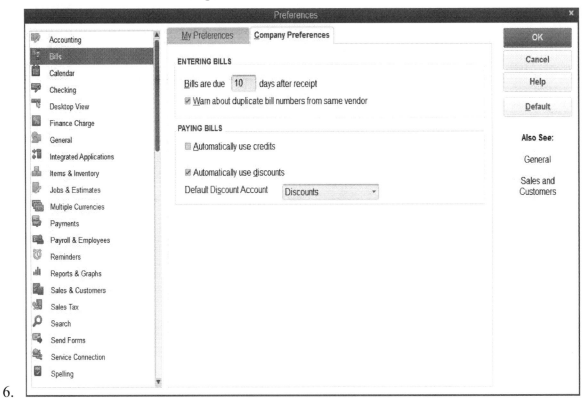

6.

Now that you have set up preference for the Discounts you will need to go into Vendors to apply the different discounts to each Vendor.

Applying Discount to each Vendor

1. Click on Vendors at the top of the Main Menu Bar.
2. Click on Vendor Center
3. Select a Vendor to apply Discount. In My example I chose Keen Law and selected 2% 10 Net 30. There are some preset payment terms. You can add more Payment terms if what you need is not listed as an option.
4. When finished with your selection click ok.

5.

To see the discount applied click on Pay Bills from the home page vender area. Then select Keen Law or the Vendor you chose.

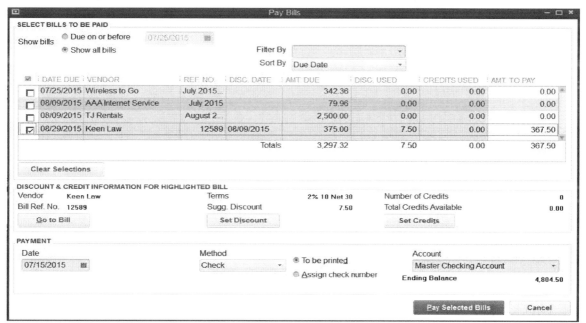

See once Keen Law was selected the Discount used applied to the payment. To pay the bill click Pay Selected Bills. Click Done or you can print the check now.

Printing Checks

You can print one check at a time if you need or you can print in batches.

1. Click on File at the top of the Main Menu Bar.
2. Select Print Forms
3. Select Checks and Click ok. Make sure your Check number is correct.

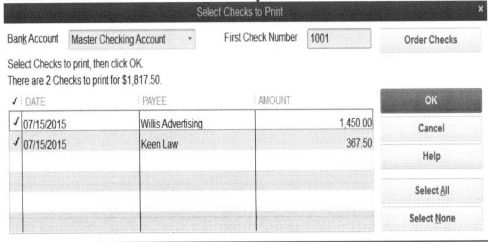

4. _____

The following screen is the Print Checks screen. Make sure you have the correct printer and correct check style and have your checks loaded in the printer then click on the print button.

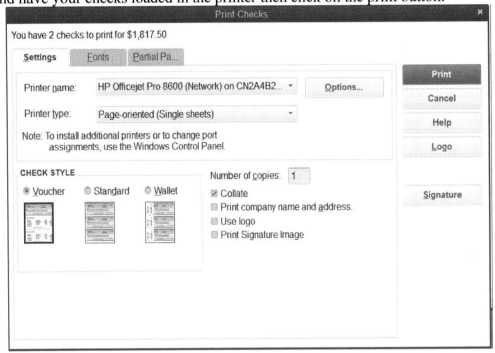

Writing Checks

You can just quickly enter information into a check and print on the spot. So for example if you need to go pick up business cards being printed at the printer you can enter the vendor and amount take the check with you to pay for the business cards.

1. Click on Banking at the top of the Main Menu Bar
2. Click Write Checks.
3. Enter vendor name, amount and other necessary data.
4. Click Print in the ribbon icon area just below Main and Reports to the right.
5. Click print on next screen then click ok when done. Press Esc to exit out of screen.

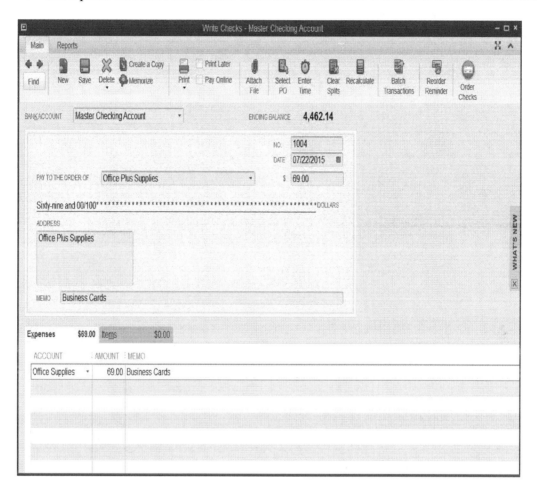

1099 Vendor Setup

A 1099 forms are required to fill out at the end of the year for the IRS if you paid for services over $600.00 to a company or person who is not incorporated. By setting up this company or individual as a 1099 vendor QuickBooks will track the amount paid to this 1099 vendor and print the 1099 forms. It's a good idea to contact your Accountant for the tax laws or go directly to the IRS website to review the laws.

How to setup a 1099 Vendor
1. Click Edit at the top of the Main Menu Bar.
2. Scroll down to almost the bottom of the preference choices and choose Tax: 1099
3. Click on Company Preferences
4. Click Yes on Do you File 1099 MISC Forms. Click Ok when done.

Setup an existing Vendor you do business with.
1. Click on Vendors at the top of the Main Menu Bar. Select Vendor Center
2. Double Click on existing Vendor to add 1099 Information.
3. Click on Tax Settings and enter their Vendor Tax ID/Social Security Number
4. Click the Box for Vendor Eligible for 1099
5. Click OK when done.

You can also set the Vendor ID when setting up new Vendor.

Split Transactions

Often times when paying a bill you will need to divide the amount into two or more categories.

How to Write a Split Transactions Check
1. Click on Banking at the top of the Main Menu Bar, select Write Checks.
2. Type in All Insurance Company. Enter 550.00 for the amount
3. Click into the accounts below Insurance for General Liability 325.00
4. Click the second line in accounts for Professional Liability 225.00
5. When finished Click Print then Print again.
6. Click OK and Press Esc Button to get out of the screen.

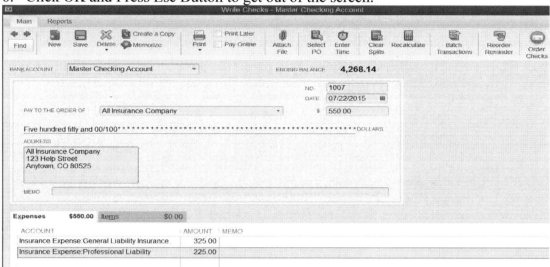

Set up Accounts in a Vendor for Split Transactions
1. Click on Vendors at the Top of the Main Menu Bar, Click on Vendor Center
2. Double Click on All Insurance Company, Select Account Settings
3. Click on Drop Down lists to add General Liability then second drop down for Professional Liability. Click Ok when finished.

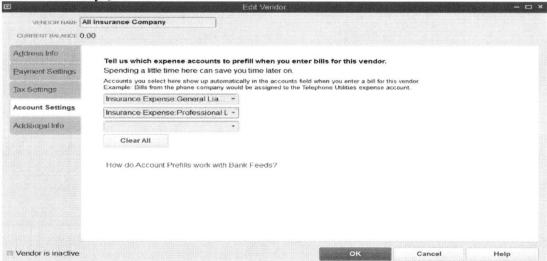

Note: You can set up any and all Vendors with prefill accounts. This is great especially if the account doesn't change. If you set the accounts up and need it to be a different account occasionally you can change it when entering bill or check.

Voided Checks

Sometimes we need to void checks and QuickBooks makes it super simple.

How to Void a Check

1. Click on Banking at the top of the Main Menu Bar, Select Use Register.
2. The Use Register screen comes up to select account, make sure it's the right account and click ok.

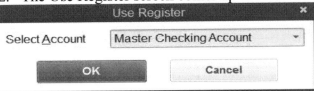

3. Double Click on Computer Plus, check number 1006, to open.
4. Click on Edit at the top of the Main Menu Bar.
5. Click Void Check, then Click Save in the Ribbon bar above the Check.

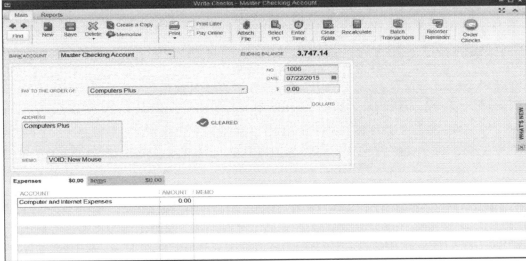

Press the Esc Button to exit out of this screen. Notice it says VOID: New Mouse in the memo and it shows cleared.

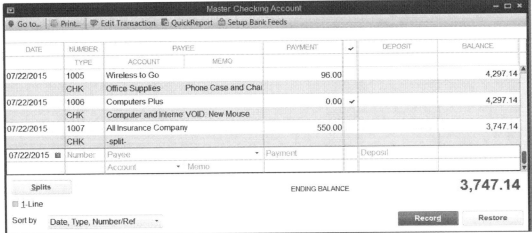

See in the Checking Register the Voided Check shows 0.00 and has check mark next to it to indicate it's cleared and that's to always show and know that every check is accounted for.

Using a Check Register

Let's take a look at the check register. You can use the check register to enter checks you have written by hand and any other withdrawals from your account such as a debit checking card.

1. Click on Banking at the top of the Main Menu Bar, Select Use Register.
2. The following screen comes up next, so click ok if this is the account you are going to look in.

3.

Here's the check register in QuickBooks. It is an electronic resemblance of your pocket book check register. This is where any money in or out transactions go. You can print checks, enter hand written checks, deposits printed or hand written and all other money in or out transactions. This is two line view of the check register and you can see more on the screen by viewing in one live view.

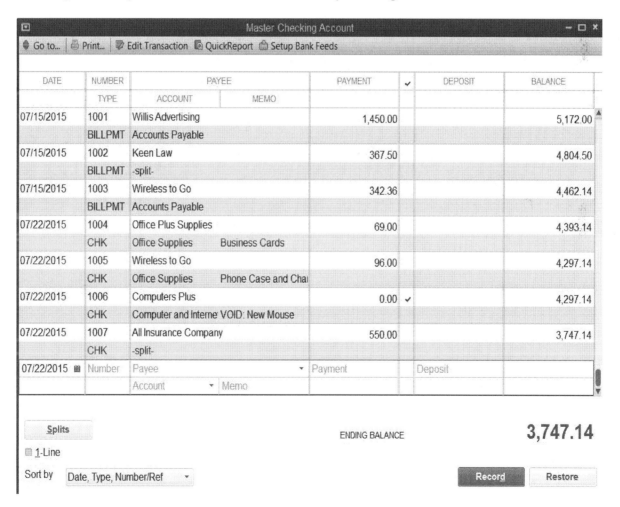

Here's the one line view. To view this way just click on the little box next to 1-Line bottom left corner.

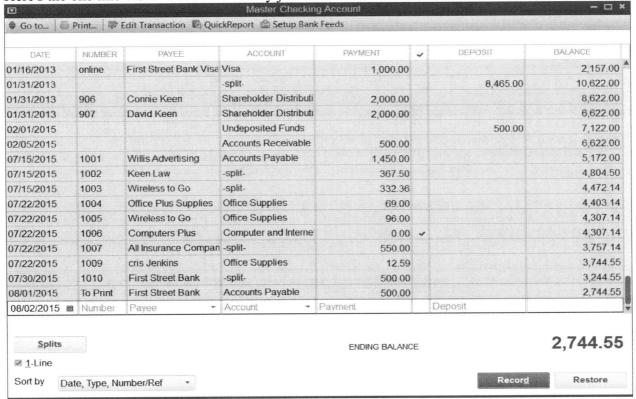

DATE	NUMBER	PAYEE	ACCOUNT	PAYMENT	✓	DEPOSIT	BALANCE
01/16/2013	online	First Street Bank Visa	Visa	1,000.00			2,157.00
01/31/2013			-split-			8,465.00	10,622.00
01/31/2013	906	Connie Keen	Shareholder Distributi	2,000.00			8,622.00
01/31/2013	907	David Keen	Shareholder Distributi	2,000.00			6,622.00
02/01/2015			Undeposited Funds			500.00	7,122.00
02/05/2015			Accounts Receivable	500.00			6,622.00
07/15/2015	1001	Willis Advertising	Accounts Payable	1,450.00			5,172.00
07/15/2015	1002	Keen Law	-split-	367.50			4,804.50
07/15/2015	1003	Wireless to Go	-split-	332.36			4,472.14
07/22/2015	1004	Office Plus Supplies	Office Supplies	69.00			4,403.14
07/22/2015	1005	Wireless to Go	Office Supplies	96.00			4,307.14
07/22/2015	1006	Computers Plus	Computer and Interne	0.00	✓		4,307.14
07/22/2015	1007	All Insurance Compan	-split-	550.00			3,757.14
07/22/2015	1009	cris Jenkins	Office Supplies	12.59			3,744.55
07/30/2015	1010	First Street Bank	-split-	500.00			3,244.55
08/01/2015	To Print	First Street Bank	Accounts Payable	500.00			2,744.55
08/02/2015	Number	Payee	Account	Payment		Deposit	

Splits

☑ 1-Line

Sort by Date, Type, Number/Ref

ENDING BALANCE **2,744.55**

Record   Restore

Moving around the Register

1. Click on the Go To button in the left corner of the screen on the icon bar.

This is the screen that pops up. You can search for a transaction dollar amount, search by payee name, by memo or Number Reference/Check Number.

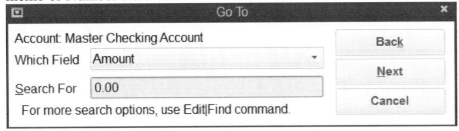

Go To

Account: Master Checking Account

Which Field Amount

Search For 0.00

For more search options, use Edit|Find command.

Back

Next

Cancel

Click on the Print Button in the left corner of the screen on the icon bar. You can enter date range for a report of the check register.

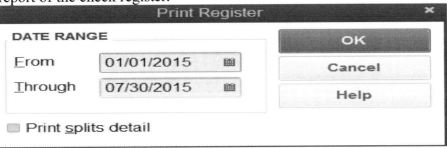

Print Register

DATE RANGE

From 01/01/2015

Through 07/30/2015

OK

Cancel

Help

☐ Print splits detail

Editing Transaction in the Check Register

1. Highlight a transaction in the Check Register
2. Click on Edit Transaction in the Icon Bar of the Check Register

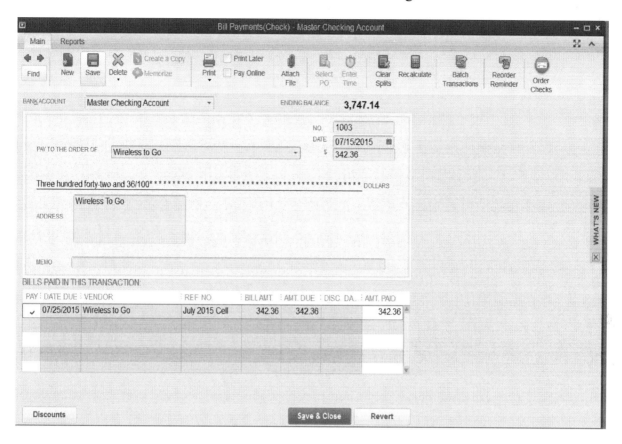

To run the Quick Report
1. Highlight a transaction of a vendor that you want more history on.
2. Click on Quick Report
3. This is the report you will get. You can sort by dates etc just as you would from the reports menu.

Setup Bank Feeds

By clicking on the Setup Bank Feeds button in the Icon Bar of the Check Register this is the screen that pops up. This is to setup banking to where you can download information from your banking directly into you check register. Most banks have the Bank Feeds capability, but not all do offer this.

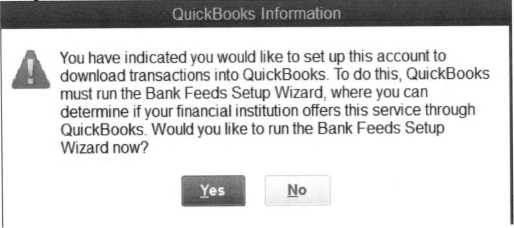

Entering Transactions in the Check Register

1. Click on Banking in the top Main Menu Bar
2. Select Use Register
3. Go to first blank line, enter date
4. Tab to number field and the next check number will automatically appear. If that is what you want then you tab to the next field and if not then change to another number or value you need.
5. Tab to the name field and fill in the name. If the name is not already a vendor then type the name and tab, a screen will pop up and just hit Quick Add and ok.
6. Tab to account field, click on drop down list and select account or type in account.
7. Enter the Amount
8. Click the Record Button. If you are finished just click the Esc button to exit out of the check register or add more transactions.

Additional Sorting in the Check Register

Click on the Sort by drop down list at the bottom left hand side of the check Register

You can sort by
1. Date, Type, Number/Ref
2. Amount (Largest Amount first)
3. Amount (Smallest Amount First)
4. Number/Ref
5. Order Entered
6. Date and Order Entered
7. Cleared Status

Recording Loan Payments

I will show you both ways you can enter a loan. If you have the QuickBooks version that has the Loan Manager included that is such a great tool and if you don't have it you can enter everything and will still get the job done.

Before setting up the Loan Manager payments, but sure to have your loan documents at hand. Next we need to set up three chart of accounts.

1. Click on Lists at the Top of the Main Menu Bar
2. Select Chart of Accounts
3. Click on the Account Button at the bottom of the Screen on the Chart of Accounts window.
4. Select New, Click Fixed Asset and Click Continue
5. Enter Name of County Line Road Land, Enter the opening balance and date
6. Click Save and New
7. Change the Account Type to Long Term Liability
8. Enter the name as Land Payment and enter the opening balance and date.
9. Click Save and New
10. Change Account Type to Expense
11. Enter Name as Land Interest
12. Click save and Close

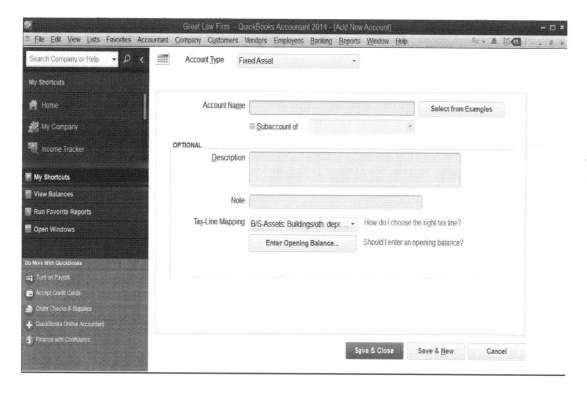

Ok we have now set up the three accounts to make your new Loan payment. Each loan payment will be different, depending on what the loan is for. The example I am setting up is for Land Acquisition to build a new office building on. The loan is just for the land right now. Remember when you set the chart of account up for this loan you entered the loan amount in the beginning balance, so in the loan manager you won't have to enter that nor will you have to set up a journal enter by entering the beginning balances.

Setting up Loan in Loan Manager

1. Click on Banking at the top of the Main Menu Bar
2. Click on Loan Manager
3. Click on Add a Loan
4. This is what the loan screen looks like with loan entered.

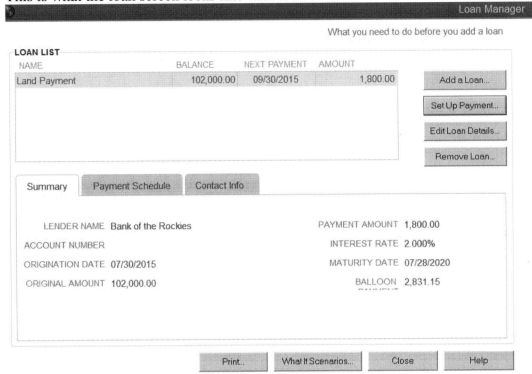

As you can see I entered, amount, lender, date and term of loan. Click Next

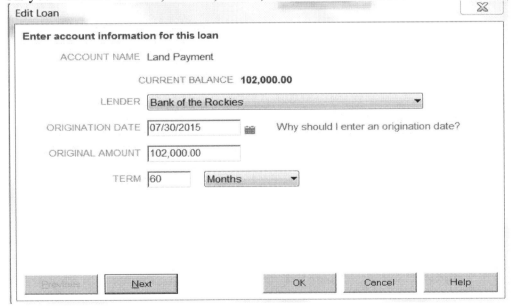

Here it has the next payment due date, payment amount with principal and interest. Click next.

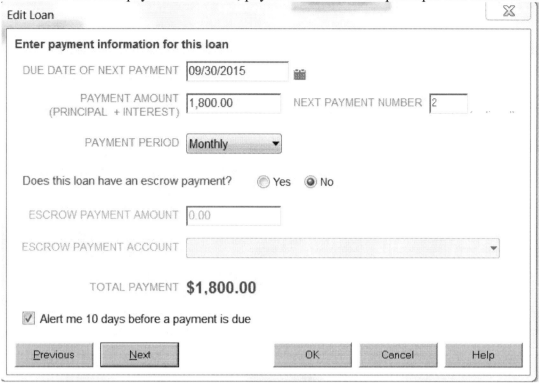

This screen has the interest rate, payment account, Interest Expense Account, Fees Acct. Click ok.

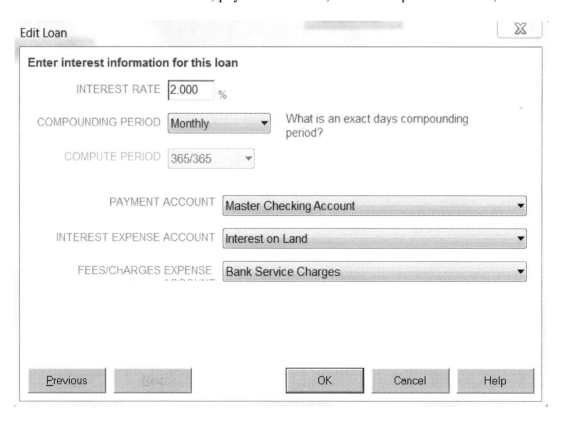

This screen shows you the payment schedule that includes principal and interest and a running balance as it gets paid down. You can print this as well.

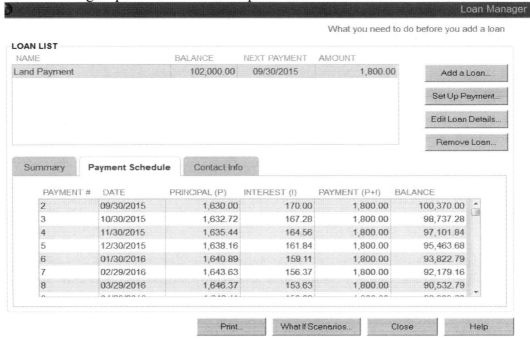

Setting up Payment

Click on Set up Payment in the Loan Manger screen. Make sure the loan you are setting up for a payment is highlighted. Click ok.

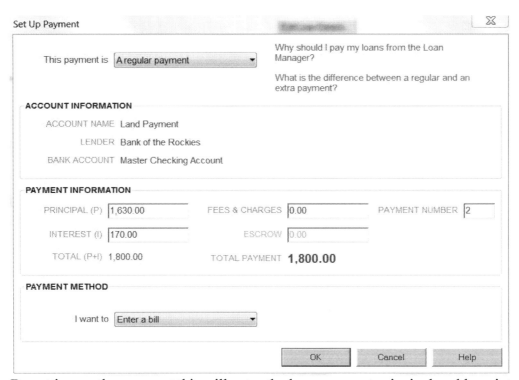

By setting up the payment this will enter the loan payment principal and loan interest into the correct accounts. You can enter a bill or you can choose to write a check.

Recording a Loan Payment without Loan Manager

Set up other current liability as a line of credit for 5,000.00
1. Click on Lists at the top of the Main Menu Bar
2. Select Chart of Accounts
3. Click on Accounts at the bottom of the page
4. Click New and select Other Current Liability
5. Name it Line of Credit
6. Give it Opening Balance of 5,000.00 and 7/1/2015 date.

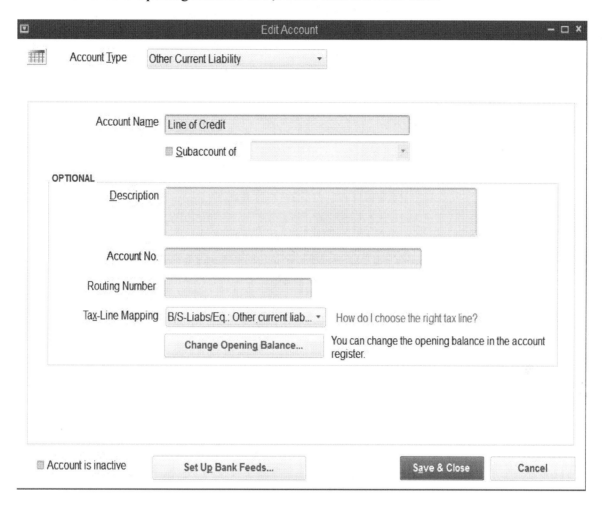

Write a Check for Loan Payment

1. Click on Banking at the top of the Main Menu Bar.
2. Select Write Checks.
3. Enter the lender name, the amount and date.
4. Tab down to the accounts area, enter the line of credit account and enter 450 amount.
5. Tab down to the next line in the accounts area and enter Interest Expense and amount of 50
6. Click Print

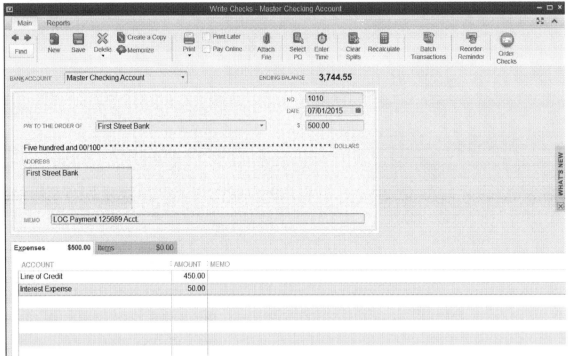

See the line of credit in the Check Register, Check 1010.

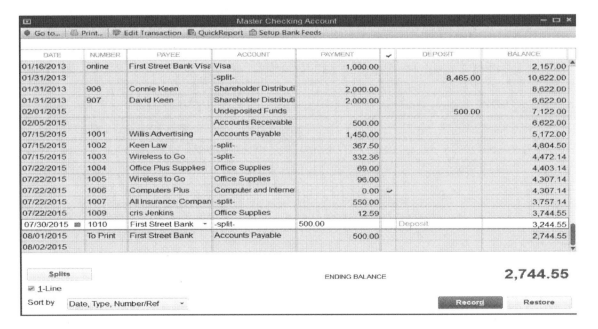

Enter Loan Payment as a Bill

1. Click on Vendors on the top Main Menu Bar
2. Select Enter Bills
3. Enter Vendor, Ref No., the amount and enter the line of credit account and the interest expense account. Amounts as shown.
4. Click Save & Close.

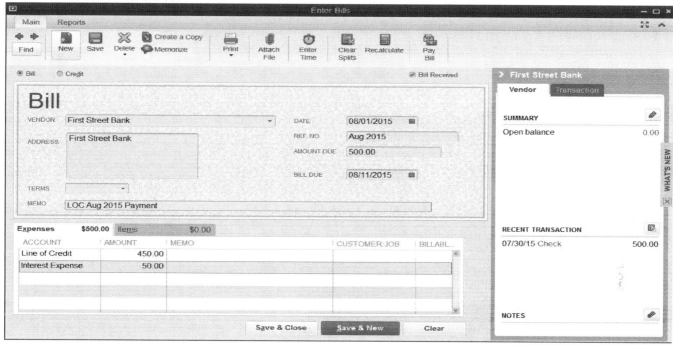

You can see the bill you just entered is now in the Bills to Pay. If you pay now click on the First Street Bank Bill. Click the Pay Selected Bills. Click Done to Print Check later.

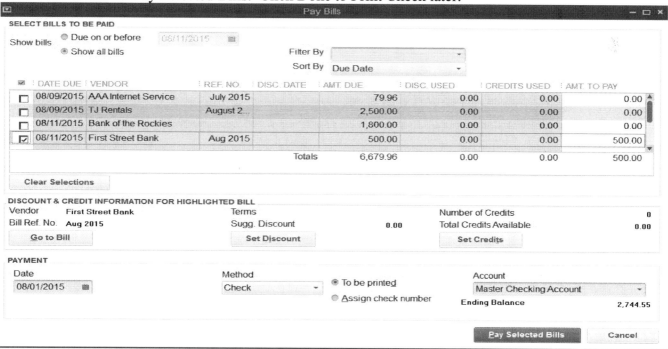

Chapter 4
Clients/Customers

In this chapter you will learn about setting up all information about clients/customers and their cases/matters. Some of the steps pertaining to clients/customers were introduced in basic form in the setup company file stage. You will learn more in depth in this chapter.

Customers/Clients

The Customer/Client list holds all their pertinent information. Within each Client list is the Job List that keeps all the Clients Cases/Matters. You can add customized information that you define to your needs, and notes about specific conversations and decisions. You can assign different prices levels for your clients, depending on the version of QuickBooks you have. I will go over much more about price levels in the next chapter. I highly recommend you go over the next few chapters to get ideas and a feel of how you want to set up clients billing, items and price levels. Once you go over the next few chapters you should know and thus probably make less setting up mistakes.

1. Click on the customers tab in the middle of your home page, or customers in your short cuts or the top of the Main Menu Bar and select Customer Center.
2. Click on the New Customer & Job Button at the top
3. Select New Customer

Here's the New Customer Screen to start entering Client information.

When finished entering information on this tab click on Payment settings to enter information.

Here's the information entered on Payment Settings Tab. No price level set since that will be added next chapter. When finished entering information on this Tab then click on Sales Tax Settings.

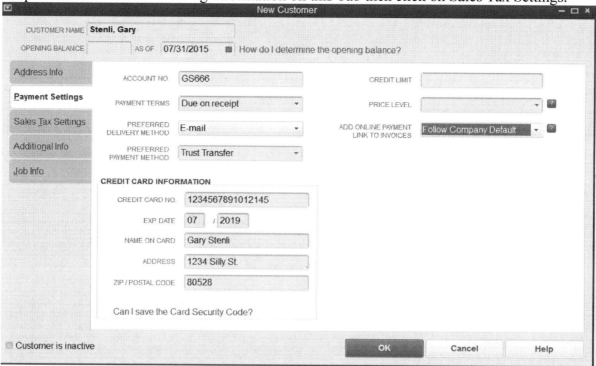

This Tab is obviously not necessary for this Practice since we don't sell any products. If you sell products then enter the pertinent information and when done click the Addition Info tab.

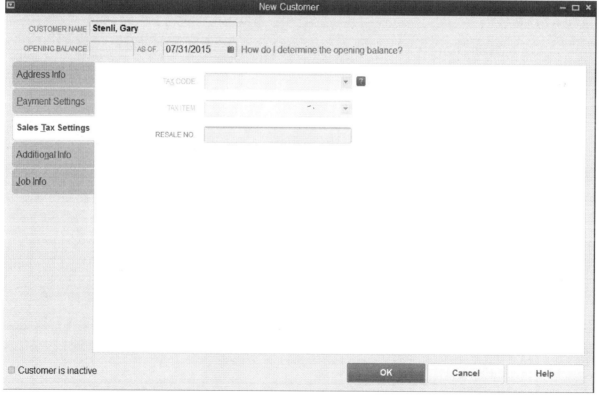

Information filled in on the Additional Info and as you can see he is a referral. His attorney is CK. Click on Define Fields next in the custom fields section.

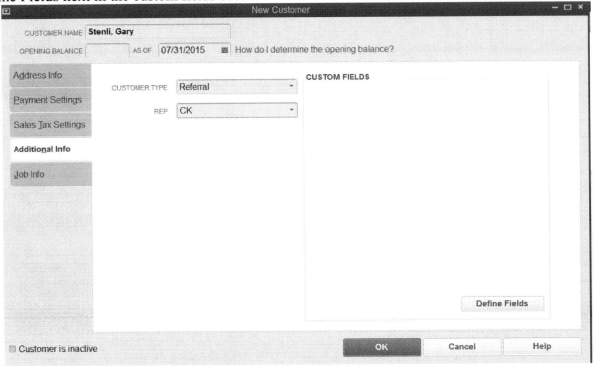

I added Opposing Party as an additional field for clients and vendors. You can any more and when done click ok.

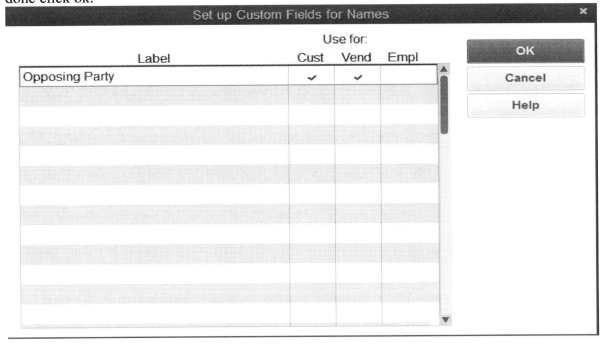

As you can see the new custom field, Opposing Party is now ready for information that has been entered. Click on Job Info next.

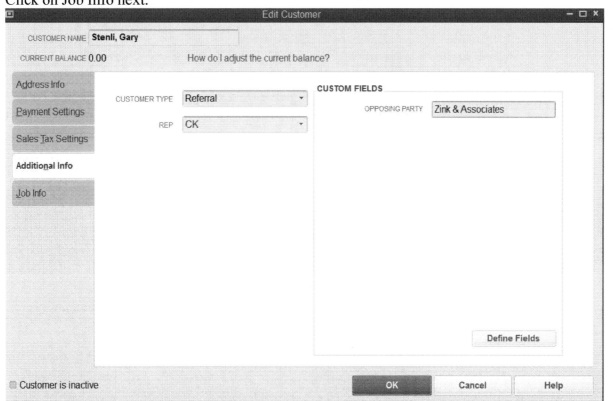

The Case/Matter information has been entered under the Job Info Tab. Click ok when done.

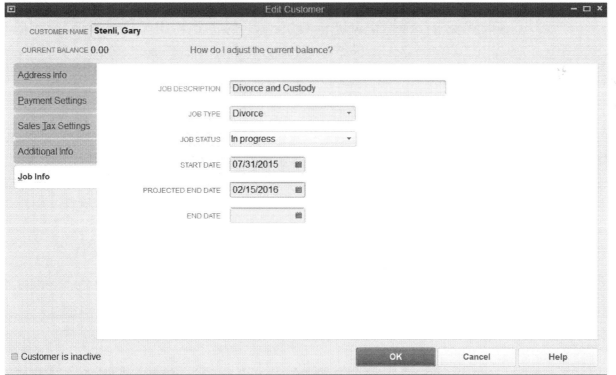

This Job was automatically entered at Job 1, so you will have to edit them name to the case/matter.

Adding Additional Cases/Matters

You will be adding most of the information for the new case again. The Clients address pretty much stays the same, but as always check that to make sure you are up-to-date.

1. Click on New Customer & Job at the top of the icon in the customer center. Make sure you have the customer highlighted that you are adding a Case/Matter to.
2. Click on Add Job.

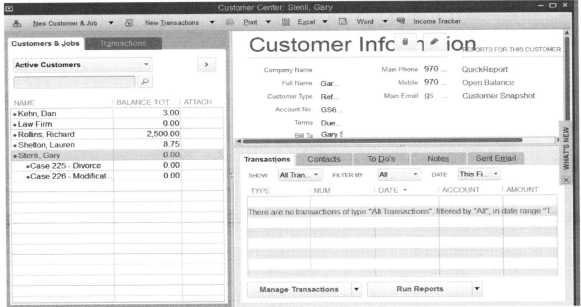

1. Give the Case/Matter a name in the Job Name field.
2. Check to make sure all the Address Info is correct
3. Click Payment settings. You will have to refill this information.
4. Click Additional Info and you will have to fill in the custom fields.
5. Click on Job Info Tab and enter your Case/Matter Information and click ok when done.

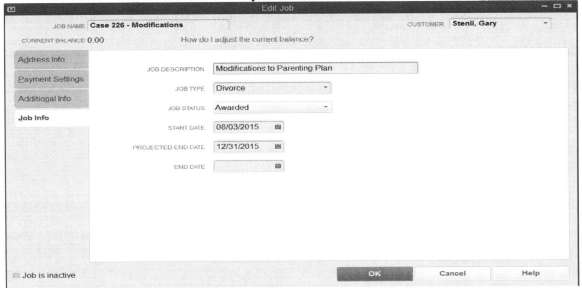

Note: If this client changes attorneys in your Practice just enter the new information under the correct Case/Matter.

Job Types

As you can see on the Job Info Page is a drop down list of Job Type. This is for the kind of case a Client has hired you for his/her legal representation.

1. Click on Job tab and enter Job Description
2. Click on drop down list on the Job Type and if the Job Type you need is not listed click on add new from the top of the drop down list.
3. Finish entering necessary information and click ok.

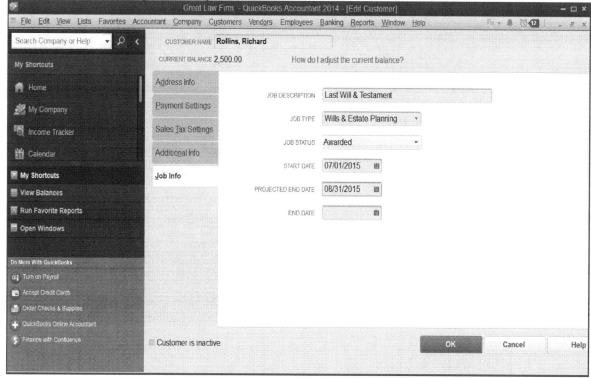

Clicking on adding New Job Type. This screen pops up and this is where you enter the new name. Click ok when done.

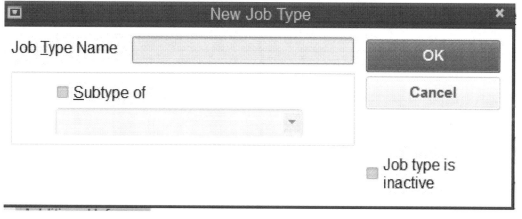

Add/Edit Multiple List Entries

To save time you can use the Add/Edit Multiple List Entries to update multiple entries at time. Make sure your Customer Center Window is open before using this list entries.

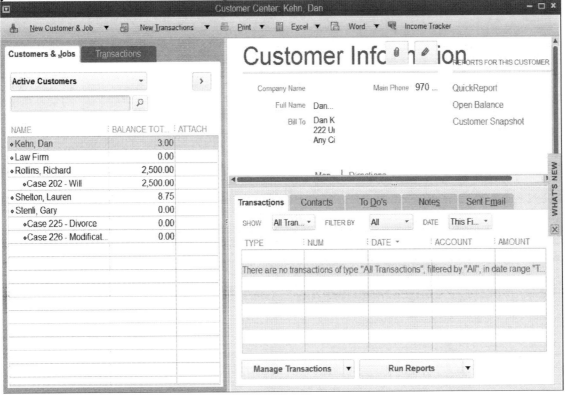

1. Click on Lists from the top of the Main Menu Bar.
2. Click on Add/Edit Multiple List Entries.
3. Start adding new clients and/or editing existing clients.
4. Click Save Changes when done. Click Close.

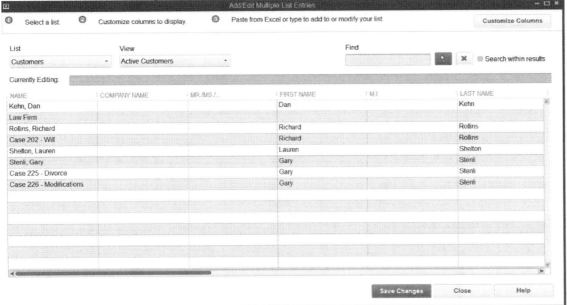

Chapter 5
Items, Levels & Rates

In this chapter you will learn how to setup your Service Items, Price Levels and Billing Rates that you bill your clients for. These things need to be setup before billing your Clients.

Setting up Items

Items are the Services and Products a business offers Clients/Customers. With this and most Law Practices are Service only items along with Discounts you may or may not offer. Items are used when you create invoices, statements and tracking time. They are a much easier faster means of data entry once setup.

You can create an Item for each type of work, such as different attorneys, paralegals, partner, associate, law clerk or administrator. Also, you can setup items for charge type items to handle things like faxes, postage and copying for clients.

I will show you how to set up a list and later show you how to customize this list to your needs.

Another thing that you may want and that is to set up employees with different rates and if so you will need the premier version. Let's say you want to set up an employee that is a paralegal with different billing rates you could place these different rates as sub items under that employee. Same thing to set up an attorney and you set up sub items under the attorney for more detail. A huge advantage to having everyone have their own item is you can run income reports based on them. This will allow you to see where the income is coming from.

Remember if you are not sure on a name you want for an account you can always Edit that name later and change it to a more appropriate name for you.

Keep in mind that I am taking you through the steps of entering Items from the top Menu Bar to stay consistent, but that there are a multitude of ways to enter Items such as from the Home Page under Company section. Another Way is under Edit at the top Main Menu Bar enter New Item. Last but not least with the Item List open you can enter a new Item by right clicking anywhere on the page and choose New.

Service Items

Service is what it says, it's a service you or someone in your company performed for a person or another business. Service Items are the items needed when tracking time and entering on an invoice to be billed to your client.

1. Click on Lists at the top of the Main Menu Bar
2. Select Item List
3. Click on Item and the bottom of the Item List Page.
4. Select New and choose Service as the Type and press enter or tab.
5. Type in Legal Fees for the Item Name Box and press enter or tab.
6. Type in Legal Fees in the Description Box and press enter or tab.
7. Enter a rate of 300.00 in the rate field and this will be your standard rate.
8. Choose the account you want this service item to store and record your data by clicking on the arrow. For this exercise we will choose Legal Fee Income.
9. Click Ok when done or if you are entering more than one Item then Click Next until you are done and then Click Ok.

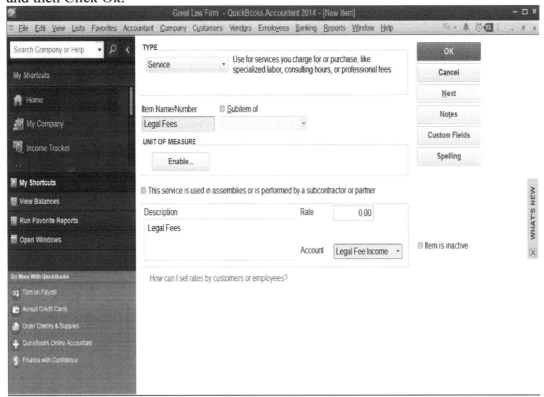

Now that you have set up Legal Fees when you are creating an invoice or statement charges the amount/transactions will be listed under the Legal Fee Income Account on your income statement and Chart of Accounts.

If you have more than one attorney I have found it beneficial for you to have a Service Item for each Attorney so you can track the income by each attorney. For Example attorney CK would have an item CK and then maybe, most likely, have some sub items under each attorney Service Item. By doing this you can place CK's billing rates for his/her time on the items. To track this you can pull a report on sales by item. We will go over how to create and modify reports later in another chapter. You can set up administrative time at a $0.00 rate to track this time even though you don't bill out for that time, but want to track the administrative/employee time.

Other Charge Items/Type

Like everything there more than one way to handle Items and transactions. When creating items you may want to record them in and income account called Client Reimbursed Expense Income. You will want to decide beforehand on the way you are going to bill your clients before choosing which way to go. If you are going to go Statement method then set up this Item like the screen below.

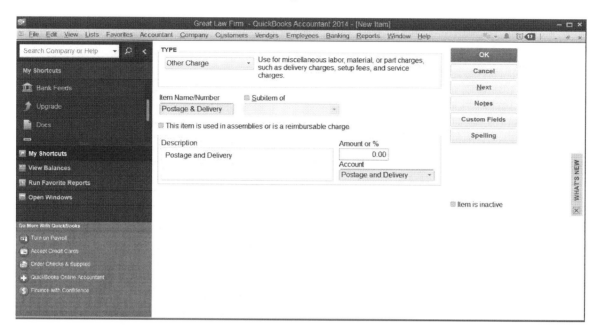

Use the method below if you are going to use the Invoice billing for your Clients. You will want to click on the box that states this item is used in assemblies or is a reimbursable charge. As you can see by the example you need expense and income account. This example is Postage and delivery. If you need to add Reimbursed Client Expenses Income Account see example on next page.

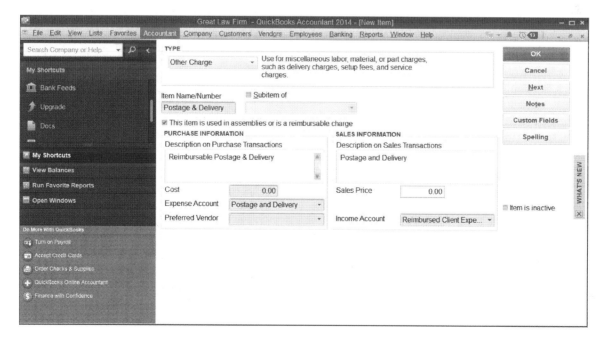

Setting up Reimbursed Client Expenses Income Account

1. Click on Company at the top Main Menu Bar
2. Select Chart of Accounts
3. Select Income and click Continue
4. Enter Reimbursed Client Expenses
5. You can enter a Description or Note.
6. Consult your CPA on which Tax Line to assign it to.
7. Click Save and Close.

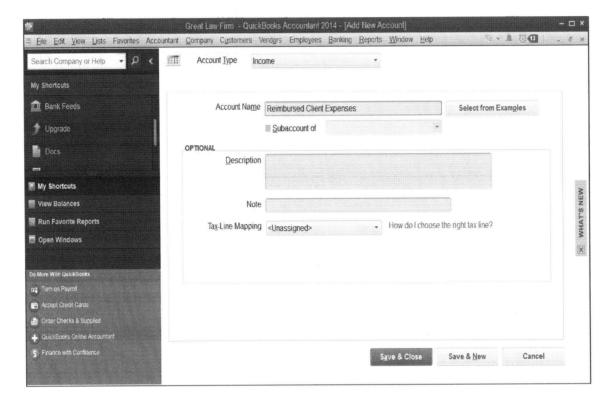

Price Levels

There are many good reasons to use Price Levels. One reason is some Clients may have an extended case and maybe they have been a lifelong client you want to keep them at a special rate. You may also charge different rates for different kinds of cases such as Family Law one charge and Criminal Law a different charge. QuickBooks Premier Programs works great with Price Levels this way.

Remember we just entered a Service Item for $300.00 under Legal Fees. Now where the Price Level will come in valuable is if you have say a long time client that is billed $225.00, so you want to have that rate show up for this particular client when do your billing. **THIS only works when using invoices or time data with statement charges. It does not work using it in the register.** Make sure you have the preference set to use Price Levels, assuming your QuickBooks Edition allows this.

Setting up Price Levels

1. Click on Lists at the top Main Menu Bar
2. Select Price Level List
3. Click on the Price Level Button at the bottom of the Price Levels Screen
4. Select New
5. Price Level Name is 225
6. Click on Legal Fees
7. You will need to decide which way to set your Price Level first.
8. Go to the line that says "Adjust price of marked items to be"
9. Click on the drop down list and choose either, Current Custom Price, Standard Price or Costs. If you choose Standard Price then you will enter a percent value in the 0.0% box and click adjust. If you choose Current Custom Price then you will enter the amount you want to bill in the custom price column of 225.00 in this exercise. Click ok when done.

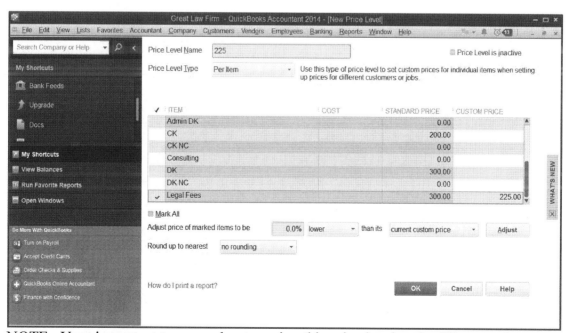

NOTE: Very important to remember to assign this price level to the Client you have to receive this rate. We will go over setting up this price level with the Client on the next page.

Setting up Clients with Price Levels

Steps to setting up Clients with a different Price level. You will do this after you have Price Levels setup.

1. Click on Customers at the top of the Main Menu Bar
2. Select Customer Center
3. Highlight the client that you are going to set up a Price Level for. In this exercise I am selecting Dan Kehn.
4. Double Click on the Clients name to Edit/Adding Price Levels to this Client
5. Select the Payment Settings Tab.
6. Click on the Drop Down Menu on Price Level and choose 225
7. Click Ok when finished. Push the Esc button to get out of this screen.

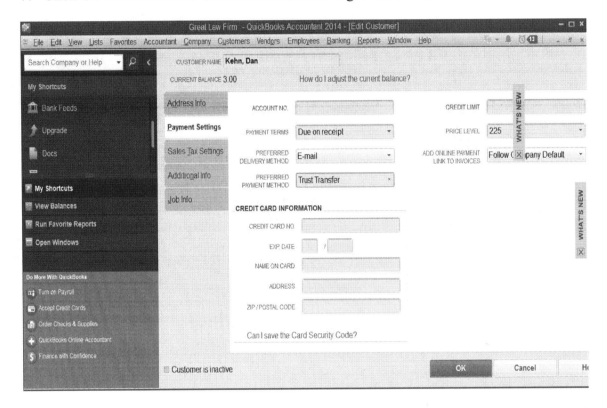

Depending on the Version and Year the year of your QuickBooks Program you may only have the fixed % method. In this case it will allow you to reduce or increase your standard rate for the items you have setup.

If you are doing a PRICE INCREASE just make sure you have billed all your time under the rate before the increase to avoid unhappy Clients. To do the increase go into the Price Levels Screen and edit to change the % rates to match what you want to bill. This will only apply to the clients you said you would work for a certain rate other than your standard rate. This feature is much more time consuming if not using the Premier Editions, so for a little more money to upgrade it's well worth it. You can use the Pro Version, but I don't recommend using this feature with Pro.

Once you have setup your price levels and assigned them to clients or jobs then run a test to make sure you have them set up right. Enter some data and then you go back and delete the test data.

Billing Rates

The billing rates are a great feature and you will access to these in the Accountant, Professional and Contractor Editions. Using the Billing Rate levels allows you to set custom service item rates for different employees/attorneys and vendors. For Example you may have several employees/attorneys that do the exact same service, but bill at different rates. Keep in mind Billing Rates are only used if you track time in QuickBooks and use the Add Time/Costs window. You can use Price Levels and Billing Rates together. As always when setting Billing Rates or anything else in QuickBooks do a test run to make sure its setup right for you.

When you use Billing Rates with Price Levels and you invoice Clients with a fixed percentage price level, the adjustment is applied to the employees/attorneys billing rate. If the invoice is for a client with a per item price level the client price is always used. You can always adjust the rate on the invoice whenever you want.

Just a matter of caution, especially at first setting up Billing Rates and Price Levels, pay attention to the rates to your clients so that you don't bill out the wrong rates.

How to Setup Billing Rates
1. Click on the List from the top Main Menu Bar
2. Click the Billing Rate Level
3. Click on drop down Billing Rate Level box located at the bottom of the Billing Rate Level Screen
4. Choose New
5. Enter a Billing Rate Level Name. In this case we are assigning the name Paralegal.
6. Choose Fixed Hourly Rate if you want all services performed by employees/Paralegals with this billing rate to be billed at this rate.
7. Choose Custom Hourly Rate per Service Item if you want a different hourly rate for each Service Item performed by employees/Paralegals with this billing rate.
8. Click Ok when done. NOTE: Be sure to assign this Billing Rate to employees/attorneys. See how to on the next page.

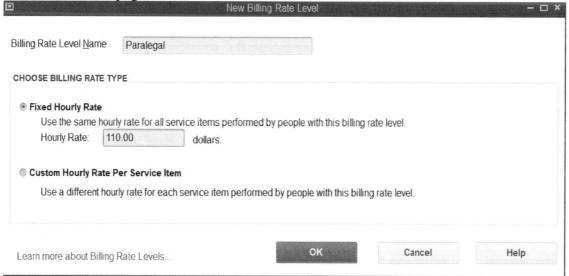

This feature is not available in the Pro Version of QuickBooks, so if you want this feature I recommend you upgrade to the Premier Professional Version for a Law Practice. When setup run a test to make sure your Billing Rates and Price Levels are working as needed.

Assign Billing Rates to Employees

How to assign Billing Rates to Employees/Attorneys

1. Click on Employees at the top of the Main Menu Bar
2. Choose Employee Center
3. Highlight and Double Click on the Employee to assign a Billing Rate Level.
4. Click on the Additional Info Tab
5. Click on the arrow for the drop down list next to Billing Rate Level and select Paralegal for this exercise.
6. Click Ok when done.

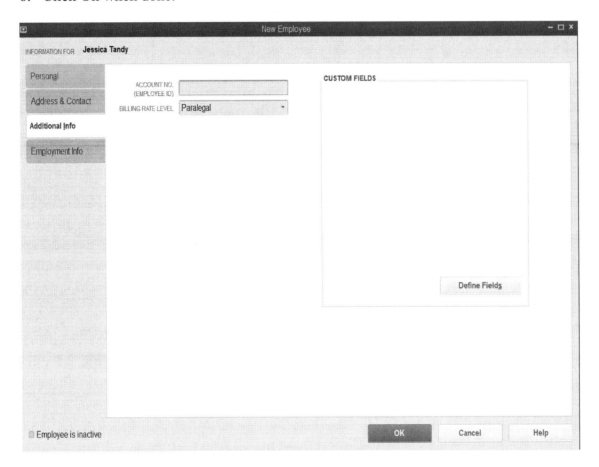

Chapter 6
Tracking Time

We are ready to tackle the Tracking Time feature to bill for your time or just track time spent on projects.

Tracking Time

Most Professionals are selling their time and knowledge. QuickBooks lets you track your time on Cases/Matters, and analyze your time by Client or case, the person who did the work, or by the type of work done.

You can enter time for an owner, partner, or employee. On the time entry form, you choose the client and case for which the work was done in the Customer: job field. You then select the service item, which represents the type of work you did. Later you can bill the charges to your client on statements or invoices, depending on which way you bill. You need to make sure time tracking is turned on in your Preferences.

QuickBooks offers an online time tracking solution that will allow employees to enter time online and it will pull into your company file.

Setting up Time for Employees

To track time in QuickBooks you need to setup employees, subcontractor, owner or partner.
1. Click on Employees from the top of the Main Menu Bar
2. Select Employee Center
3. Click on New Employee on the Icon Ribbon just above Employees Tab

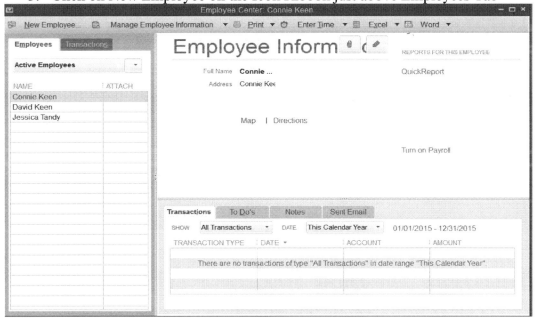

Fill out the personal information for the employee, continue through each tab filling out the necessary information. You don't have to fill in the payroll information if you are not planning to use QuickBooks for payroll.

Continue on filling out the information if you are using payroll and you may want to fill this in just to have each person in the company's information even if you don't use QuickBooks Payroll.

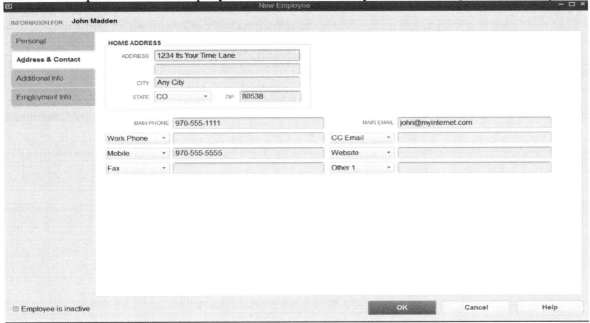

You can fill in all four tabs show to your left, Personal, Address & Contact, Additional Info and Employment Info even if you have Payroll turned off. If you want to run Payroll then you have to turn the feature on in Preferences and sign up for QuickBooks Payroll or, QuickBooks Online Payroll and you can even sign up for QuickBooks to take care of Full Payroll duties. Last but not least you can find someone like me, an accountant Pro Advisor to take care of Payroll and more for you.

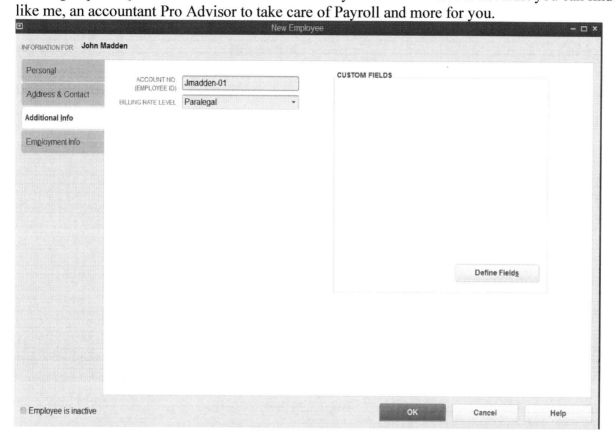

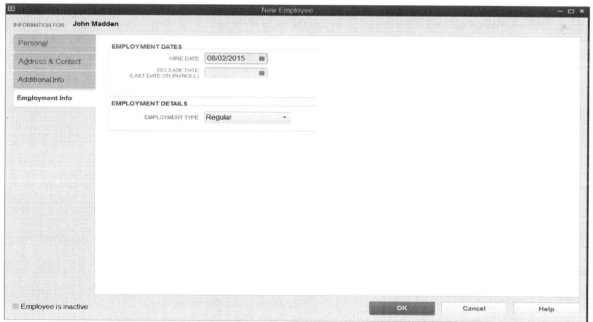

We will go through setting up Payroll in the next Chapter. We will finish Time Tracking in this chapter.

We are now ready to start entering time. You have two options of entering time and they are single activity form, this is for entering individual activities or you can use the weekly Timesheet. You can switch back and forth between both/either method at any given time. Always be sure to enter complete and accurate information as possible if you want your time to accurately and completely transfer to invoices and statements or show on reports.

Single Activity Form

Like everything the Single Activity way to enter time is great for some and the Weekly Timesheets will work better for others. The Single Time Activity are convenient to use if you will be continuously running QuickBooks, and entering each activity as you do it, rather than entering all your time at the end of the week from a paper timesheet. One bonus is you can see and enter more of your notes on the single time entry form.

1. Click on Enter Time from the Home Page in the Employees Section
2. Click Time/Enter Single Activity
3. Enter the date or make sure the date is correct.
4. Enter the Payroll Item and make sure the Billable box is checked (if this to be billed)
5. Enter Name
6. Center the Customer: Job
7. Enter Class if you are using Class Tracking
8. Enter the Service Item
9. Enter the time
10. Enter in the Notes the Description of the work you performed for this client to bill out.
11. Click the Save & Close Button when done or Click on Save & New if you are entering more time.

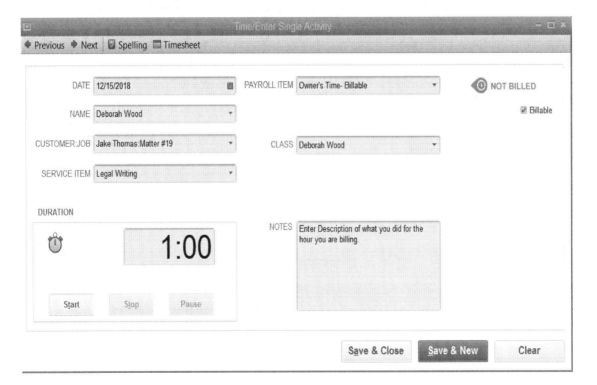

Weekly Timesheet

The weekly timesheet in QuickBooks is the way to go if you need and want to enter time at the end of each week or for a certain period, working from a paper time record.

1. Click on Enter Time on the Home Page under the Employees Section and select Weekly Timesheet.
2. Click on Name and enter the Employee name. You may need to change the date and if so click on the small calendar icon next to date.
3. Click on the Customer: Job and enter a client/Case.
4. Tab to Service Item and enter the item name if you know it and if not choose from the drop down list.
5. Tab to Notes and enter the work you performed for the time you are entering.
6. Tab over to Class and enter Class/Employee name
7. Tab over to the day of work performed and enter time worked.
8. Place a check mark in the Billable box if it's billable.
9. Continue until you have entered your time for this person for the week
10. Press save and close if finished or save and new if need to enter more Timesheets.

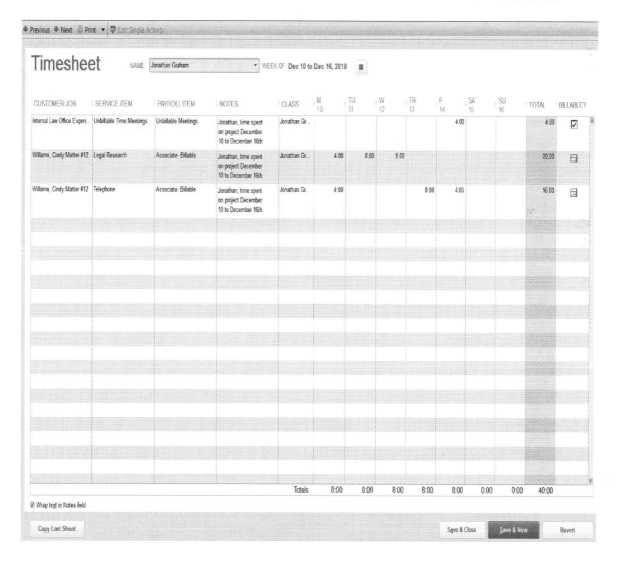

Reports on Time

By looking at this report you can see how much of time was spent on billable vs non-billable.

1. Click on Reports at the top Main Menu Bar
2. Select Jobs, Time & Mileage
3. Select Time by Item

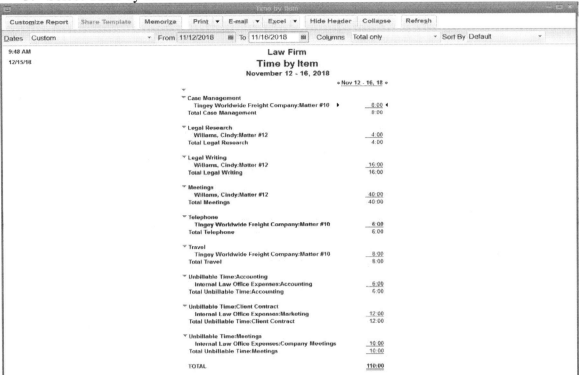

By clicking on Customize Report you can not only get the report by % of each service by placing a check in the % column option box or % of Row box. As you can see you have many more options to choose from to customize to your needs. Click OK when done.

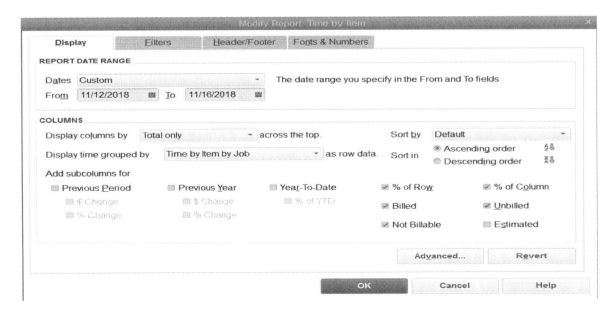

Memorize Report

Upon closing the customized report, a box will pop up asking if you want to memorize this report. If you click yes you can save time and be able to pull this new memorized report up anytime. If you do click yes it will give it the name Time by Item and you can leave as is or give it a different name or you can go back and rename it later.

To pull up your new memorized report or any other memorized reports, click on Reports, then Memorized Reports. The new report will be listed. Later in the book I will show you how you can create report groups, like Time Reports, Billing Reports or Income Reports. Once you have a report like you want it then memorizing them and putting into groups will save you so much time.

If you happen to have the Professional or Premier editions of QuickBooks you can go into Reports and find Memorized Reports to see some pre-setup reports they have designed for the Professional Services. I highly recommend looking at these reports to see if they can help you with your Practice. You can even tweak them.

Here is the memorized Report List in the Accountant Edition geared to Law Practices. What great reports already set up, so be sure to check it out if your edition offers this.

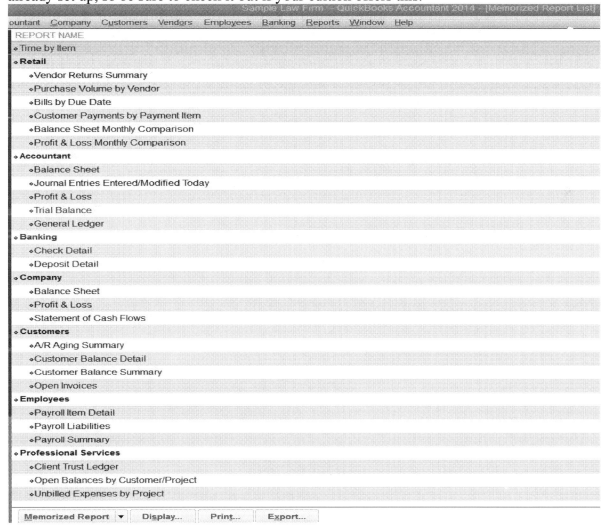

Employee Reports

In the previous examples we ran a report on Time by Item with billable and non-billable. Now we are going to create a report to see what cases your employees are working on.

1. Click on Reports from the top Main Menu Bar.
2. Select Jobs, Time & Mileage
3. Choose Time by Name.

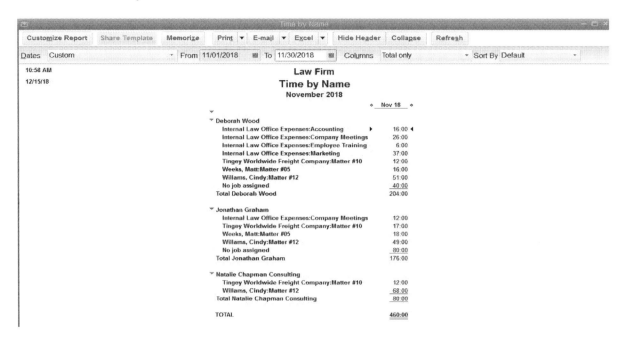

You can modify this report by clicking on the button Customize Report in the top left of the report screen. As you can see by this screen shot you have many ways to change this report to your needs. Remember to memorize it if you want after you have made your changes.

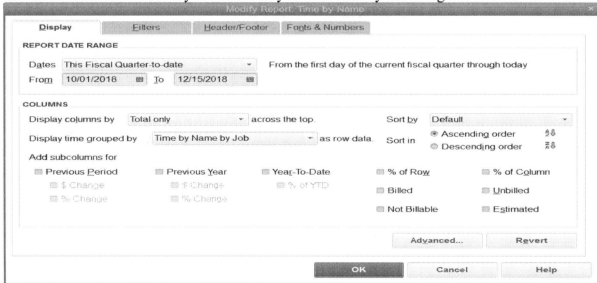

There are more reports to create/run such as Time by Job. To run this report Click on Reports, Jobs, Time & Mileage, and then select Tim by Job Summary or Details. You can customize this report as well and memorize it too.

Client Reports

Reports on Clients is a great report as well to have at your fingertips.

1. Click on Reports at the top Main Menu Bar
2. Click on Jobs, Time & Mileage
3. Select Time by Job Detail

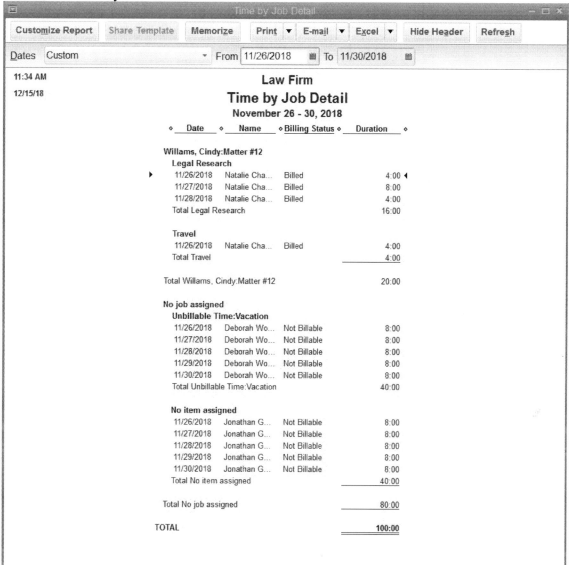

Let's say you want to print out just one case you can do that. To print out one case just double click on the Total under the particular case you want to print. Then click the print button to print on a printer or you can save as a PDF for your files or email.

This report, as all or most reports, can be customized. For this report let's say you want to include the notes for the client, you can do that.

Screen shot for the customizing the client report to add Notes. See how I placed the check mark next to notes?

Here's the report with the notes added. If the notes column does not show the full line just adjust your diamond icons next to each heading.

Here's the report for Total on one case for a certain time frame, double click on the total in report.

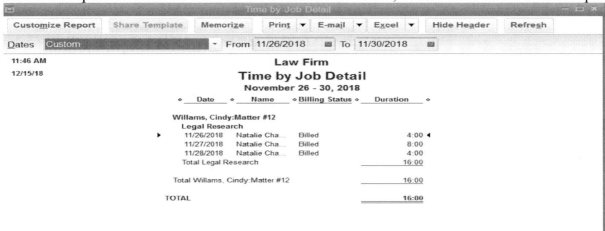

Unbilled Time Report

Another great report to have at your fingertips is a report solely for Unbilled Time. This will help you stay on top of being sure all your services get billed in a timely manner.

1. Click on Reports at the top Main Menu Bar
2. Click Jobs, Time and Mileage
3. Click Time by Item
4. Click Customize Report at the top left of report screen
5. Place a checkmark next to the Unbilled and click ok.
6. Change dates to the dates you need.
7. Memorize this to save time.

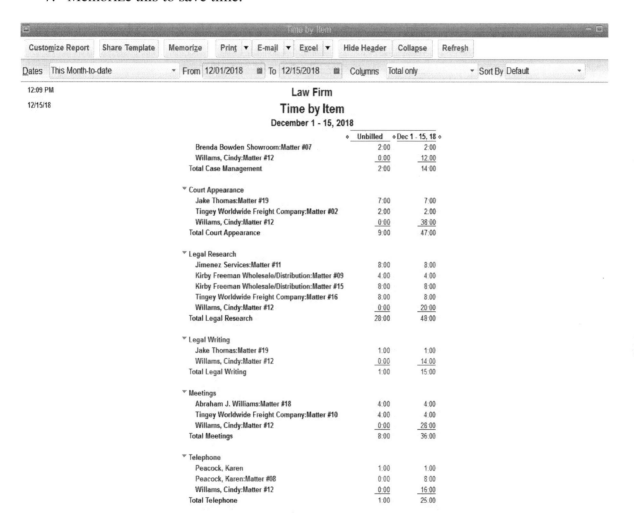

Reports for Unbilled Time for Clients

This is another great report to have at your fingertips.

1. Click on Reports at the top of the Main Menu Bar
2. Select Jobs, Time & Mileage
3. Select Time by Job Detail.
4. Click the Customize Report button in the top of the Report screen
5. Click on the Filters tab
6. Click on Billing Status and select unbilled, see in the screenshot below.
7. Click OK

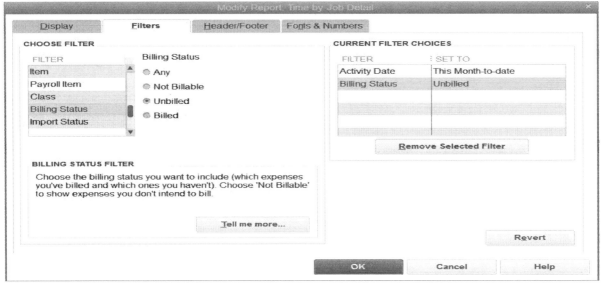

Here's the Report. It's a short report, but I chose custom date for 1 week. You can use this report to create invoices. Change the dates to include all dates and memorize this report as Unbilled Time.

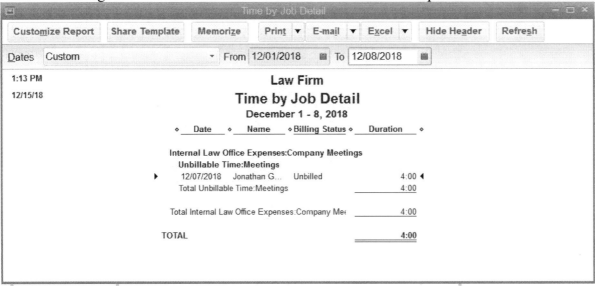

Note: By figuring out the Reports you need and work with if you will memorize these then all you have to do is go straight to your memorized reports instead of all the other steps. This means more time for other things.

Chapter 7
Payroll

I will take you through setting up Payroll and all the options QuickBooks has to offer for Payroll. There are several options. If you use QuickBooks for any of these options you will have to sign up and pay for QuickBooks Payroll. I will tell you it's worth it to go with any of their options. The Three options are Basic, Enhanced or Full Service and they are as follows.

- You can run all of your payroll yourself with the Desktop version or the online version
- You can run all of your payroll yourself except let QuickBooks Run your Tax Reports and pay your employment taxes.
- You can let QuickBooks Run your whole payroll including Tax Reporting and pay your employment taxes. Full Service Payroll and you enter the hours.
- You could hire someone like me, Accountant QuickBooks Pro Advisor, as well.

How to setup and run Payroll from QuickBooks

1. Click on Employees at the top of the Main Menu Bar
2. Click on Payroll Center
3. Click on the Preferences tab on the Payroll Center Icon Ribbon on top right to make sure your payroll is turned on. Seen the Screenshot on the next page for your options.

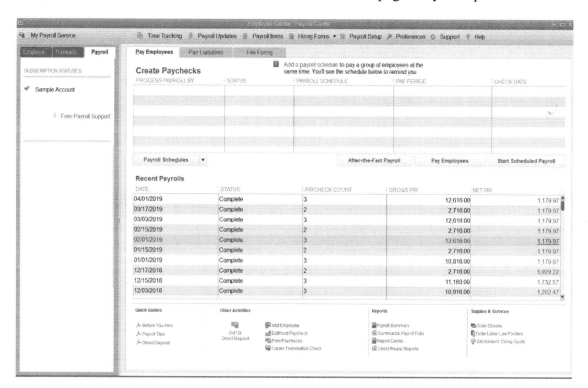

Here's the payroll preference window and as you can see you have three choices to make, Full Payroll, No Payroll or online Payroll. For this payroll exercise I chose Full Payroll. Once you have selected your options then click ok.

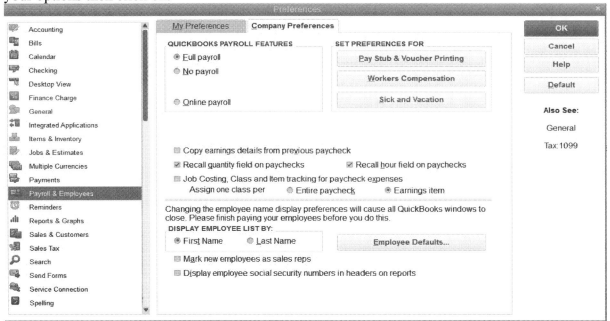

Next step is to sign up for QuickBooks Payroll. The best way to do this and to look at your options, talk with someone over the phone or chat on line is to click on the Support button on the Payroll center open screen. The Support Icon is on the upper right top in the Icon Bar on the Payroll Center screen. This will take you to Payroll signup and support. You can choose your options, talk to someone and signup.

Here's the support screen. Click on Payroll Services at the top of the menu and click on Compare Products. See on the Next Screen the products.

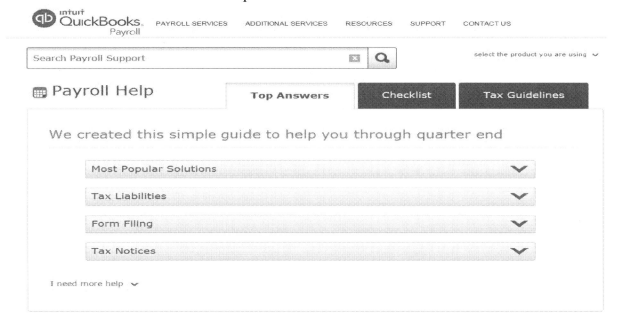

This task may look daunting, but it's not as bad as you think. There are a fair amount of steps to take, but once you are setup it is easy and fast. The hardest part is making sure your payroll/timesheets are correct after you are setup and going.

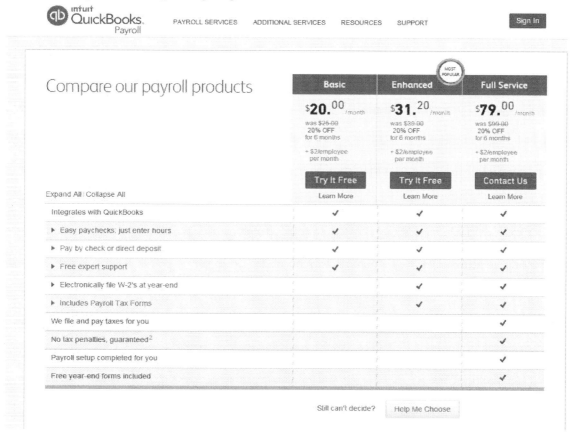

1. Once you have made you selection and paid for your payroll service you will receive a Payroll key that you will need to activate it within QuickBooks. I chose the Enhanced Service, since I am doing my full payroll.
2. Click on Employees at the top of the Main Menu Bar
3. Select My Payroll Service
4. Choose Activate Service Key
5. Click Add and enter the your Payroll Service Key Number
6. Click next and follow the prompts and finish.
7. Last step before starting the actual Payroll Setup is to make sure QuickBooks Update is turned on. See the next page.

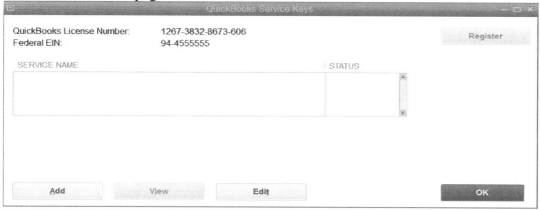

To turn on Payroll Updates and make sure Payroll is up-to-date
1. Click on Help at the top of the Main Menu Bar
2. Select Update QuickBooks
3. Choose the Options tab as shown below
4. Click the Mark All Button to sign up for all the payroll updates
5. Click Save
6.

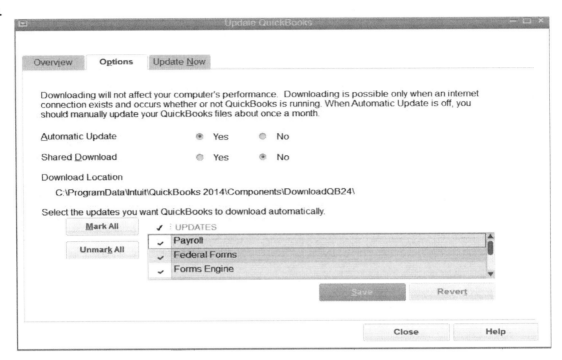

Click on the Update Now tab as shown below. Click on the Button Get Updates. You have to wait for all the updates to down load. Once the updates are done then click close and you are ready for Payroll Setup.

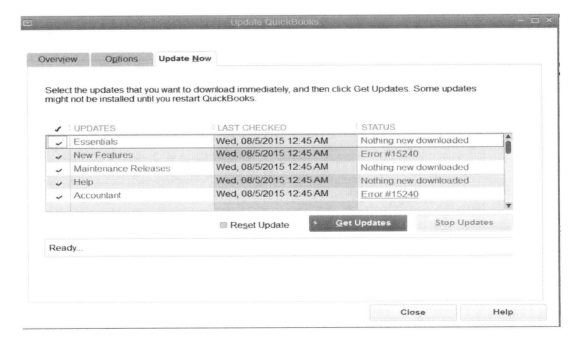

Payroll Setup

We are now ready to setup up your Company Payroll. You have turned the payroll feature on in the Preferences, you went online/called/signed up for Payroll. You activated your Payroll Service Key and you turned your payroll updates on, downloaded to latest updates. Now take the following steps.

1. Click on Employees at the top of the Main Menu Bar
2. Click on Payroll Center (this is if you closed out the window before and if you didn't then you are already ready to this point)
3. Click Payroll Setup in the Icon bar in your Payroll Center screen.
4. Click Continue and follow the prompts in the introduction.

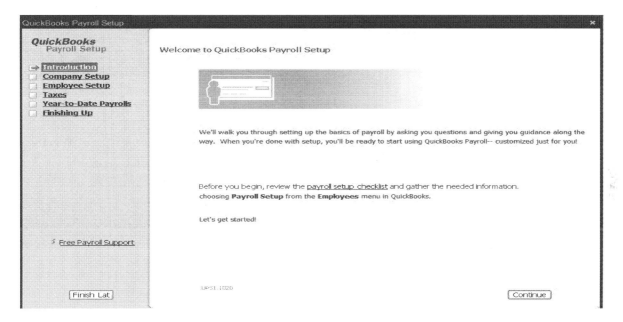

After clicking Continue on this first screen and clicked continue on the next screen the following screen came up. You need to make sure your accounts look right. You can see the buttons on the bottom left of your screen you can add, edit or delete. Once you made your changes, if any, click continue.

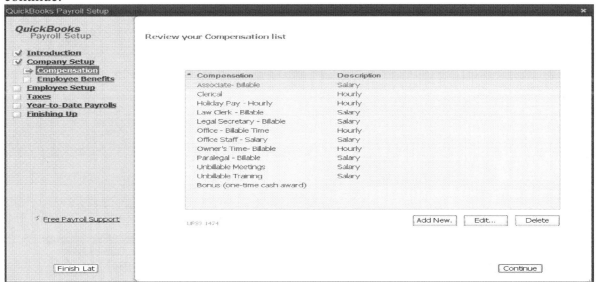

Employee Benefits

Read and follow the Employee Benefits and click on Continue. You will need to have a liability account and other accounts you will notice as you go through setup. If you go through setup and decide you need to set up accounts you can hit the finish later button in the bottom left hand of your screen. Each state has different laws and rules to abide by, so you will need to know these laws and since they are all different I can't begin to cover that plus laws change. Either talk to your CPA, or get help from QuickBooks Payroll support if you need it. For the sake of this exercise let's click continue to go through all the setup process.

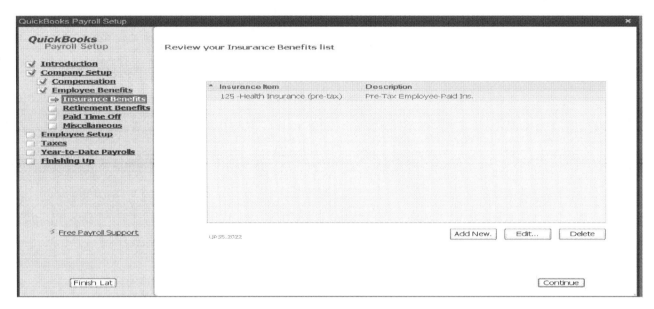

As you can see the Retirement Benefits has a 401(k) set up. Here again each company has different benefits and you will need to go through the steps to set this up. Your CPA or QuickBooks Payroll support can help with this process if you need it. It's not a bad idea once you are setup to have your CPA check everything out to be sure you have it setup properly just as a precaution measure. Click Continue.

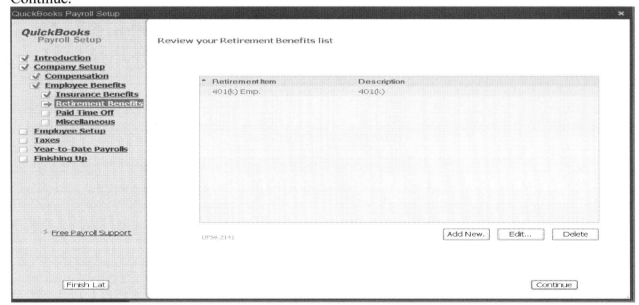

Paid Time Off in Payroll

Here again this is all different with each company and you will need to enter your company's paid time off data. Look at the accounts and even if they look right you need to click on the Edit Button to check out the information and if the Description on your screen looks right then click continue.

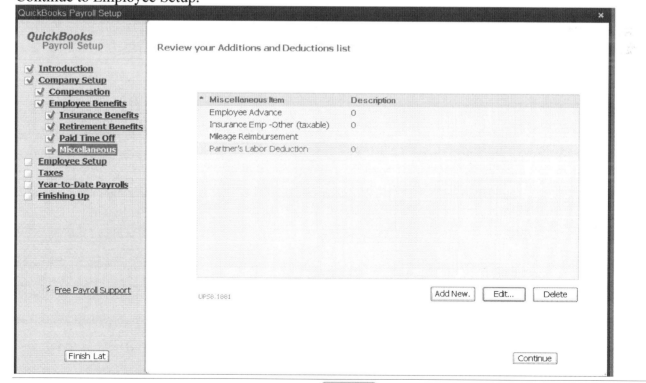

Here's the miscellaneous setup. Check it out and if it's right or you make changes then when done click Continue to Employee Setup.

Employee Setup in Payroll

Click Continue to the Employee Setup and read the prompts then click continue. The next screen should look like this other than your employees will be different since this is a sample company.

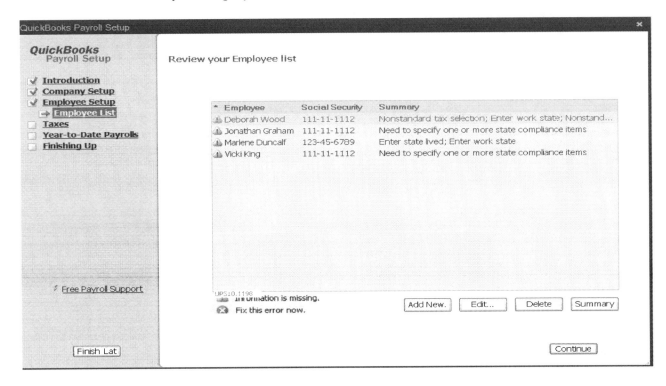

Notice at the bottom of this screen it says information missing fix this error now. Either click the Edit button or double click on the employee(s) needing updating. If you haven't entered any employees then just hit add new now. Once done click continue.

This is the Next Screen for Taxes. Read and click Continue

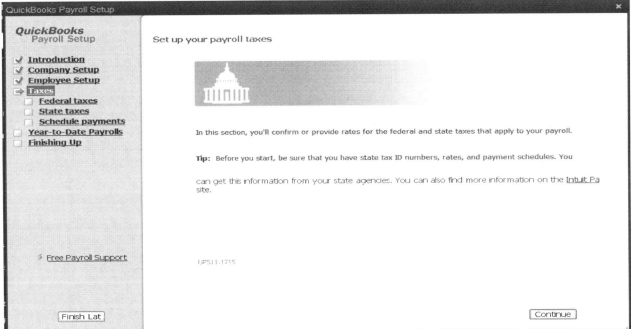

Setup Taxes in Payroll

After clicking continue this is the next screen. If everything looks right click Continue if not click on what needs editing and click the edit button. When done Click Continue.

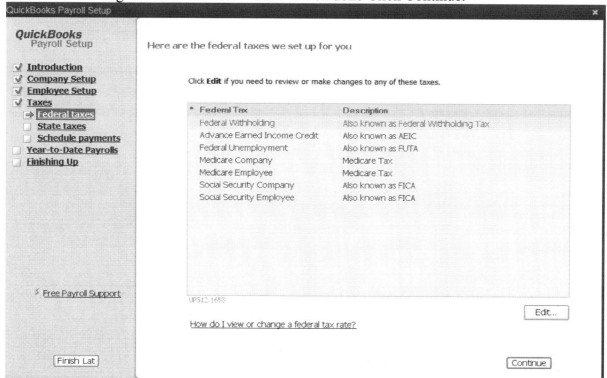

Here's the screen for your state Taxes. Here again all States are different, so check to make sure your state tax information is correct. Make any and all necessary changes, if any, and click Continue.

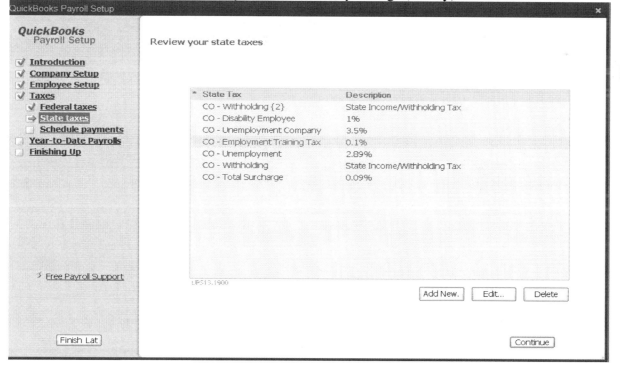

Payroll Scheduled Payments

This is where you set up the dates, and liability payments to be made monthly, quarterly and annually. If everything looks ok Click Continue and if not make the necessary changes and click Continue.

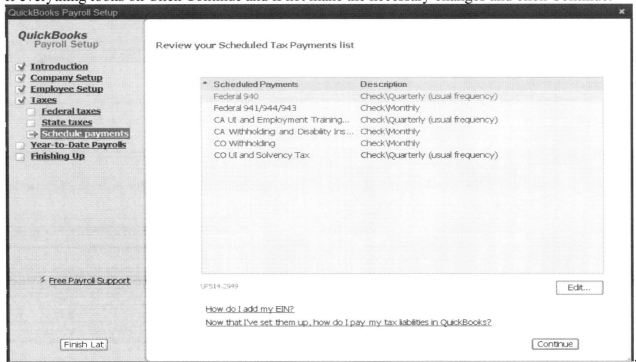

This has to do with your Year-to-date Payroll. This is where maybe you are setting up QuickBooks in the middle of the year and you need to enter months of previous payroll for the current year. Read and Click Continue.

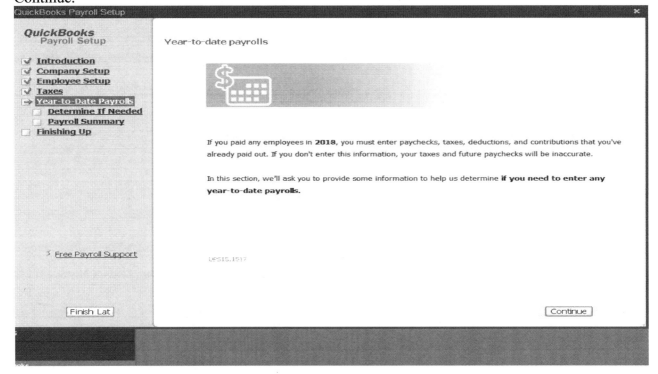

Here is asks if you have issued paychecks this year, so give the correct answer and click Continue.

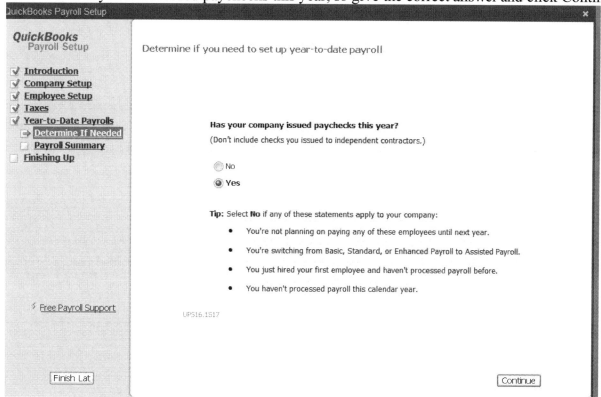

Here is where you will enter your historical payroll. It's on like a spreadsheet. Click edit and it gives you step by step instructions. You will want to enter any tax payments as well. When done click continue.

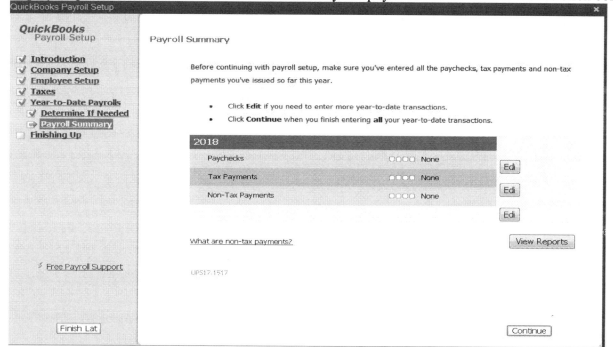

You have finished payroll setup. Click button, Go to Payroll Center.

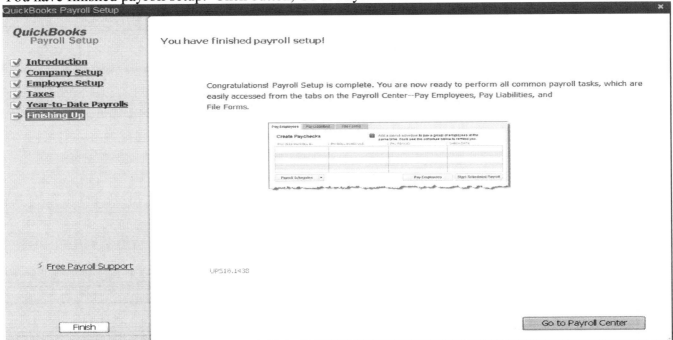

Setting up Payroll Schedule

Click on the link, add a payroll schedule in the middle of the screen to the right of the Create paychecks heading.

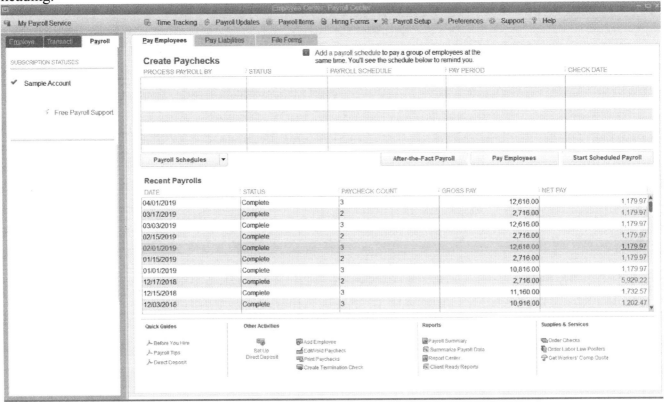

This is what it looks like after setting up a schedule. Click ok when done. If you need to set up more click on the drop down tab that says Payroll Schedules and select new. If you need to edit a schedule just highlight the schedule to Edit and click on the Payroll Schedules drop down list and click edit or delete if you need to delete a schedule.

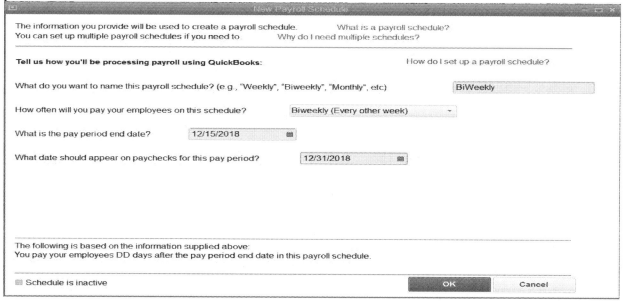

Setup Payroll schedule in Each Employee File

1. Click on Employees at the top of the Main Menu Bar
2. Select Employee Center
3. If the Employees Tab is not clicked on then click on the Employees Tab
4. Highlight the first employee and double click their file open
5. Go to the Payroll Info Tab and pull down the drop down list next to the Payroll Schedule Tab and select the schedule for the employee.
6. Enter any other pertinent information that you may still need to enter and click ok
7. Continue steps 4 through 6 until all employees are on a schedule that need to be and that all pertinent information is entered and click ok.

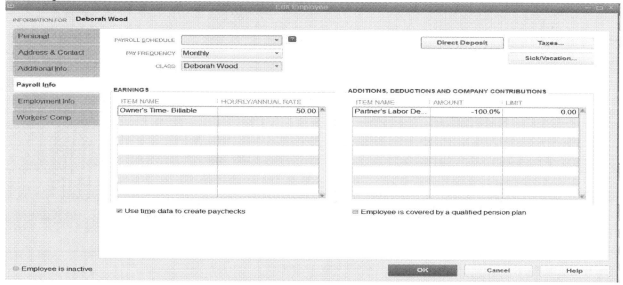

Pay Employees

The last chapter we did Time Tracking. Enter your time and we will pay the employees. If you are not using a sample file you can use a sample file to go through this exercise or come back when you're ready to run paychecks.

1. Click on Employees at the top of the Main Menu Bar
2. Select Pay Employees then choose Scheduled Payroll
3. Click on Scheduled Payroll and click continue
4. If everything looks right Click Continue
5. Click Create Paychecks. Click on Print now or Print Later.

Pay Liabilities

Check to see if you have any Payroll taxes due that need to be paid. Let's say the top entry in tax liabilities needs to be paid, so place a check mart next to the top line, select view/Pay. If everything looks ok then click button save and close. Print checks or close and print later. Run Reports that you need and you are done with payroll.

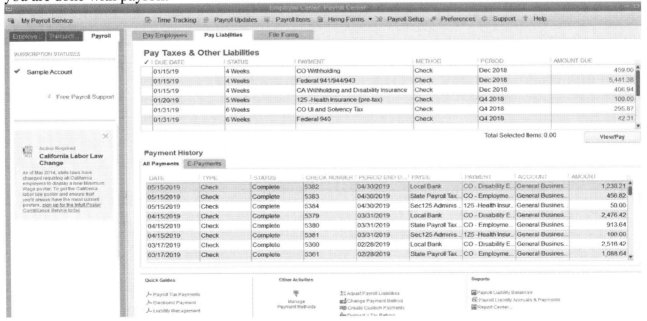

Other Payroll Options

This is the Employees Section on the Home Page. As you can see the Process Payroll Forms below. This is to file and pay, depending on your schedule, taxes for Quarterly, Monthly or Annually.

Employee Forms is another good source. To access them see instructions below.

1. Click on Employees at the top of the Main Menu Bar.
2. Select Employee Forms
3. Employee forms consist of Federal I9, Federal W-4 and Federal W-9 (1099 Vendors) and Direct Deposit Authorization
4. You need each employee to fill out the Federal I9 and Federal W-9 forms. If you want to set up direct deposit then they need to fill out the Direct Deposit Authorization form too.

Edit/Void Paychecks

If you need to void or edit a paycheck do the following
1. Click on Employees at the top Main Menu Bar
2. Click Edit/Void Paychecks and the following window will come up. If the check you want to void or edit is not in the window, then go to your employee and pull it up that way.
3. Click Void on Highlighted check and it voids it right away.
4. Highlight employee you want to edit and Click Edit. Then Click Paycheck Detail Button and make your changes. Click on unlock net pay or Enter Net/Calculate gross and make your changes and click ok. Click done when you're done.

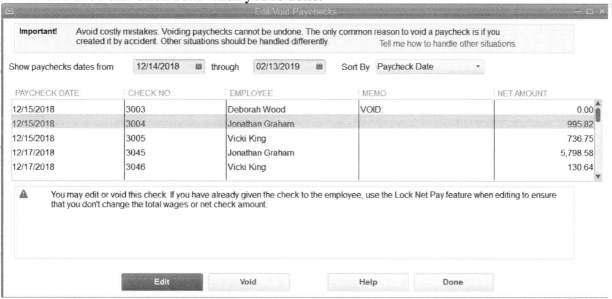

Payroll Items

We didn't cover Payroll Items here because you should have setup them up during setup and the rest of them when you enrolled in Payroll. Here is the list of Payroll Items in my Sample Company File. This needs to be done before running any paychecks if you did not do this.

To Access this list, Edit, add or delete or modify in any way do the following.

1. Click on Lists and the top Main Menu Bar
2. Select Payroll Item Lists
3. Bottom of the Screen select the drop down list Payroll Item and make your selection of New or Edit or whatever your needs are.

ITEM NAME	TYPE	AMOUNT	LIMIT	TAX TRACKING	PAYABLE TO	ACCOUNT ID
Associate- Billable	Yearly Salary			Compensation		
Law Clerk - Billable	Yearly Salary			Compensation		
Legal Secretary - Billable	Yearly Salary			Compensation		
Office Staff - Salary	Yearly Salary			Compensation		
Paralegal - Billable	Yearly Salary			Compensation		
Sick - Salary	Yearly Salary			Compensation		
Unbillable Meetings	Yearly Salary			Compensation		
Unbillable Training	Yearly Salary			Compensation		
Vacation - Salary	Yearly Salary			Compensation		
Clerical	Hourly Wage			Compensation		
Holiday Pay - Hourly	Hourly Wage			Compensation		
Office - Billable Time	Hourly Wage			Compensation		
Owner's Time- Billable	Hourly Wage			Compensation		
Sick - Hourly	Hourly Wage			Compensation		
Vacation - Hourly	Hourly Wage			Compensation		
Bonus (one-time cash award)	Addition	0.00		Compensation		
Employee Advance	Addition	0.00		None		
Mileage Reimbursement	Addition	0.00		None		
125 -Health Insurance (pre-tax)	Deduction	0.00		Premium Only/125	Sec125 Administrator	Acct# 870547
401(k) Emp.	Deduction	0.00		401(k)	401K Administrator	45632010
Insurance Emp -Other (taxable)	Deduction	0.00		None		
Partner's Labor Deduction	Deduction	0.00		Other		
Advance Earned Income Credit	Federal Tax			Advance EIC Payment	Local Bank	94-4555555
Federal Unemployment	Federal Tax	0.6%	7,000.00	FUTA	Local Bank	94-4555555
Federal Withholding	Federal Tax			Federal	Local Bank	94-4555555
Medicare Company	Federal Tax	1.45%		Comp. Medicare	Local Bank	94-4555555
Medicare Employee	Federal Tax	1.45%		Medicare	Local Bank	94-4555555
Social Security Company	Federal Tax	6.2%	113,700.00	Comp. SS Tax	Local Bank	94-4555555
Social Security Employee	Federal Tax	6.2%	-113,700.00	SS Tax	Local Bank	94-4555555
CO - Withholding	State Withholding Tax			SWH	Colorado Department of Revenue	88254625
CO - Withholding {2}	State Withholding Tax			SWH	State Payroll Tax Agency	501-2683-2
CO - Disability Employee	State Disability Tax	1.0%	-100,880.00	SDI	State Payroll Tax Agency	501-2683-2
CO - Unemployment	State Unemployment Tax	2.89%	11,300.00	Comp. SUI	Colorado State Treasurer	125896 69-3
CO - Unemployment Company	State Unemployment Tax	3.5%	7,000.00	Comp. SUI	State Payroll Tax Agency	856-6593-2

Payroll Item ▼   Activities ▼   Reports ▼   ☐ Include inactive

Chapter 8
Client Billing

In this chapter we will go over Client Billing. You will learn how to bill a client and the options you have. You have to options with QuickBooks for attorneys to bill clients. The two options are the invoicing or billing with Statements. I have found that most of my attorney clients prefer the Statement charge way for billing their clients. The reason they like it is you can print a statement for a time frame. However, even if you invoice you can send statements as a reminder to pay your bill. It all depends on your needs.

Invoicing

Invoicing used to be used if you charged a flat rate for services and if you bill for your time, but not anymore. You can bill for different rates, you just need to upgrade to Premier Professional services edition. You can bill choosing Time & Expenses or Create Invoice and if you have Pro version Create Invoice is what will come up. If you have the Premier edition and it does not come up the way I explained be sure to check your preferences to make sure they are turned on. Go to Edit, then Preferences and Time & Expense and choose the option to create invoices from a list of time and expenses. See Screen below.

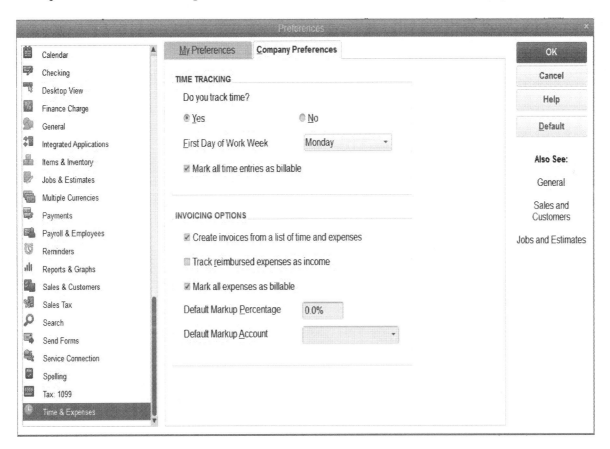

As you can see with this screen you have other options. Choose your options then click ok when done. See the next page for creating invoices by Time and Expenses.

Invoice for Time and Expenses

Here's Screen shot for Invoice for Time & Expenses. You can see this will have other expenses along with Mileage. At the bottom of the screen is a box you can check to let you select specific billables for this Customer: Job.
1. Choose the client you want to bill for.
2. After making choice then click the create invoice button at the bottom of the screen.

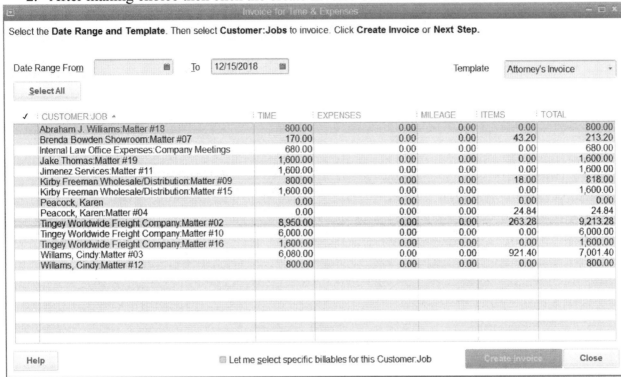

Here's an invoice created by Time & Expenses. You can modify this invoice if needed. You can add additional information. We will now print this invoice, see on next page. As you can see just above the invoice in the Icon Ribbon Bar there is a print button, so click on that and choose print.

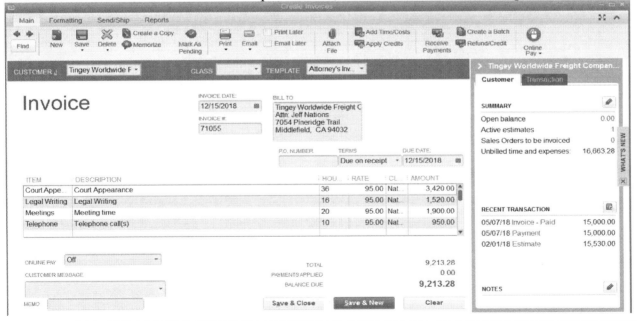

I selected Preview and this is a good idea to make sure it looks like you want. If it's all good click on the print button and print how many copies you need.

Print	Prev page	Next page	Zoom In	Help	Close

Law Firm
110 Sampson Way
Middlefield, CA 94521

Invoice

Invoice #:	71055
Invoice Date:	12/15/2018
Due Date:	12/15/2018
Case:	Matter #02
P.O. Number:	

Bill To:

Tingey Worldwide Freight Company
Attn: Jeff Nations
7054 Pineridge Trail
Middlefield, CA 94032

Description	Hours/Qty	Rate	Amount
Court Appearance	36	95.00	3,420.00
Legal Writing	16	95.00	1,520.00
Meeting time	20	95.00	1,900.00
Telephone call(s)	10	95.00	950.00
Legal Research	8	95.00	760.00
Court Appearance	2	200.00	400.00
Overnight Mail/Fed Ex/ Airborne etc.	1	15.00	15.00
Filing and court fees	1	35.00	35.00
Overnight Mail/Fed Ex/ Airborne etc.	1	12.00	12.00
Filing and court fees	1	60.00	60.00
Filing and court fees	1	45.00	45.00
Overnight Mail/Fed Ex/ Airborne etc.	1	12.00	12.00
Mileage reimbursement	123	0.36	44.28
Filing and court fees	1	40.00	40.00

Total	$9,213.28
Payments/Credits	$0.00
Balance Due	$9,213.28

We will now bill more than one client, do batch Invoices. See on the next page.

Batch Invoicing - Invoice for Time & Expenses

You can create one, two or many, including all you have ready for invoicing this well. Click on the button that says Invoices, choose Invoice for Time & Expenses.

This screen comes up next. Select Clients to bill and click button Next Step located bottom of screen.

This screen comes up after client to invoice selection. You can Edit or Review if needed. If everything looks ok then click on button Create Invoices.

After you hit Create Invoices the screen will be this screen. If you do not have each client set up in their personal file to mail or email and it's left to none then you will have to go to File, Print Forms, and Print Invoices to print the ones that didn't get printed.

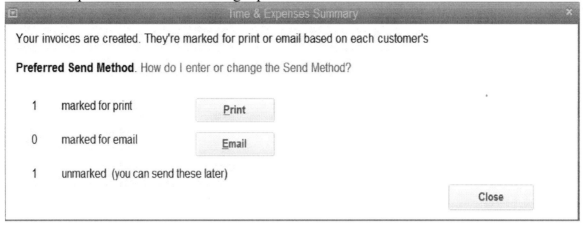

1. Click on Customers at the top of the Main Menu Bar
2. Click on Customer Center
3. Double Click on a Client to pull up their file. Click on each Job under your client.
4. Click on Payment Settings Tab.
5. See Preferred Delivery method? It shows none. This needs to be changed to Mail or E-Mail. If you set to Mail this will print right away if you choose to print instead of going to the print later file. If your client decides they want it emailed you can change this at that time.
6. Click Ok when you are finished.

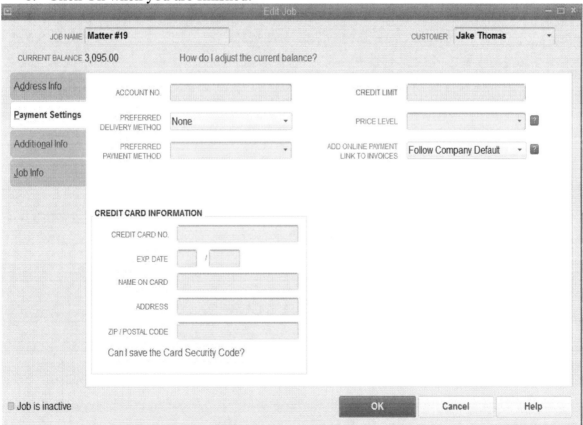

Create Invoices - Single Invoice at a time.

We are now going to create an invoice by clicking on Invoices and selecting Create Invoices as shown below where the red arrow is.

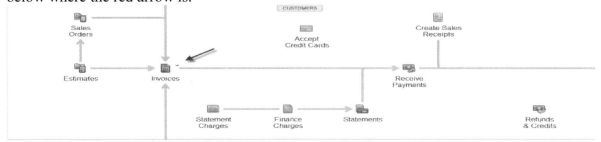

This screen comes up after selection Create Invoices. Go to the Customer Job drop down box and choose a client to bill.

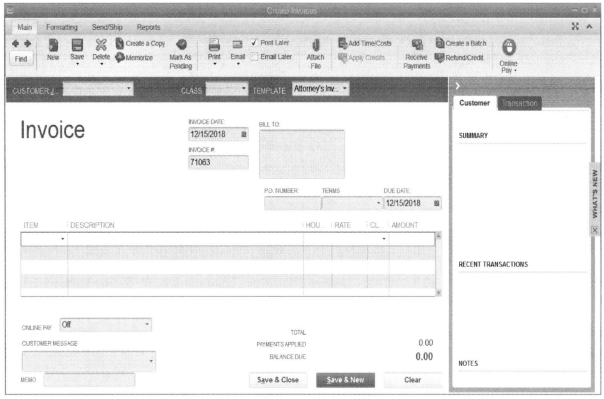

This screen will pop up. You have two choices. Make your choice and click ok.

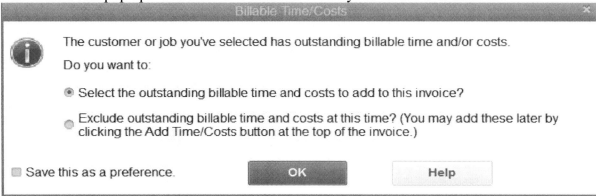

After clicking ok from the previous screen this is your next screen. Select items, by placing a check mark by each line, you want to bill out for. If you have expenses and mileage and other items you can bill for that right now too. To bill out for expenses, mileage or items, just click on each tab and do the same thing as you are for the Time.

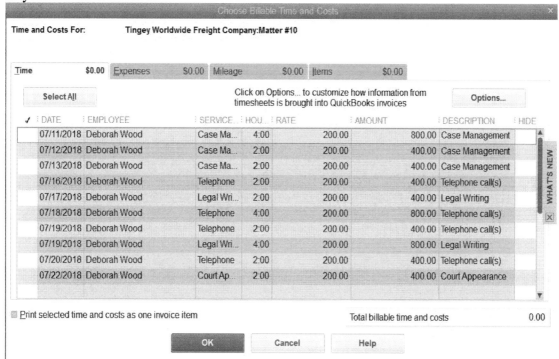

You may want to group your time/items by activity type or maybe by the service such as Legal Research. You have total control on how your invoices look by having it setup properly and deciding how you want it. It's always a good idea, if you don't know, to test drive some of these options. A great way is use the Sample Law File that comes with your QuickBooks Desktop Program.

I just billed out the case management hours. This is just a quick example of ways to invoice.

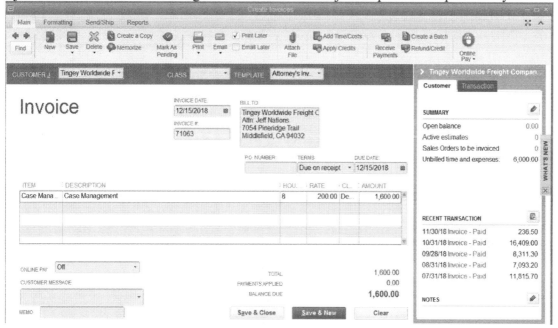

You can add subtotal at the bottom of a section(s) to total each group if you want to. See Below.

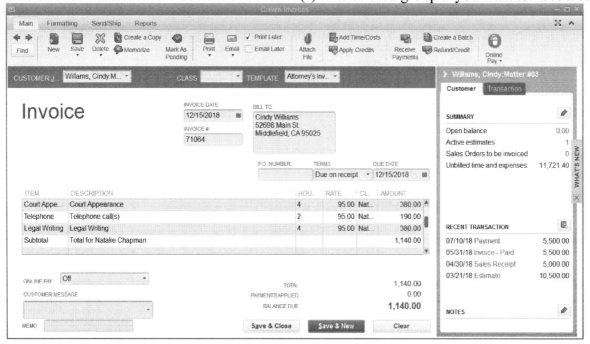

See Invoice with subtotaled by groups

Law Firm
110 Sampson Way
Middlefield, CA 94521

Invoice

Invoice #: 71064
Invoice Date: 12/15/2018
Due Date: 12/15/2018
Case: Matter #03
P.O. Number:

Bill To:
Cindy Williams
52698 Main St.
Middlefield, CA 95025

Description	Hours/Qty	Rate	Amount
Legal Research	2	95.00	190.00
Consulting meeting with client			
Court Appearance	4	95.00	380.00
Consulting meeting with client			
Telephone call(s)	2	95.00	190.00
Consulting meeting with client			
Legal Writing	4	95.00	380.00
Consulting meeting with client			
Total For Natalie Chapman			1,140.00
Legal Research	4	65.00	260.00
Legal Research on Project			
Legal Research	4	65.00	260.00
Legal Research on Project			
Legal Research	6	65.00	390.00
Legal Research on Project			
Legal Research	5	65.00	325.00
Legal Research on Project			
Legal Research	6	65.00	390.00
Legal Research on Project			
Total for Vicki King			1,625.00

Total	$2,765.00
Payments/Credits	$0.00
Balance Due	$2,765.00

Here is an example of the same invoice, but with added and grouped reimbursable Expenses.

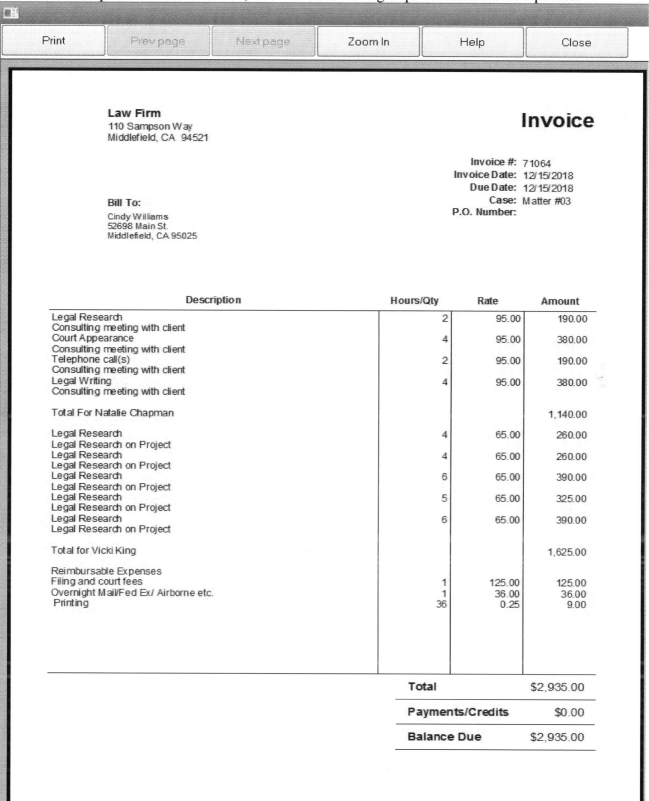

| Print | Prev page | Next page | Zoom In | Help | Close |

Law Firm
110 Sampson Way
Middlefield, CA 94521

Invoice

Invoice #:	71064
Invoice Date:	12/15/2018
Due Date:	12/15/2018
Case:	Matter #03
P.O. Number:	

Bill To:
Cindy Williams
52698 Main St.
Middlefield, CA 95025

Description	Hours/Qty	Rate	Amount
Legal Research	2	95.00	190.00
Consulting meeting with client			
Court Appearance	4	95.00	380.00
Consulting meeting with client			
Telephone call(s)	2	95.00	190.00
Consulting meeting with client			
Legal Writing	4	95.00	380.00
Consulting meeting with client			
Total For Natalie Chapman			1,140.00
Legal Research	4	65.00	260.00
Legal Research on Project			
Legal Research	4	65.00	260.00
Legal Research on Project			
Legal Research	6	65.00	390.00
Legal Research on Project			
Legal Research	5	65.00	325.00
Legal Research on Project			
Legal Research	6	65.00	390.00
Legal Research on Project			
Total for Vicki King			1,625.00
Reimbursable Expenses			
Filing and court fees	1	125.00	125.00
Overnight Mail/Fed Ex/ Airborne etc.	1	36.00	36.00
Printing	36	0.25	9.00

Total	$2,935.00
Payments/Credits	$0.00
Balance Due	$2,935.00

Flat Fee Invoicing

Creating a flat fee invoice is really simple. Say you have many services like you charge 400 for a Will drawn up or you charge 900 for a Bankruptcy. Here's how to do that.

Home Page for customers

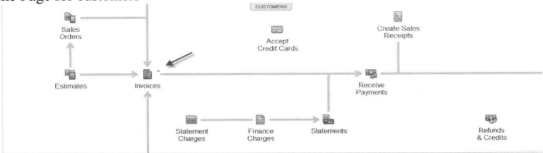

1. Click on the Invoices button like shown above on the home page. Click on Create Invoices
2. Type in the Clients name in Customer: Job box. If your client is not in your customer list then you can quick add or you can choose setup customer. Quick add just adds the name whereas setup opens the screen to add name, address and other pertinent information.
3. Click on the item area and choose Legal Fees or something like I did, Bankruptcy. Note how the description and rate are already filled in? It's because it was setup as an Item.
4. Type in 1 in the Quantity/Hours field.
5. Print or email now or later and save and close or save and new if you are billing more.

Remember if you are going to use jobs/cases/matters for your clients you need to choose the job/case/matter for the client in the customer job box when creating invoices.

Notice the Print and email buttons in the Icon Bar along with the Print later and Email later, so you can email or print now or later in batch's. The invoice can be saved as a PDF to attach to emails. If you are emailing be sure to have set up your company email address and the email address of your client. QuickBooks will send it through Outlook or default email account.

Here's a Flat Fee Invoice

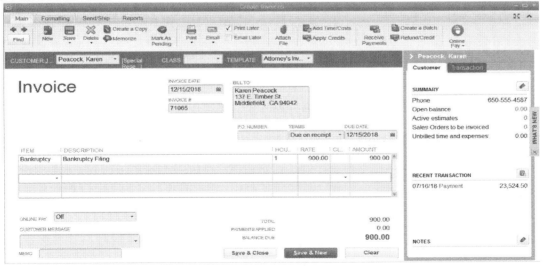

Setting up Payment plans with Invoicing

You may, probably do, have clients that have to pay you weekly, biweekly or monthly. Let's say they are going to pay 1,000 down and 1,000 biweekly until they have paid you 10,000 to have you represent them. We are going to bill 1,000 now and create the remaining invoices individually with the date that they are due to make a payment. Use the terms as Due Upon receipt. This will allow you to create an aging report in the future so you can forecast what is coming in that month and even months.

Here's the invoice for down payment.

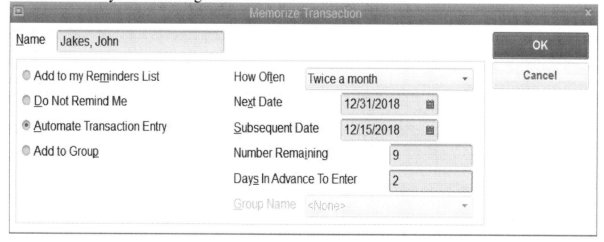

Here's copy of the memorized invoice to come due twice a month for nine more invoices until he has 10,000 in his trust account to have enough for legal representation. This is just a sample and there are multitude of ways to use this great feature.

Printing Invoices

We have hit and missed on Printing, so I will go over the ways to print your invoices.

1. Click on the print button on the invoice to print it right at the time you create an invoice.
2. Print later by placing check mark in the box that says Print Later.
3. Printing later. Click File then Print Forms and choose Invoices then select all or choose which ones you want to print now.

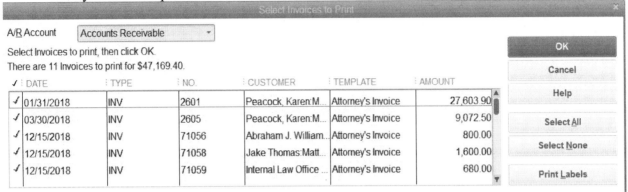

E-mailing Invoices

This invoice/email was generated by QuickBooks and you can edit the content in the email. It also, as you can see, attached the QuickBooks generated invoice.

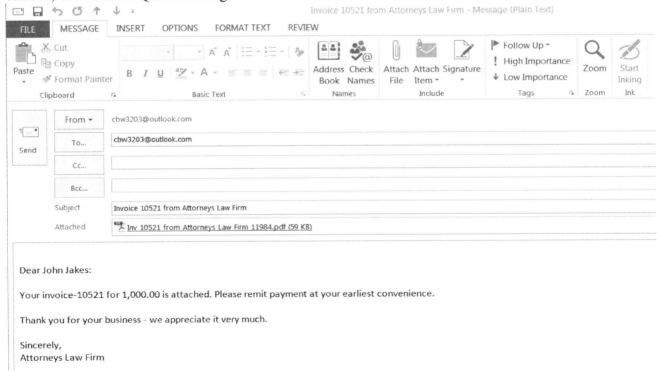

 To email just check this box on the ribbon to email later or don't check it and click on the email button with the icon to email right then not later.

To Send Invoice Later

If you chose to send the invoice later here's how.

1. Click File at the top of the Main Menu Bar
2. Select Send Forms
3. Click on all or choose the ones you want to send.
4. Click Send Now
5. Click Close when finished.

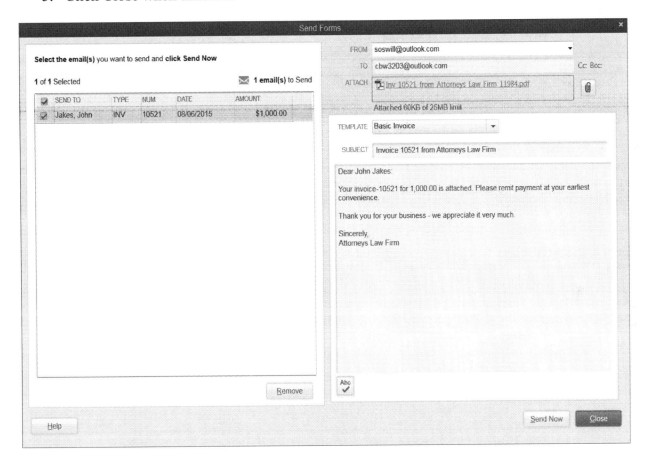

Note: You can change/edit the body of the email right on this screen. This is generated by QuickBooks and you can change it every time or add additional information.

Invoice Customizing

The Invoice Templates that come in the QuickBooks already formatted templates are great, but you may want to add/edit or delete somethings to fit your specific needs.

1. Click Lists from the top of the Main Menu Bar
2. Select Templates
3. Click on the button Templates at the bottom of the screen
4. Select Edit Template

Lists of Templates

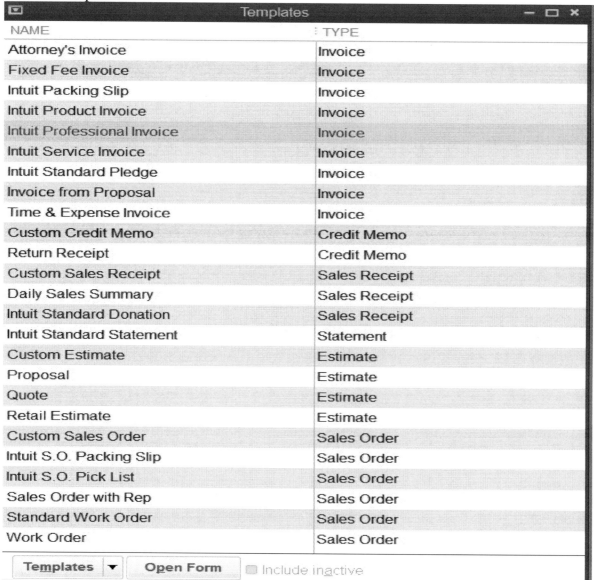

NAME	TYPE
Attorney's Invoice	Invoice
Fixed Fee Invoice	Invoice
Intuit Packing Slip	Invoice
Intuit Product Invoice	Invoice
Intuit Professional Invoice	Invoice
Intuit Service Invoice	Invoice
Intuit Standard Pledge	Invoice
Invoice from Proposal	Invoice
Time & Expense Invoice	Invoice
Custom Credit Memo	Credit Memo
Return Receipt	Credit Memo
Custom Sales Receipt	Sales Receipt
Daily Sales Summary	Sales Receipt
Intuit Standard Donation	Sales Receipt
Intuit Standard Statement	Statement
Custom Estimate	Estimate
Proposal	Estimate
Quote	Estimate
Retail Estimate	Estimate
Custom Sales Order	Sales Order
Intuit S.O. Packing Slip	Sales Order
Intuit S.O. Pick List	Sales Order
Sales Order with Rep	Sales Order
Standard Work Order	Sales Order
Work Order	Sales Order

Templates ▼   Open Form   ☐ Include inactive

See on the next page the Basic Customization Window for the QuickBooks Attorney's Invoice.

Basic Customization Screen

You can choose the information you want to appear on your invoices and change the fonts or apply a color scheme.

Click on the Additional Customization button. A popup screen will appear telling you to make a copy, make a copy. With the additional customization you can choose what will print on the invoice and the order the columns are in. You can select what you see on the screen as well. Click on the different tabs to see what is available for you to add/change/edit. When you are done click the OK button.

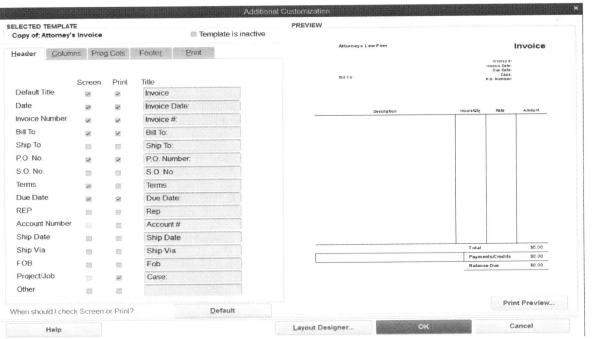

You can change the layout by clicking on the layout designer, this will bring the form up so you can change the appearance, such as borders, the font type and the size and alignment.

Layout Designer in Additional Customization

Double click on the item you want to move, edit, or delete. Click on the Add button if you want to add an item. Click OK button when you are done making changes.

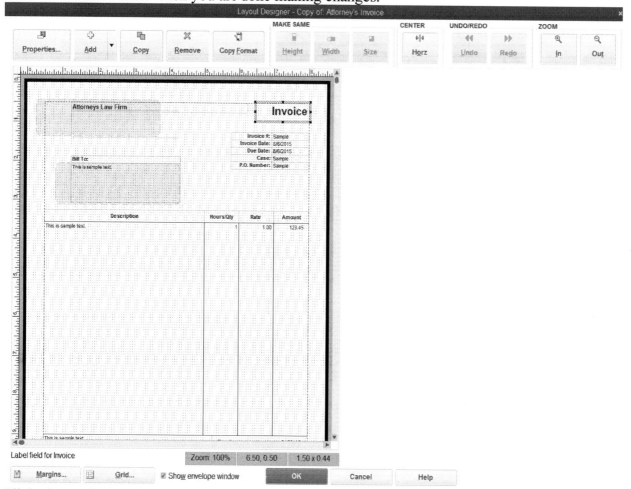

Click ok to exit out of the additional customization window and click ok again to exit out of the Basic customization window.

There are many templates to choose from and change if you want. QuickBooks also has other templates you can download and some are for a fee, but really nice. It's worth a look.

Entering Statement Charges

I want to go over using Billing Statements now. You may use these and you may not. A billing statement lists the charges a client has accumulated over a period of time. By choosing this method you will be able to print a statement with the detail description notes you enter in the charges. I have found this to be the preferred method for attorneys that work on cases over an extended period of time. However, billing statements have limitations like everything does. The main limitation is that they do not allow you to use the sales tax option and you can't use price levels when you enter charges directly into the register, but you can override the charge. The drawback is you have to remember to override the clients with special rates each time.

Home Page - Customers

To enter statement charges Click on Statement Charges in the Customers section on the home page. See below with the red arrow pointing to Statement Charges.

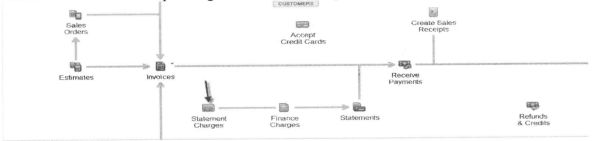

To pull up a client's Register as shown below to enter statement charges.

1. Highlight client in the Customers Center and right click on that customer name then select Enter Statement Charges.
2. Enter the Date, item, Qty and Rate. Enter the Description you want to show on statement.
3. If you put a due date it also lets your clients know how much is past due from a previous billing cycle.
4. To add Time/Costs to Billing Statements, Click on the Time/Costs Button on the Icon Bar below.

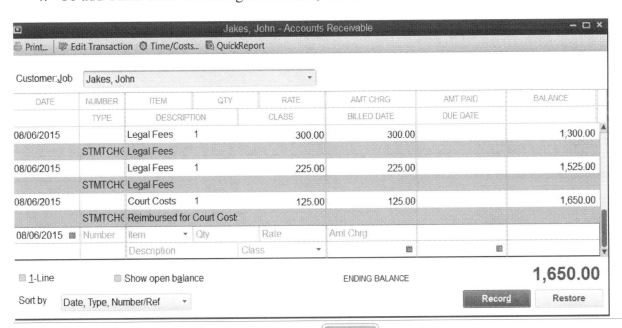

After Clicking on the Time/Costs button on the Clients Register this window pops up. To transfer the Time/Costs to the Clients Register click on the options button on the screen.

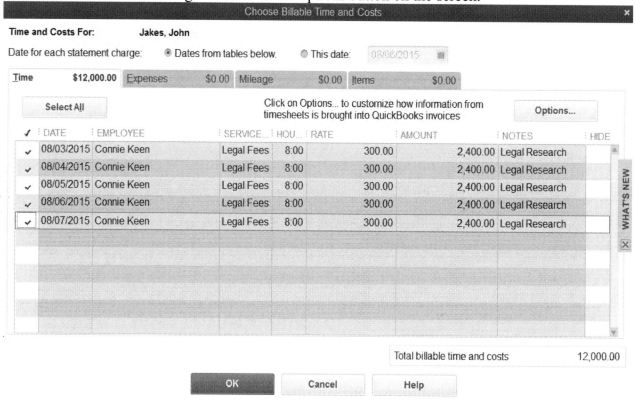

Here are your choices from the Options button. Make your choices and click ok.

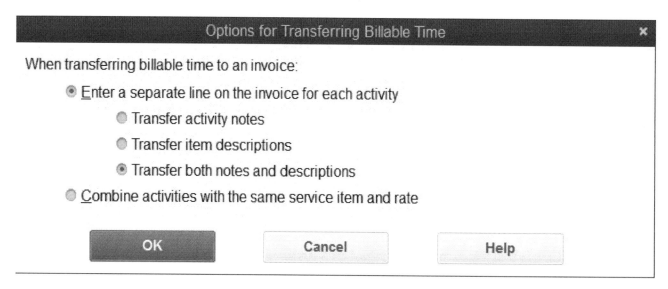

Billing Clients for Postage, Copies, Mileage and Other Items using the Statement Method

You can enter other charges like Postage and copies directly in the client register. All you have to do is enter the date, select the postage item and enter a quantity and amount. You can enter a memo describing what you mailed or what the charge is for.

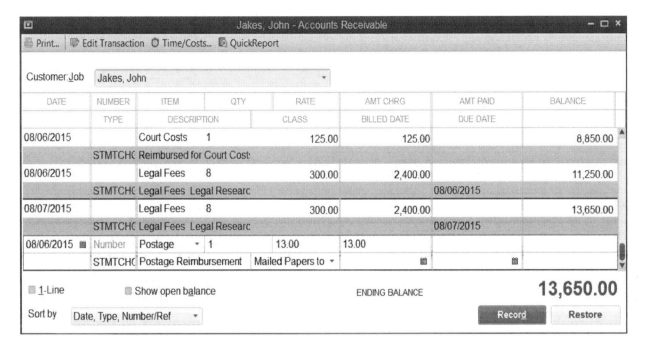

Setting up Payment Plans with Statements

You may have clients that cannot pay the necessary amount to have you represent them, so you can set up a payment plan for them using statement charges automatically.

Pull up the Customer center, highlight the client you want to enter statement charges. Enter the date, Legal Fees, Qty, and description Record. Right click on this charge to memorize it. See Below.

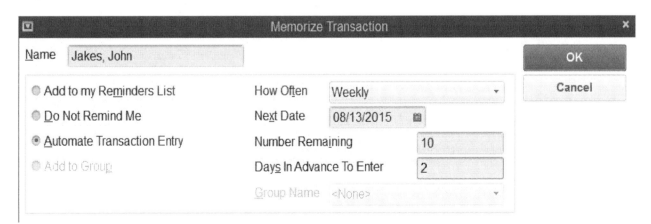

You can email or print these weekly statements for payments from your clients. You can also run an aging report in the future so you can forecast what is coming in that month.

Printing Statements

You can print statements by clicking on the Statements icon on the Home Page under Customers. Choose the statement date and the statement period from. Select Additional Options section select any items that you want. I checked off the most common.

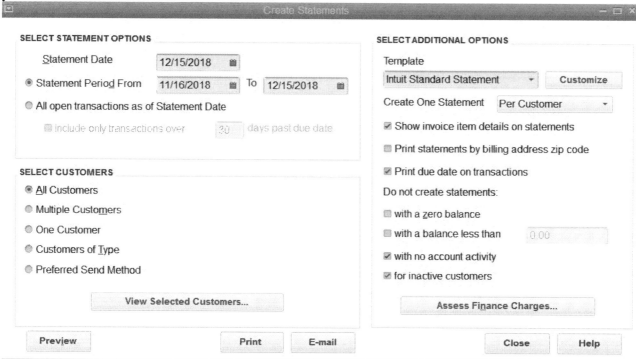

You can also customize your statement basically the same way you do your invoices or other forms. Click on Layout Designer Button to add, edit or delete anything or move things around. You can find more templates from QuickBooks to download. Click Ok when done.

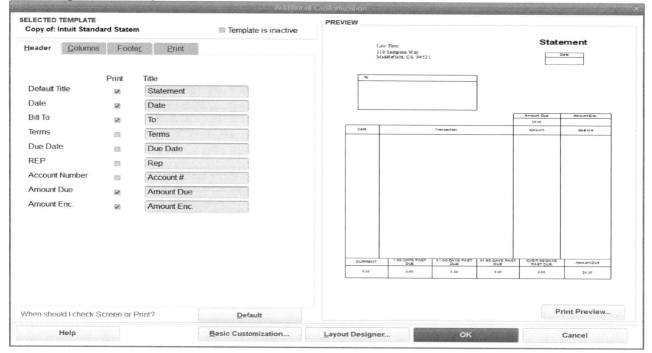

Tracking Billable Expenses

Track expense you have paid for upfront for your clients so you can get reimbursed for them. Some of these expense may be for postage, printing, Long Distance telephone charges and other things. The easiest and best way to track these expenses is to enter them when you write the check or when you enter the bill. All you need to do is allocate each expense for each client when writing the check or entering the bill. If you are using a trust account for the costs **DO NOT DO THIS SEE CHAPTER 12** for how to handle trust money.

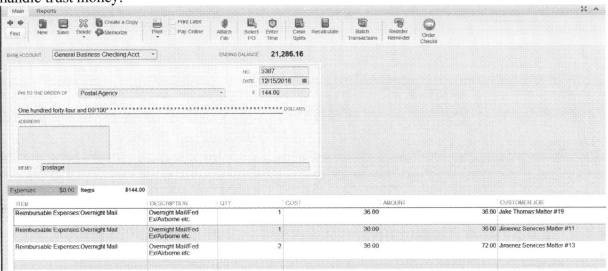

1. Click on Banking from the top of the Main Menu Bar and select Write Checks.
2. Enter the vendor name, date, amount and the check number should be the next check number.
3. Enter in the amounts under the items tab.
4. Enter the item, description, Qty, cost, amount and the customer to bill to.
5. When finished Click Save at the top of the screen, Print the check now or later.

Invoice for Time and Expenses for the Reimbursements you just wrote a check for. Either Click on Invoice Button and Invoice for Time and Expenses or bill from the Clients Statement Register by clicking on Time/Costs button on the Clients Register. Click on items to bill then click Next Step & Click Create Invoices. Click ok to print them later.

Select the **Date Range and Template**. Then select **Customer:Jobs** to invoice. Click **Create Invoice** or **Next Step**.

Date Range From _____ To 12/15/2018 ▦   Template: Attorney's Invoice

Select All

✓	CUSTOMER:JOB ▲	TIME	EXPENSES	MILEAGE	ITEMS	TOTAL
✓	Jake Thomas:Matter #19	0.00	0.00	0.00	36.00	36.00
✓	Jimenez Services:Matter #11	0.00	0.00	0.00	36.00	36.00
✓	Jimenez Services:Matter #13	0.00	0.00	0.00	72.00	72.00
	Kirby Freeman Wholesale/Distribution:Matter #15	1,600.00	0.00	0.00	0.00	1,600.00
	Peacock, Karen	0.00	0.00	0.00	0.00	0.00
	Peacock, Karen:Matter #04	0.00	0.00	0.00	24.84	24.84
	Tingey Worldwide Freight Company:Matter #10	4,400.00	0.00	0.00	0.00	4,400.00
	Tingey Worldwide Freight Company:Matter #16	1,600.00	0.00	0.00	0.00	1,600.00
	Willams, Cindy:Matter #03	8,385.00	0.00	0.00	921.40	9,306.40
	Willams, Cindy:Matter #12	800.00	0.00	0.00	0.00	800.00

Help   ☑ Let me select specific billables for the Customer:Job   Next Step   Close

See a Sample Invoice to email for expense reimbursement charge on the next page.

This was only one charge as a sample. In a Law Practice there will most likely be more on the billing. This can be combined with time as well and billed out on the monthly billing.

Law Firm
110 Sampson Way
Middlefield, CA 94521

Invoice

Invoice #:	71068
Invoice Date:	12/15/2018
Due Date:	12/15/2018
Case:	Matter #19
P.O. Number:	

Bill To:
Jake Thomas

Description	Hours/Qty	Rate	Amount
Overnight Mail/Fed Ex/ Airborne etc.	1	36.00	36.00

Total	$36.00
Payments/Credits	$0.00
Balance Due	$36.00

Contingency Cases

When taking on Contingency Cases you will want to track the expenses for these cases differently. It could be that these expenses are not deductible until you actually get paid for the job. In this case these expenses will be on your balance sheet as an Other Current Asset. When you get ready to bill your clients, you will be able to bill for these expenses. You should ask your CPA or tax professional to find out if this is the best method for you.

Tracking Billable Expenses

First make sure you have the asset account setup.

1. Click on Lists at the top Main Menu Bar
2. Select Chart of Accounts (If you don't see account for Advanced Client Costs then continue to add this account and if you have it then move on to next steps of writing a check.
3. Click Account button at the bottom of the screen and Select New
4. Select other Account Types towards the bottom and choose Other Current Asset, click Continue
5. Enter Advanced Client Costs as shown below. When finished adding information click save & close.

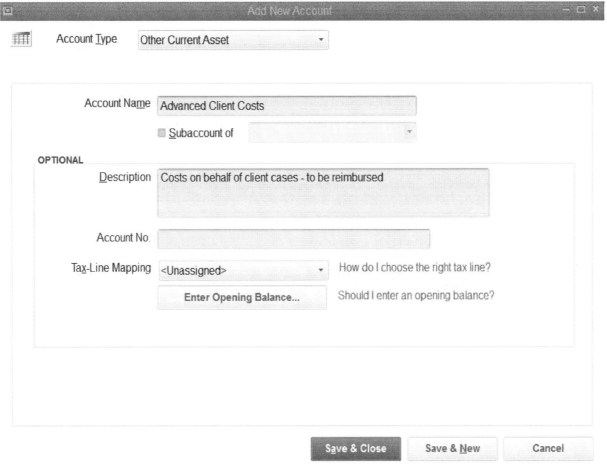

Next we will setup a contingency case client

Contingency Case Client Setup

Now that we set up an account for reimbursement of expenses on Contingency Cases we need to set up the Contingency Case Client.

Set Up Client
1. Click on Customer at the top of the Main Menu Bar
2. Select Customer Center
3. Click add new customer on the New Customer & Job tab at the top left of the Customer Center screen.
4. Fill in the necessary information for the client and click Save & Close.

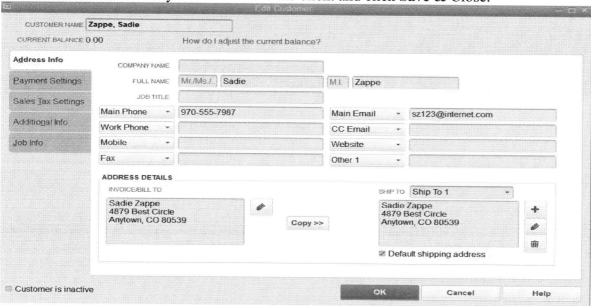

Highlight new Contingency Case Client and Click New Customer & Job tab and Select Add Job.
1. Click the Job Info Tab and enter the necessary information.
2. Add new job type, Contingency
3. When finished entering all the data click ok

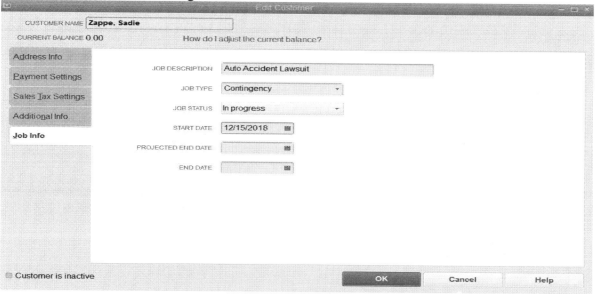

Writing Checks for Contingency Cases

Now that we have set up Accounts for Advanced Client costs and setup the client we are ready to write some checks to be reimbursed for expenses when the time comes.

1. Click on Banking at the top of the Main Menu Bar
2. Select Write Checks.
3. Enter the Vendor, amount and date
4. Enter account/Item, description, Qty, amount, and Client/Job
5. Click print, if printing now, or save if entering more checks and printing later.
6. Press Esc button after saving or printing.

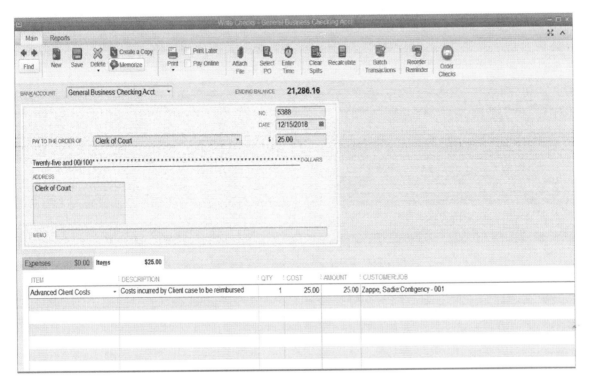

We are going to setup, run and memorize reports for Contingency Cases next.
Keep in mind, depending on the version you are using, to track each client contingency reimbursements you may have to set up an Item Called Advanced Client Costs and then bill out time and costs.

Reports for Contingency Cases

To stay on top of the costs being incurred in your contingency cases and for each client, you can create a report showing you this information. To save time we will memorize the report, so that at any time with the click of a button you can see what is going on.

1. Click on Reports at the top of the Main Menu Bar, select Customers & Receivables.
2. Click on Customer Balance Detail, Click on Customize Report Button on the top of the report.
3. Choose the filters tab and select the account advanced Client cost or Choose Item, then the Advanced Client Cost. See Below.

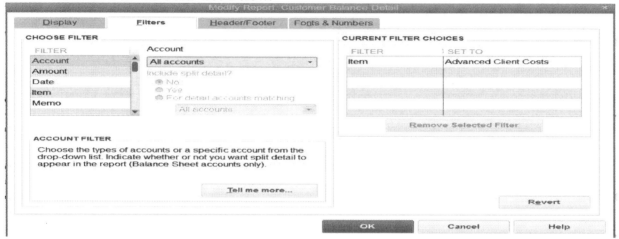

Report for Contingency Costs per Client.

Click on Memorize in the top of the Report to Memorize this report as shown below.

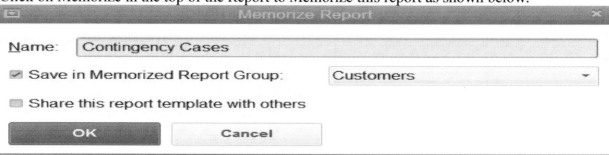

Billing Contingency Clients with Invoice Method

Enter a bill for an easy way to bill clients for postage and copies with invoice method.

1. Create an Item for Postage Charges to be reimbursed. (Set this up if not setup yet)
2. The Item Type needs to be Other Charge.
3. Check the box, This Item is used in assemblies or is a reimbursable charge.
4. The expense account will be Postage and Delivery, and the Income Account will be Reimbursed Client Expense Income account.
5. Do not put a value in the cost or price because this will probably be different often times.
6. Click Ok when finished.

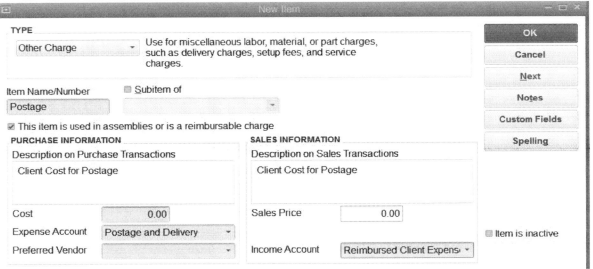

Entering Bill for the postage
1. Click the Vendors at the top of the Main Menu Bar, Select Enter Bills
2. You can enter Postmaster, USPS or set up your law firm as a vendor.
3. On the items tab enter the postage item & Qty & Cost, select client, mark billable & class.
4. Click Save & Close when finished.

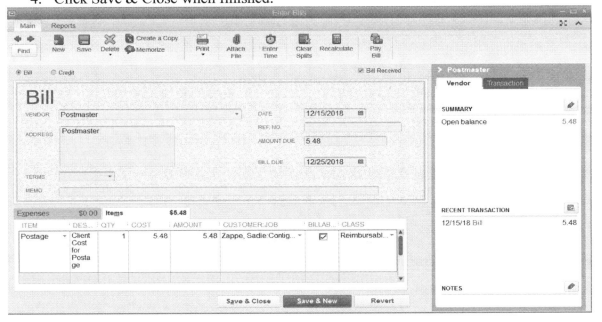

Next be sure to enter the amount as a negative in the expenses tab as shown below. Notice when doing that it is marked as paid, but will still go into unbilled account to be bill to the client.

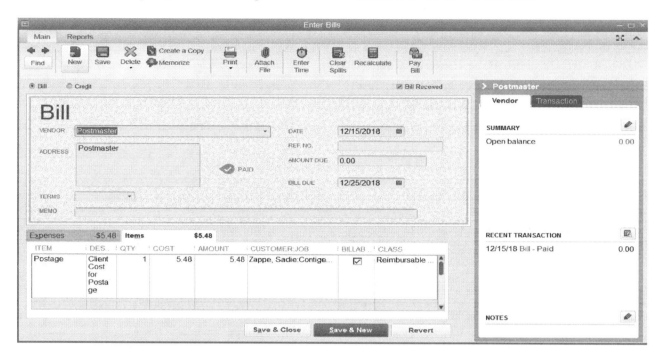

Now let's run an unbilled costs by job report. When you go to invoice your clients it will pop up and let you know you have expenses to bill. You can go to Reports, Jobs, Time & Mileage and select Unbilled Cost to see who you need to bill for these types of charges as I just did in the example below. See the bill we just entered below in report.

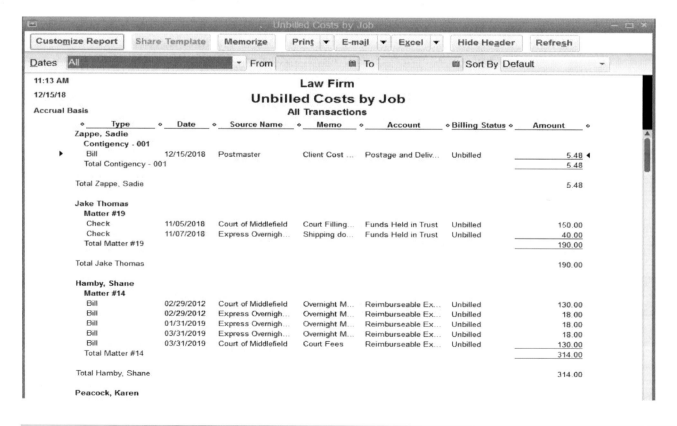

Chapter 9
Receiving Account Payments

In this chapter you will learn how to receive payments from your clients against their accounts.

Receiving Payments on Client Accounts

We have created invoices and statement charges, so we need to collect payments on these accounts.

1. Click on Customers at the top of the Main Menu Bar
2. Select Receive Payments
3. Type In Williams in the Received From and Select Williams, Cindy
4. Type in 12,000.00 in the Payment Amount Field and click on Check as form of payment.
5. QuickBooks will automatically put a checkmark next to the invoices it thinks the money is for. Sometimes is totally right and sometimes not. You can uncheck some or all and re check them to the correct invoices.
6. They underpaid the one big invoice by 583.10, so leave as underpayment unless you are supposed to write it off or for other reasons.
7. Click Save & Close if finished entering payments or Save & New if you have more to enter.

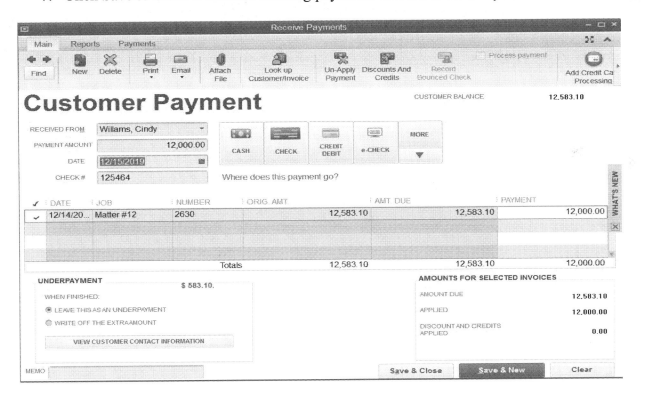

I have many Clients ask where do the payments go. QuickBooks created a payment account called Undeposited Funds. When you receive and enter a payment the payment will go into Undeposited Funds. This is like the in-between bag getting to the bank, basically your bank bag.

When you are ready to take your deposit(s) to the bank you will click on Make Deposits from the Home Page and a list will pop up with all your checks ready to go to the bank.

Recording Deposits

Now that you have entered receiving payments we are now ready to deposit them into your bank account.

1. Click on Banking at the top Main Menu Bar
2. Select Make Deposits
3. Click the Select All Button if you want to deposit all checks. If you only want to deposit some of them just place a check mark next to the ones you want to deposit by clicking on those checks.
4. Click Ok when selection is made.

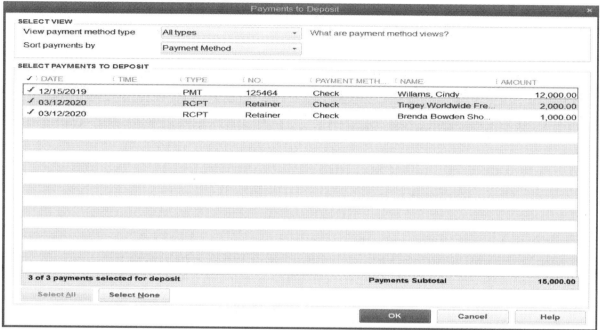

Here's the Make Deposits Screen see From Account is the Undeposited Funds. You can either click save and close if you are done or save & new if you have more. Make sure the Deposit to is going to the **correct Checking Account and the date is correct**. You can hand write your deposits and enter like this or you can enter and print on deposit slips you can purchase. It is so worth getting the deposit slips to print.

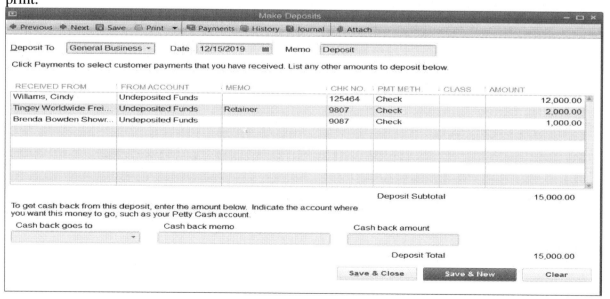

Accounts Receivable Register

After the payments have been received and entered into the Undeposited Funds. Next you make your deposit and the payments finally make their final resting place and that is the Accounts Receivable Register.

As you can see in this register there is the payment made by Williams, Cindy that had an underpayment. You can see as well when you invoice a client they end up here.

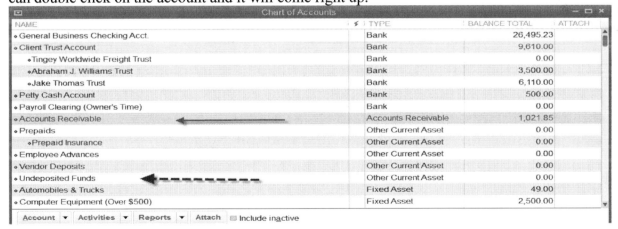

DATE	NUMBER	CUSTOMER	ITEM	QTY	RATE	AMT CHRG	AMT PAID
	TYPE	DESCRIPTION		CLASS		BILLED DATE	DUE DATE
12/14/2019	68421	Willams, Cindy:Matter #					17,161.70
	PMT						
12/15/2019	125464	Willams, Cindy:Matter #					12,000.00
	PMT						
12/17/2019	32322	Tingey Worldwide Freig					236.50
	PMT						
01/31/2020	2631	Kirby Freeman Wholesa				6,487.60	
	INV						Paid
01/31/2020	2632	Jimenez Services:Matte				11,837.60	
	INV						Paid
02/14/2020	999	Jimenez Services:Matte					11,837.60
	PMT						
02/14/2020	2519	Kirby Freeman Wholesa					6,487.60
	PMT						

1-Line   Show open balance   ENDING BALANCE   **1,021.85**

Sort by   Date, Type, Number/Ref   Record   Restore

To look at the Accounts Receivable Register. Pull up the Chart of Accounts and its located there and you can double click on the account and it will come right up.

NAME	TYPE	BALANCE TOTAL	ATTACH
◦ General Business Checking Acct.	Bank	26,495.23	
◦ Client Trust Account	Bank	9,610.00	
◦ Tingey Worldwide Freight Trust	Bank	0.00	
◦ Abraham J. Williams Trust	Bank	3,500.00	
◦ Jake Thomas Trust	Bank	6,110.00	
◦ Petty Cash Account	Bank	500.00	
◦ Payroll Clearing (Owner's Time)	Bank	0.00	
◦ Accounts Receivable	Accounts Receivable	1,021.85	
◦ Prepaids	Other Current Asset	0.00	
◦ Prepaid Insurance	Other Current Asset	0.00	
◦ Employee Advances	Other Current Asset	0.00	
◦ Vendor Deposits	Other Current Asset	0.00	
◦ Undeposited Funds	Other Current Asset	0.00	
◦ Automobiles & Trucks	Fixed Asset	49.00	
◦ Computer Equipment (Over $500)	Fixed Asset	2,500.00	

Account ▾   Activities ▾   Reports ▾   Attach   Include inactive

Notice the Red arrow is the Accounts Receivable, see the balance in the open Register match's in the Chart of Accounts. Also see the Blue Arrow pointing to the Undeposited Funds Account. See the Undeposited Funds Register on the Next Page.

Cristie Will

The Undeposited Funds Register. See the Payment of 12,000.00 received from Williams, Cindy goes into this register and leaves when the deposit is made.

DATE	REF	PAYEE		DECREASE	✓	INCREASE
	TYPE	ACCOUNT	MEMO			
	DEP	General Business Che				
12/14/2019	68421	Willams, Cindy			✓	17,161.70
	PMT	Accounts Receivable				
12/14/2019	68421	Willams, Cindy		17,161.70	✓	
	DEP	General Business Che				
12/15/2019	9087	Brenda Bowden Showroom:Matter #17		1,000.00	✓	
	DEP	General Business Che				
12/15/2019	9807	Tingey Worldwide Freight Company:Matter #1		2,000.00	✓	Payment Entered
	DEP	General Business Che Retainer				
12/15/2019	125464	Willams, Cindy			✓	12,000.00
	PMT	Accounts Receivable		Deposit Made		
12/15/2019	125464	Willams, Cindy		12,000.00	✓	
	DEP	General Business Che				
12/17/2019	32322	Tingey Worldwide Freight Company			✓	236.50
	PMT	Accounts Receivable				
12/21/2019	32322	Tingey Worldwide Freight Company		236.50	✓	
	DEP	Deposit From: Genera				
02/14/2020	999	Jimenez Services:Matter #13			✓	11,837.60
	PMT	Accounts Receivable				
02/14/2020	2519	Kirby Freeman Wholesale/Distribution:Matter			✓	6,487.60

1-Line

ENDING BALANCE

Sort by Date, Type, Number/Ref ▾

Chapter 10
Retainers

Client Retainers

You will learn how to receive and apply Retainers from Clients. This is not Trust Money. You will learn about Trusts in Chapter 12.

If you receive money in advance of a job, you don't want to show that as income until you earn it. As always follow the rules of your state regarding the professional and ethical conduct for handling client funds. Failure to abide by those rules and practices could cause administrative, civil or criminal sanctions.

You need to track money you have received as retainers as a liability on your books. This Method will not count as income until you earn it. This is money that is deposited into your operating account. We will set up an Item for Client Retainer. Check your list first and if you have the item then skip this exercise.

1. Click on lists at the top Main Menu Bar then select Item List.
2. Click on Item at the bottom of the screen and Select New
3. As the account type choose Other Charge
4. Item Name/ Number is Client Retainer
5. Description is Client Retainer
6. Account is Client Retainers, Other Current Liability
7. Amount leave as 0.00 since Retainers are different amounts.
8. Click Ok

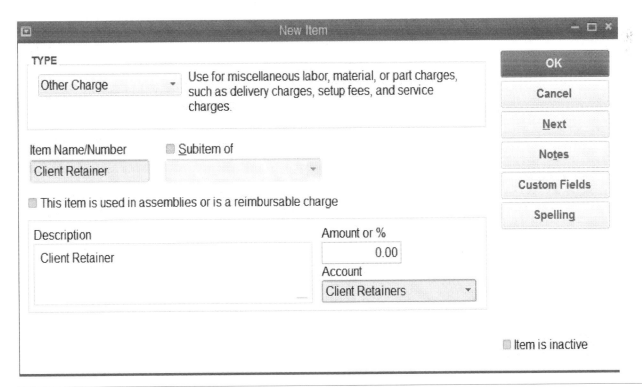

Creating Sales Receipts for Retainers

In the last chapter we talked about Receiving Payments on Account. Sales Receipts are receiving money usually when you are being paid on the spot instead of being billed out.

1. Click on Customers at the top of the Main Menu Bar
2. Select Enter Sales Receipts
3. Type in Hamby, Shane in the Customer: Job box
4. Enter the type of payment, this case check, enter the check number.
5. Item box enter client retainer, Qty 1, Class Deborah Wood and 5,000.00 as rate/Amount.
6. Print or email your client a copy.
7. Click Save & Close.

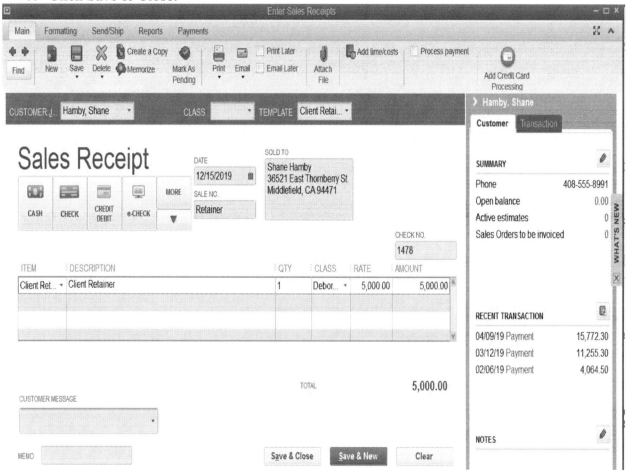

This is like all deposits and it will sit in the Undeposited Funds after entering the payment until you are ready to make the deposit and when you do you will deposit in the Operating Account.

Next we will create, run and memorize reports for Client Retainers.

Client Retainer Reports

To stay abreast as to who has money on retainers you can create a report. This report will break down the balance in your Client Retainers account by Client and Case if you are using jobs.

1. Click on Reports from the top Main Menu Bar.
2. Select Customers & Receivables, then choose Customer Balance Summary.
3. The Customer Balance Summary Report, click Customize Report button at the top of the Report Screen on the left.
4. In the Customize Report window, click the filters tab.
5. In the Filter box be sure to select Account
6. In the Account drop down list, choose Client Retainers, Other Current Liability account.
7. Go to the Header/Footer Tab
8. In the Report Title, change the name to Client Retainer Balance and click ok.

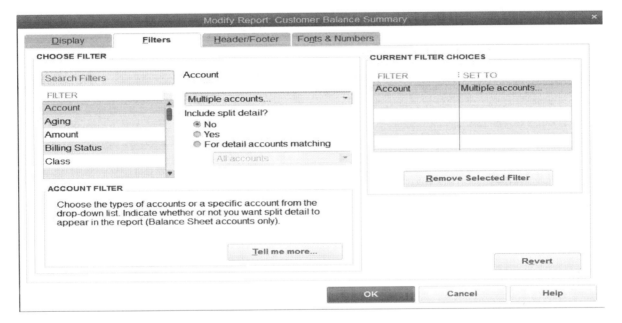

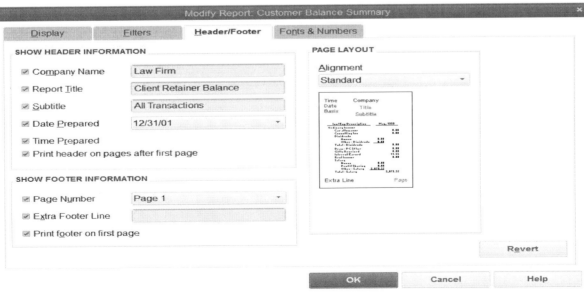

Report created, modified and Ran for Client Retainer Balances.

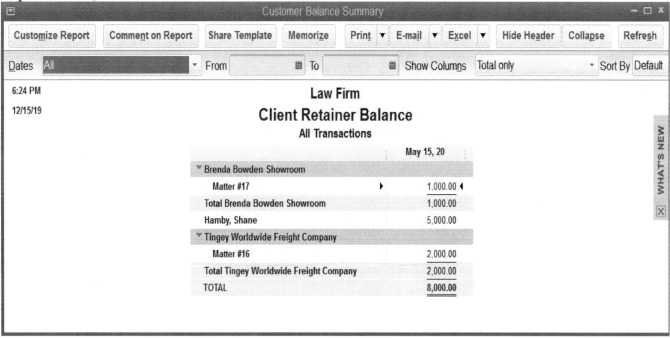

Memorize the new Client Retainer Balance report.

1. Click on the Memorize Button in the Center of the Icon Ribbon on open Client Retainer Balance Report.
2. Since we renamed the Title of the Report it will come up as the name automatically in the name field.
3. Click on save in Memorized Report Group and click the drop down arrow down and select Customers.
4. Click Ok to save it.
5. Print or Press Esc to exit the report

Applying Client Retainers

Apply Client Retainers when you have incurred costs on a case or project and are ready to move the money from the Client Retainer Liability Account to the Client's receivables account.

Invoicing for Billing and Applying Client Retainers

If you use the invoice method for billing your clients you will apply the retainer to the invoice. After you created the invoice you will add the item Client Retainers to the invoice and enter the amount. This will take it out of the client retainer liability account and apply it to the invoice.

1. Click on Create Invoices on the Home Page in the Customers Section
2. Enter Hamby, Shane in the Customer: Job drop down lists.
3. Enter Legal Fees or Legal Research and enter a description, Hours 8, Class Deborah Wood and Rate 300.00.
4. Enter Client Retainer, other Current liability account, tab over to Rate and enter -2400.00.
5. This zero outs the invoice and takes the 2400.00 from the retainer to pay the invoice.
6. Click Save & Close.

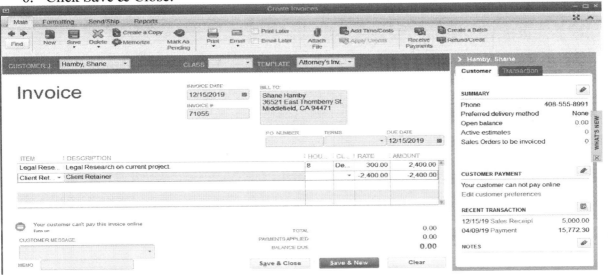

See Shane Hamby on prior report having 5,000 in retainer and now he has 2,600. See the Client Retainer Register on the next page where the 2400.00 was invoiced

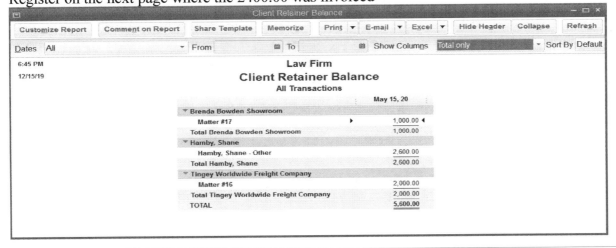

See the blue line is where we entered the sales receipt receiving the Retainer and the red line is where we invoiced Shane's Retainer Account 2,400.00 leaving him 2,600.00.

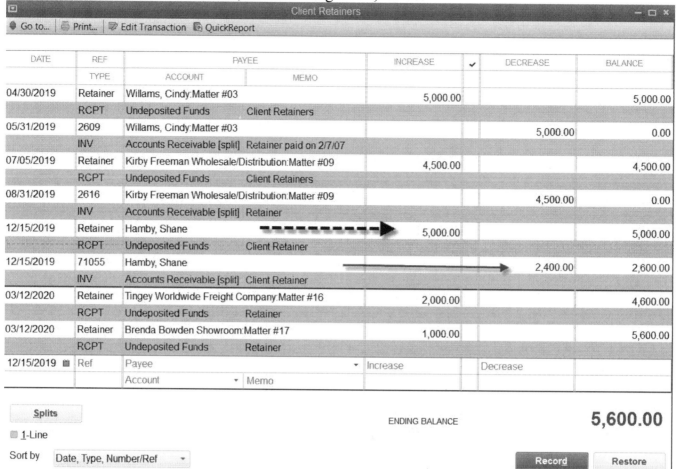

See the balance in the Client Retainers Liability Account has a balance of 5,600.00 and the memorized report ran matches.

Statement Charge Method for Retainers

With the Statement charge method you can enter charges directly into the clients register. You will apply the retainer directly into the clients register.

1. Click on Customers at the top Main Menu Bar
2. Select Customer Center
3. Choose the client from the Customer: Job list.
4. Right click on the customer and select Enter Statement Charges
5. Enter the Retainer of 5000.00 then enter the time charged as -8 in Qty and 300.00 rate and total of -2400.00.
6. When you are done entering the necessary information click Record. Press Esc button to exit out of this screen and remaining screens you don't want open.

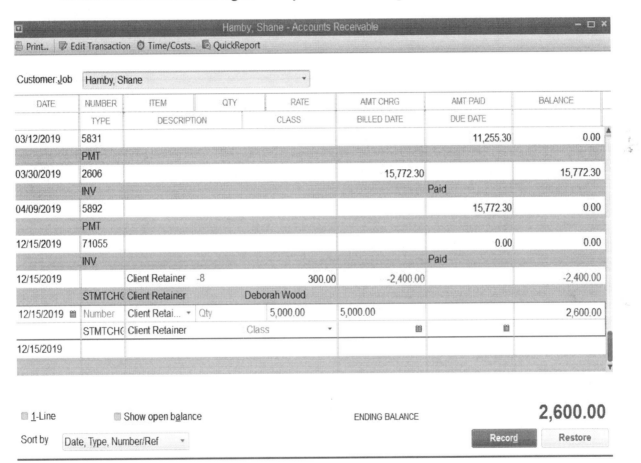

Chapter 11
Reports

This chapter is all about Reports. You will learn how to run reports. We have been over some reports for particular things, but this is about not only how to create and run reports, but to access the vast number of reports already set up.

Standard Reports

QuickBooks has well over 100 Reports that are preset that you can create and customize for your needs. The reports consists of Summary, Transaction, Detail and list reports. Click on the Report center to help you figure out what you need. Ideally after figuring out what you need you would make your own Reports Folder and memorize them and place in your folder. By setting up your own folder then you just pull up those instead of continually looking and changing when needed.

1. Click on Reports at the top Main Menu Bar
2. Select Report Center

Here's the Report Center. See all the different Standard Reports to the left of the screen. Company & Financial is highlighted and all the reports are shown on the screen. There are 20 present reports just in the Company & Financial section. In the small Ribbon area of the Report Center Screen, notice the tabs; Standard, Memorized, Favorites, Recent Contributed. There are many more just on this screen alone, scroll down to see the rest. I highly recommend you setting side time to go through all the reports to see what is available.

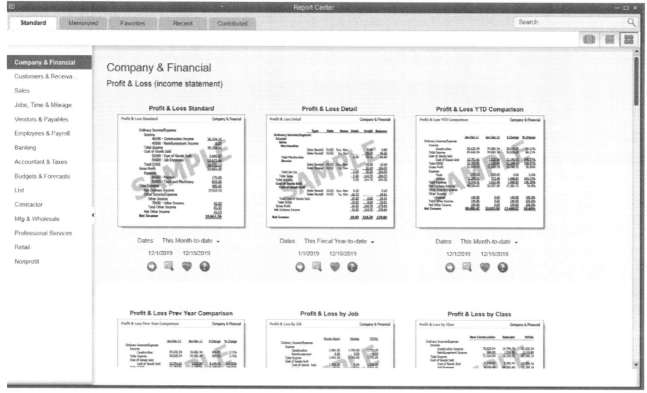

This is a Screen Shot of Contributed Reports. This is in addition to the Preset accounts. Intuit along with countless QuickBooks users has sent these in. This wills save you countless hours.

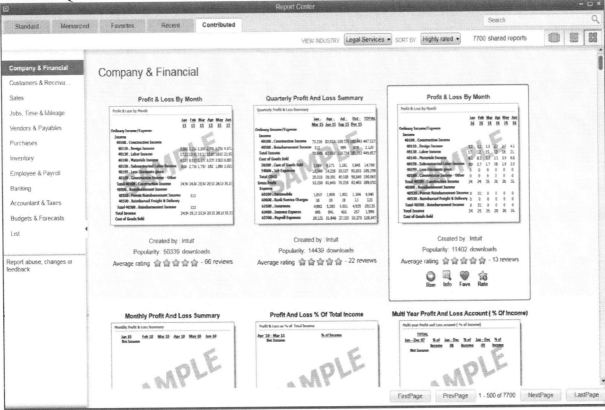

Here's Memorized Reports. This is where you can place your go to reports for quick access.

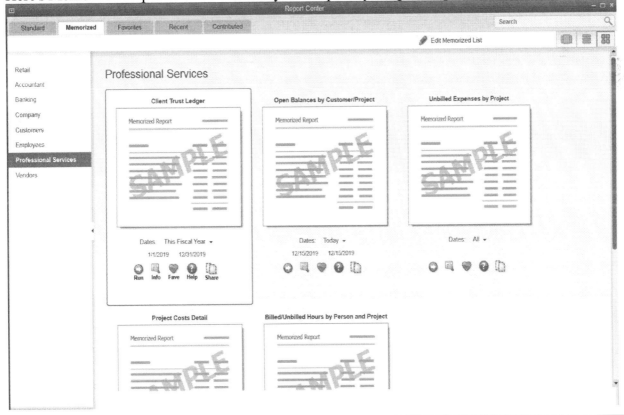

Customizing Reports

QuickBooks has given the user the ability to make almost countless modifications to reports for your needs to run and memorize to your liking. When looking at any report you will notice in the upper left hand corner of the screen you will see a button Customize Report or if you are using an older version the button would be Modify Report. The Customize Report Button is where you go to modify any report to a vast number of options.

Here's the Modify Report for Unbilled Costs by Job. This includes all dates, but I am going to change that to Last Month to make sure everything was billed out.

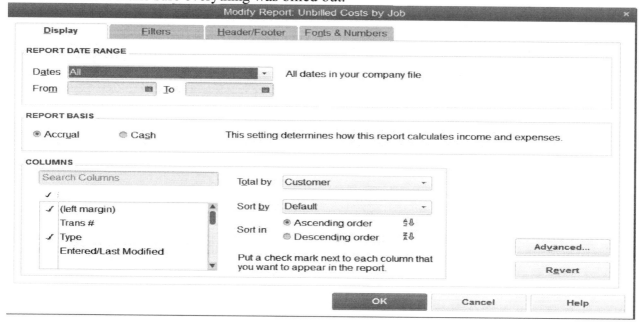

Modified Report Dates. See Report on Next Page.

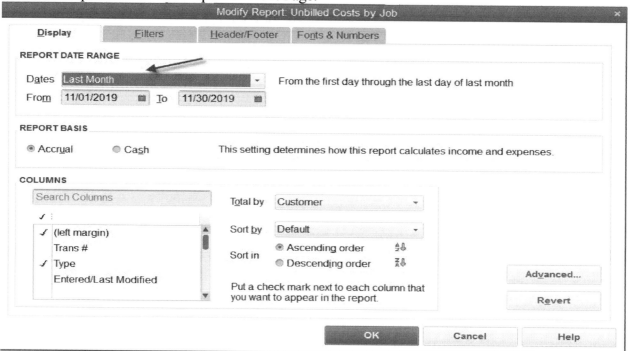

These were last month Unbilled charges.   This report is invaluable.

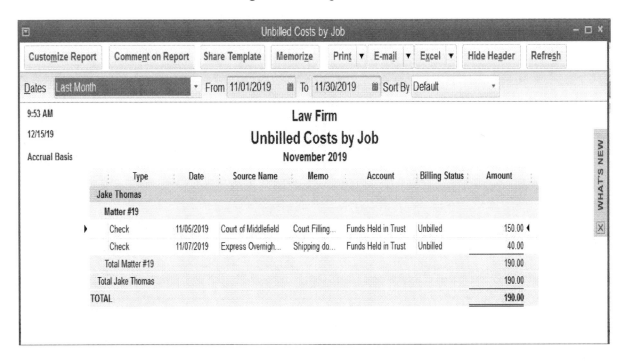

Noticed I went back for more modifying and changed the name to Unbilled Costs by Job for Prior Month. I memorized this Report in a new group I set up for my Reports. See the next Page for those steps.

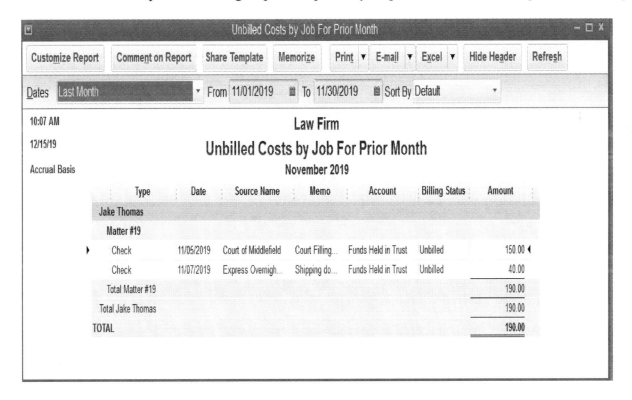

Cristie Will

Make Report Groups

To Make a New Report Group for your personal reports for quick access.

1. Click Reports at the top Main Menu Bar
2. Select Memorized Reports, then choose Memorized Report List
3. Click on the Bottom Memorized Button
4. Select New Group

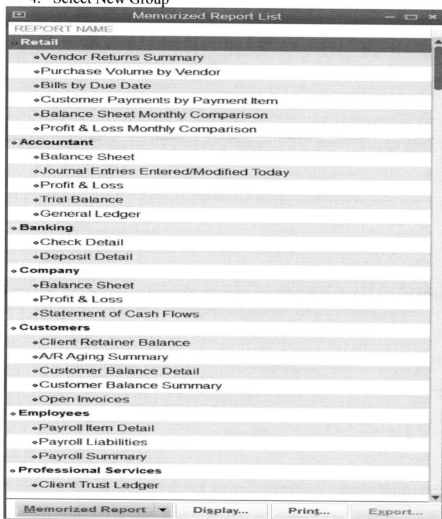

Here's the screen where you give your Group of Reports a name. Name your Group and click ok.

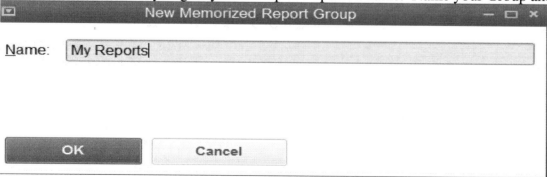

Memorize Report in your New Group

Now we setup a New Group for you. For this exercise we will use the group name I used. Here's the Report we want to memorize for the new group, My Reports.

1. Click on Memorize Report Button in the top center of the report.

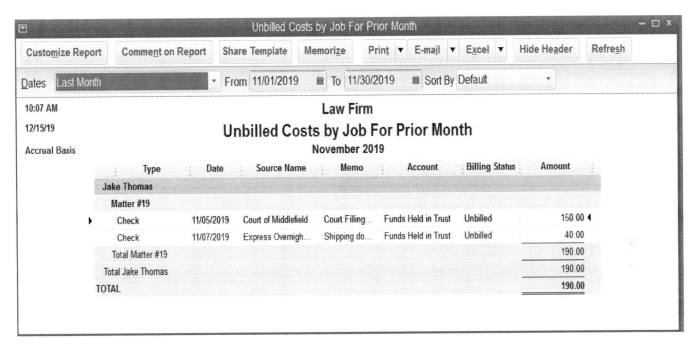

2. The name will already appear in the Name box, if the name is not what you want you need to go back and change the name. Press Esc to get out of this screen and make changes.
3. If you made changes to name or for any reason Click Memorize Button again.
4. Click the box next to save in Memorized Report Group. My Reports came up first. If your Report is not first click on drop down arrow and find your Group.
5. Click Ok when done.

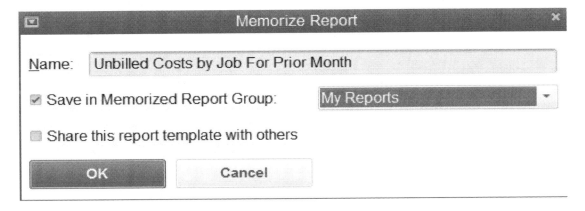

See new memorized report list on next page.

See the double arrow below pointing to the New Report Group and the New Memorized Report!

To access this go to reports at the top main menu and pull up memorized Report List or from the reports menu pull up Report Center.

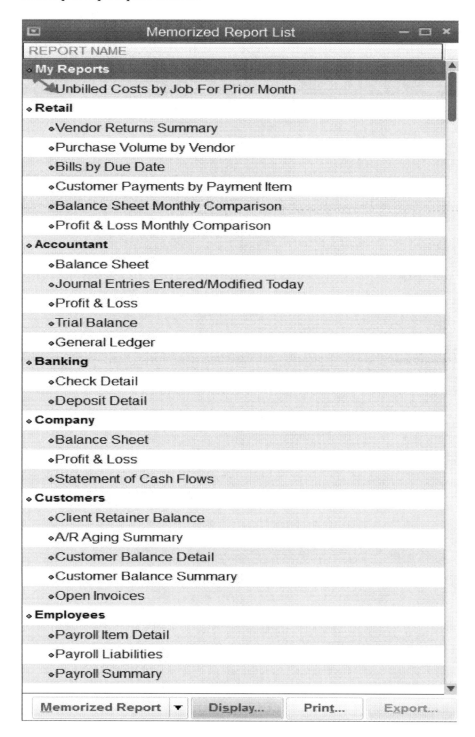

Other Report Options

QuickBooks has a lot of lists and that is great. I have saved this for the last chapter. You won't use all the lists available, but I want to show you the ones that I don't think most of us would think of using. One example is The Sales Rep List. I think of a Sales Rep as a Sales Rep in selling a product not an Attorney or anyone that works in a Law Practice.

I will show you a report run by using Sales Rep in your Law Practice. Setting up everyone as a Sales Rep you can run even more reports by that Attorney or other employee. This Sales by Rep Detail is great, but it did not group them by Sales Rep because no Sales Rep were set up. I set up a sales rep in next report.

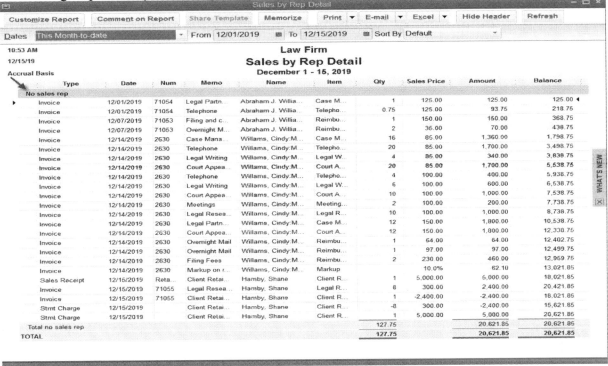

See the difference by setting up Sales Rep, Deborah Wood is grouped. I also renamed Report and memorized it.

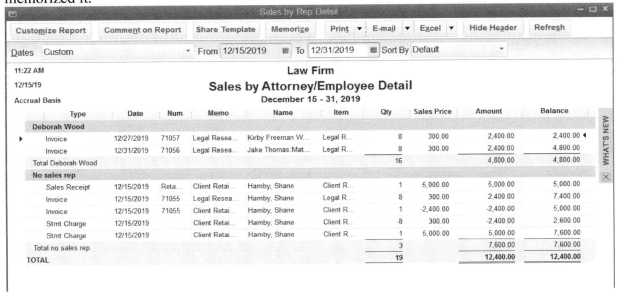

Modify Reports Screens

Notice the next four screen shots have an arrow pointing to things to go over, make changes or not. This screen is the Display on what shows on reports, so go through the columns list. Uncheck things you don't want and check things you do want. When finished click on Filters tab.

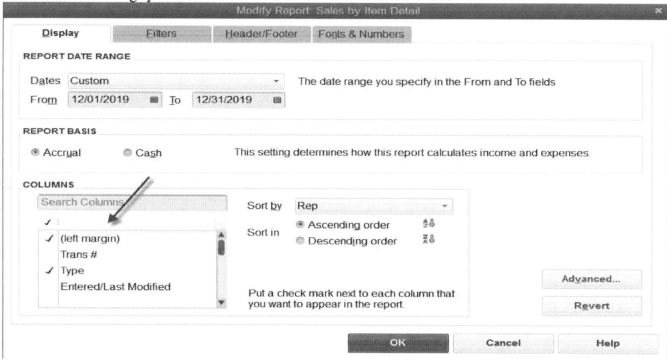

Here's the Filters Tab. Notice the red arrow pointing to current filter choices. This is what the report I set up is set to. You can change that by adding, deleting or modifying the filter choices by going down Filter list. When finished Click on Header/Footer tab.

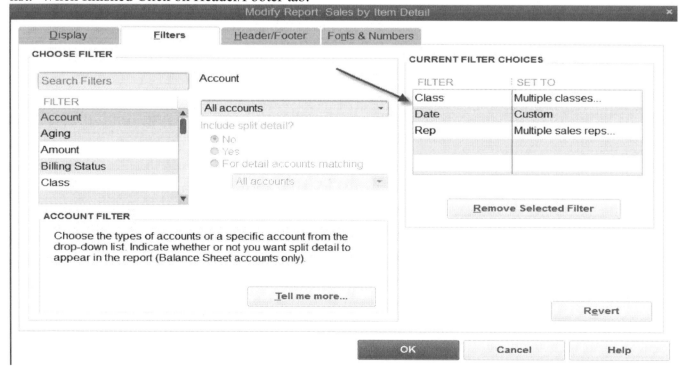

Here's the Header Footer Tab. You can change the name of the Report by changing the Report Title. You can also uncheck items you don't want on Report. When finished click on Fonts & Numbers tab.

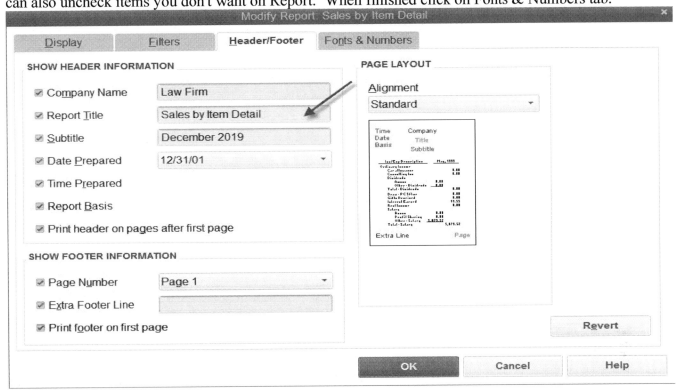

As you can see you change the fonts and maybe you want certain numbers to show up in red. Make any changes and click ok when done.

Once you are done and your report looks the way you want it then click on memorize and save for later use if desired.

Chapter 12
Trust Accounts

In this Chapter you will learn how to setup your trust account, your client's liability accounts and record IOLTA Interest. You may already have these accounts so you can skip this or follow along.

Opening Your Trust Bank Account

As you probably know that a Trust Bank Account is for holding Clients money to cover the cost of expenses. This money is to be kept in a separate bank account and cannot be commingled with other operating funds. It must be clearly identified following the law/rules and guidelines in your states rules of conduct.

To begin with the most important step is to maintaining accurate and compliant trust accounts along with making sure they are set up right with your Bank/Financial Institution.

It's important you check with your state bar association for regulations and reporting requirements. It is vital that you work with an institution that has knowledge of your states rules and regulations so that you are in full compliance. If you are unsure that a Bank meets the requirements you can contact your bar association who will be able to help in this matter.

When opening your trust account you may be required to do some of the following or other requirements depending on your states laws, so be sure to check.
1. First review your states requirements.
2. Make sure your bank knows the requirements for Trust Accounts.
3. Bank Resolution Forms - Be sure name on the account says Trust Account or IOLTA Trust Account spelled out.
4. Checks need to have Trust Account or IOLTA Trust Account spelled out.
5. Statements need to have Trust Account or IOLTA Trust Account spelled out as well.
6. NO overdraft protection is on the Trust Account.
7. NO ATM card is issued with the Trust Account
8. If you are going to accept payments with Credit Cards into the Trust Account you will have to have a separate Merchant Account for your Trust Account.
9. If it's a requirement send a letter to your Bank/Financial Institution a letter to them asking them to notify the bar in the event of a NSF or other returns, absent bank error, on the trust account. I have included an example of a letter on the next page.

Remember to check the rules in your state. As we know laws and rules can and do change.

Sample Letter to Send to Your Bank. As always check your state laws for any particular wording that needs to be in letter and/or if your state even requires it. If a letter is required your state may have its own letter Template for you.

Best Law in Town
111 Defense Street
Anyplace, State, Zip

Your Bank Name
Your Bank Street
Your Bank City, State & Zip

Date

To: Your Bank

Re: Best Law in Town Trust Account # _____

This is a letter to authorize (Insert your bank name) to automatically notify the (State Bar you reside in) Staff Council at (Your State Bar's address this letter needs to go to) in the event that a bank draft drawn upon the above mentioned trust account is returned for non-sufficient funds or otherwise dishonored, absent bank error.

Thank You,

Your Name
Your contact Info.

Trust Account Setup

Gather all your Trust Account documents such as bank statements, so we can have pertinent documents. Next check and see if you already have a bank account in your chart of accounts that is a trust account.

This Chart of Accounts List has a Client Trust setup, but if you don't see one in yours lets set one up.

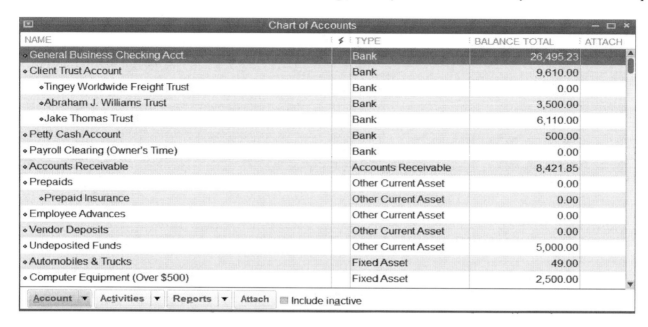

Steps to add a Trust Bank Account
1. Click on Lists at the top Main Menu Bar
2. Select Chart of Accounts
3. Click on the Account Button at the bottom of the Chart of Accounts screen
4. Click New, Choose Bank as the account type then click Continue.

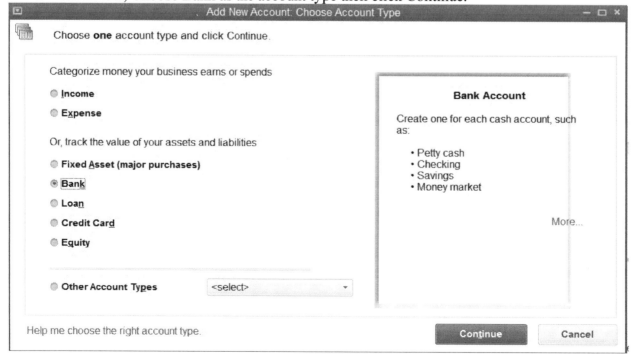

Fill in the Account Name, Description and Account number. Do Not Enter opening Balance here we will do that in this chapter a little later. Click Save and Close.

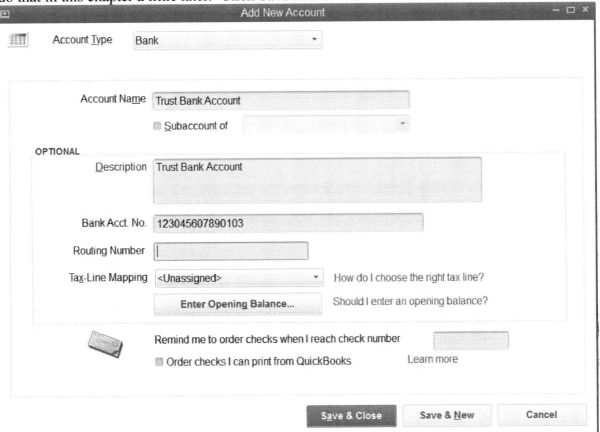

Trust Subaccount's

To make sure you keep your clients money correct and easy to check I suggest have sub account with your Trust account like the example below.

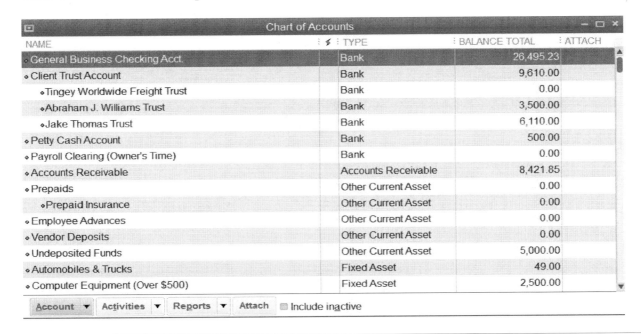

Creating Trust Subaccounts

Steps to setting up Trust subaccounts
1. Click on List from the top Main Menu Bar and select Chart of Accounts
2. Click on the Account Button at the bottom of the screen and select New
3. Choose Bank as the type and then Click Continue.
4. Type in the name of the Account Name in the Name Box (Client name that has trust money)
5. Place a check mark in the subaccount of box and choose Trust Bank Account from the drop down list. Enter a description in the Description Box.
6. Click Save & Close if you are finished or Save & New if you need to add additional accounts. In this sample exercise we will be adding 4 subaccounts.
7. Setup Subaccounts as Donald Kehn, Gary Stenli, Richard Zappe and Law Firm Funds
8. Click Save & Close when finished.

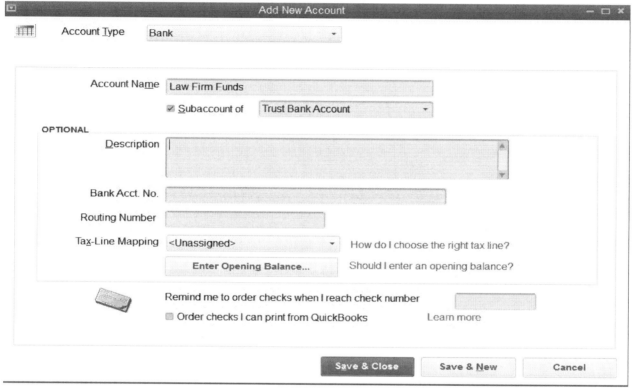

Here are the Trust Accounts we setup. We will enter balances shortly, but next we are setting up Trust Liability Accounts.

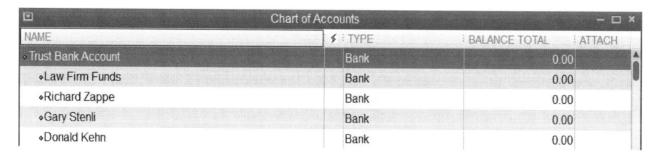

Setting up Trust Liability Accounts

Trust Liability Account is what the name says and that is its Trust money you owe your client that you have not earned. The balance in your liability accounts should be the same as the total amount you have in your bank trust account. This can be your clients money, money your firm contributed to open the account and any IOTA or IOLTA interest in the account.

During setting your company up and if you chose Law Firm/Legal as the type of business during setup then you will or should have this account. Check to see if you have an account under Other Current Liability called Trust Liability, Client Trust Liability or something similar such as my example's name is Trust Funds Held.

Steps to set up Trust Liability Account

1. Click on Lists from the top Main Menu Bar and Select Chart of Accounts.
2. Click on Account at the bottom the Chart of Accounts Screen and select New
3. Click on other type of accounts at the bottom of the screen and click on the drop down list and select Other Current Liability
4. Click Continue
5. Fill in the name and other necessary information.
6. DO NOT ENTER THE OPENING BALANCE HERE.
7. Click Save & Close when finished

NAME	⚡	TYPE	BALANCE TOTAL	ATTACH
Trust Funds Held		Other Current Liability	0.00	
Payroll Liabilities		Other Current Liability	2,753.59	
SEC125 Payable		Other Current Liability	50.00	
401K Payable		Other Current Liability	0.00	
Payroll Taxes Payable		Other Current Liability	2,703.59	
Client Retainers		Other Current Liability	8,200.00	

Trust Liability Subaccounts for Clients

To keep things as accurate and easy as possible its best to set up Trust Liability Subaccounts for Clients. This account should match The Trust Bank Account and Subaccounts.

Steps to setting up Trust Liability Subaccounts for clients
1. Click on Lists from the top Main Menu Bar and select Chart of Accounts
2. Click on the Account Button at the bottom of the Chart of Accounts screen
3. Select New
4. Click on other type of accounts at the bottom of the screen and click on the drop down list and select Other Current Liability and Click Continue
5. Type in the Client Name in the Name Box
6. Place a Check Mark in Subaccount of, click on drop down list and choose Trust Funds Held or the name of your firms account.
7. Enter a description putting case number or what you choose. When finished click Save & Close. We will enter the same names as the trust Bank Account subaccounts, Donald Kehn, Gary Stenli, Richard Zappe and Law Firm Funds as the subaccounts.
8. DO NOT ENTER BALANCES HERE

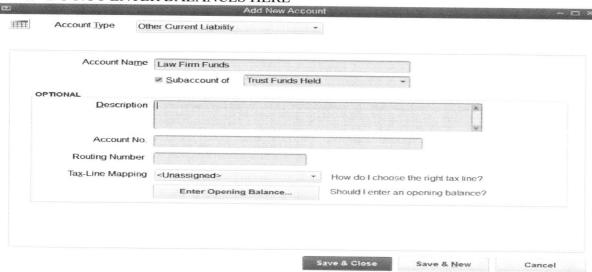

Here are the accounts we just set up.

Trust Funds Held	Other Current Liability	0.00
Law Firm Funds	Other Current Liability	0.00
Richard Zappe	Other Current Liability	0.00
Gary Stenli	Other Current Liability	0.00
Donald Kehn	Other Current Liability	0.00

Recording Interest on Trust Accounts
IOLTA/IOTA

Most all States require funds belonging to clients or third persons that are placed in trust with any member of your State Bar will be deposited into one or more interest-bearing trust accounts in an approved Bank/Financial Institution for the State Bar Foundation. With this in mind we need to be able to record the interest earned on the bank account. We will set up a subaccount to hold the interest.

1. Click on List from the top Main Menu Bar and select Chart of Accounts
2. Click on Accounts Button at the bottom of Chart of Accounts screen and choose New
3. Select other Account Types and choose Other Current Liability from the drop down list
4. Click Continue
5. Enter the Name as Client Trust - IOLTA Interest
6. Place a checkmark in the subaccount box and choose Trust Funds Held for this exercise.
7. Click Save & Close.

This is to show you the account we just set up for the interest and you enter it as shown below in your monthly account reconciliations. Remember to put in proper account, the Subaccount setup for interest.

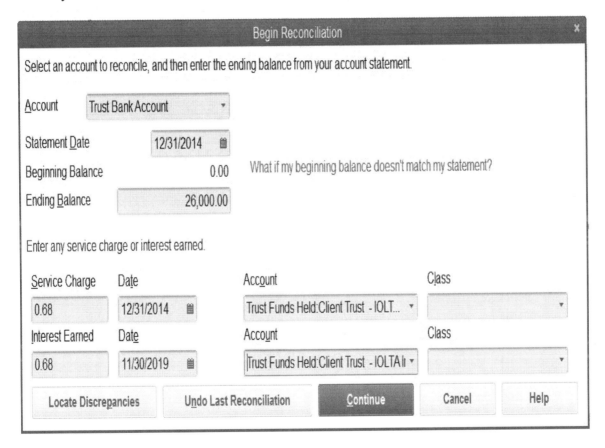

Setting up Beginning Balances

If you already have an account setup and money in the account you need to setup the beginning balances. If you haven't you can skip this section.

For this exercise/example we are going to start using this on January 1, 2015. The amount we had in our December 31, 2014 closing bank statement was $25,900.00. There were no outstanding checks or deposits.

1. Your first steps are to decide on a starting date.
2. You need to know how much money each client has in their Trust Account.
3. Donald Kehn, $10,400.00, Gary Stenli, $10,000.00, Richard Zappe, $5,500.00 and Law Firm Funds $100.00 for a total of $26,000.00

Ok now an easy way to put into QuickBooks.

1. Click Banking from the top Main Menu Bar
2. Click on Make Deposits
3. Because we set up subaccounts in the Trust Bank Accounts we have to make 4 deposits.
4. Make all four deposits the same. The Deposit To needs to be the same Client as the From Account and Received From.
5. When finished with all 4 deposits click Save & Close.

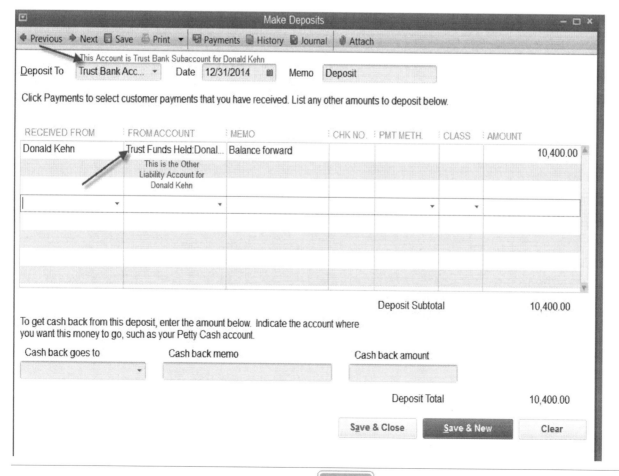

See the two red arrows match balances, plus all the subaccounts for Trust Bank Account and Trust Funds Held Liability subaccounts match.

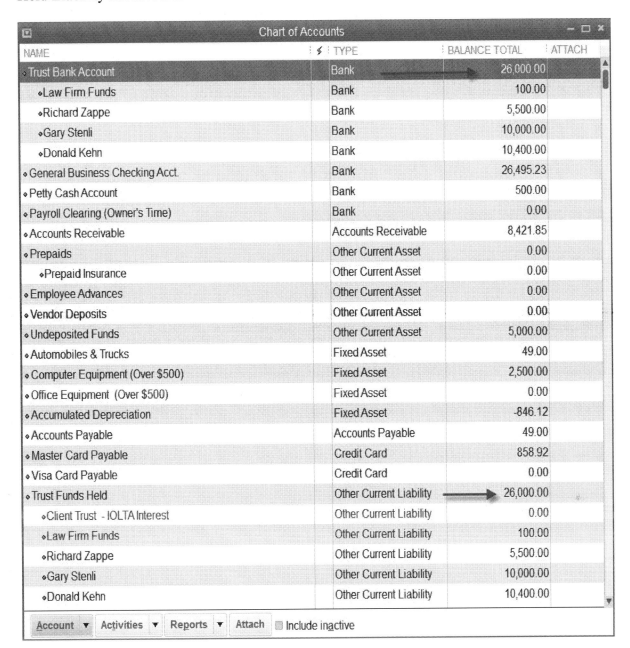

NAME	⚡ TYPE	BALANCE TOTAL	ATTACH
Trust Bank Account	Bank	26,000.00	
◦Law Firm Funds	Bank	100.00	
◦Richard Zappe	Bank	5,500.00	
◦Gary Stenli	Bank	10,000.00	
◦Donald Kehn	Bank	10,400.00	
◦General Business Checking Acct.	Bank	26,495.23	
◦Petty Cash Account	Bank	500.00	
◦Payroll Clearing (Owner's Time)	Bank	0.00	
◦Accounts Receivable	Accounts Receivable	8,421.85	
◦Prepaids	Other Current Asset	0.00	
◦Prepaid Insurance	Other Current Asset	0.00	
◦Employee Advances	Other Current Asset	0.00	
◦Vendor Deposits	Other Current Asset	0.00	
◦Undeposited Funds	Other Current Asset	5,000.00	
◦Automobiles & Trucks	Fixed Asset	49.00	
◦Computer Equipment (Over $500)	Fixed Asset	2,500.00	
◦Office Equipment (Over $500)	Fixed Asset	0.00	
◦Accumulated Depreciation	Fixed Asset	-846.12	
◦Accounts Payable	Accounts Payable	49.00	
◦Master Card Payable	Credit Card	858.92	
◦Visa Card Payable	Credit Card	0.00	
◦Trust Funds Held	Other Current Liability	26,000.00	
◦Client Trust - IOLTA Interest	Other Current Liability	0.00	
◦Law Firm Funds	Other Current Liability	100.00	
◦Richard Zappe	Other Current Liability	5,500.00	
◦Gary Stenli	Other Current Liability	10,000.00	
◦Donald Kehn	Other Current Liability	10,400.00	

Account ▾   Activities ▾   Reports ▾   Attach   ☐ Include inactive

When putting these deposits in make sure:
- Date is correct
- Deposit to Account is correct
- Received from is the correct Client
- From Account is the correct Account
- The Amount is Correct
- When done the Total on The Trust Fund Bank and Liability Account should Match
- The Subaccounts for Trust Clients should match with Trust Bank subaccounts and Trust Liability subaccounts.

Reports to verify Trust Account Balances

Ok the next step is to verify our balances to make sure the Trust bank Account matches Trust Liability Accounts.

1. Click on Reports from top Main Menu Bar
2. Click on Company & Financial
3. Select Balance Sheet Standard
4. Change the date to the date you entered your deposits into the Client Trust Bank Accounts.

Everything matches/balances

| | | Balance Sheet | | | | | | | | |

| Customize Report | Comment on Report | Share Template | Memorize | Print ▼ | E-mail ▼ | Excel ▼ | Hide Header | Collapse | Refresh |

| Dates | Custom | | As of 12/31/2014 | Show Columns | Total only | | Sort By | Default | |

3:43 PM

12/15/19

Accrual Basis

Law Firm

Balance Sheet

As of December 31, 2014

	Dec 31, 14
▼ ASSETS	
▼ Current Assets	
▼ Checking/Savings	
▼ Trust Bank Account	
Law Firm Funds	100.00
Richard Zappe	5,500.00
Gary Stenli	10,000.00
Donald Kehn	10,400.00
Total Trust Bank Account	26,000.00 ←
General Business Checking Acct.	-605.00
Total Checking/Savings	25,395.00
▶ Accounts Receivable ▶	14,170.30 ◀
Total Current Assets	39,565.30
TOTAL ASSETS	39,565.30
▼ LIABILITIES & EQUITY	
▼ Liabilities	
▼ Current Liabilities	
▼ Accounts Payable	
Accounts Payable	4,417.00
Total Accounts Payable	4,417.00
▶ Credit Cards	-204.91
▼ Other Current Liabilities	
▼ Trust Funds Held	
Law Firm Funds	100.00
Richard Zappe	5,500.00
Gary Stenli	10,000.00
Donald Kehn	10,400.00
Total Trust Funds Held	26,000.00 ←
Line of Credit	93.75
Total Other Current Liabilities	26,093.75
Total Current Liabilities	30,305.84
Total Liabilities	30,305.84
▶ Equity	9,259.46
TOTAL LIABILITIES & EQUITY	39,565.30

Detail Report for Trust Account Balance

This is a good report to have handy on a moment's notice. This shows activity in each Clients Trust Account.

1. Click on List top of the Main Menu Bar
2. Select Chart of Accounts
3. Click on the Trusts Bank Account
4. Click on the Reports button at the bottom and choose Quick Report: Trusts Bank Account

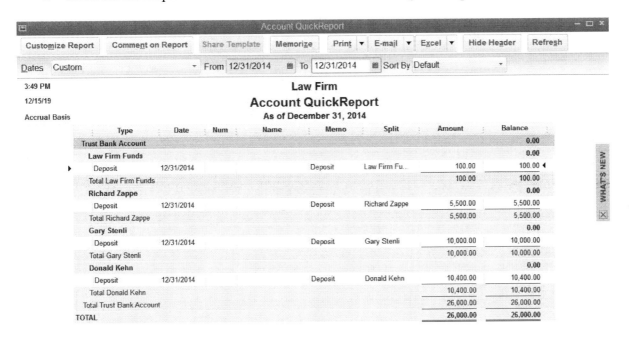

You can customize/modify this report by clicking on the Customize Report button to the top left of the report screen. For this Exercise lets remove the Num and Name columns on the customization since those two fields aren't necessary.

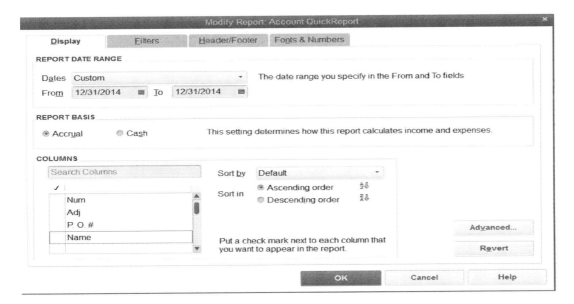

Modified Report. Removed the two columns and changed the name. Memorized Report.

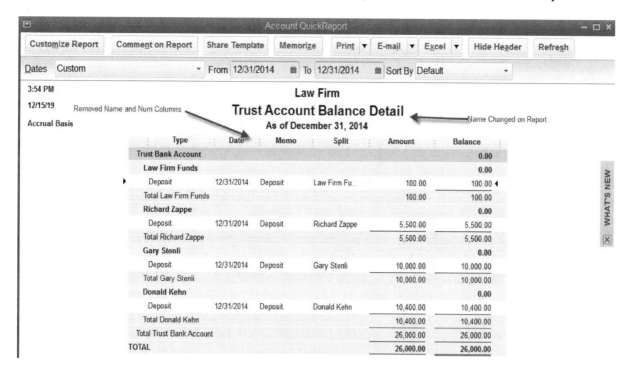

Take the same steps to create a Client Trust Liability Balance Detail Report as you did for the Client Trust Bank Account Balance Detail. The only difference is double Click on the Liability Account in the Chart of Accounts. I made same changes to this report removing Name and Num columns and changing the Title/Name of the report. I memorized this as well.

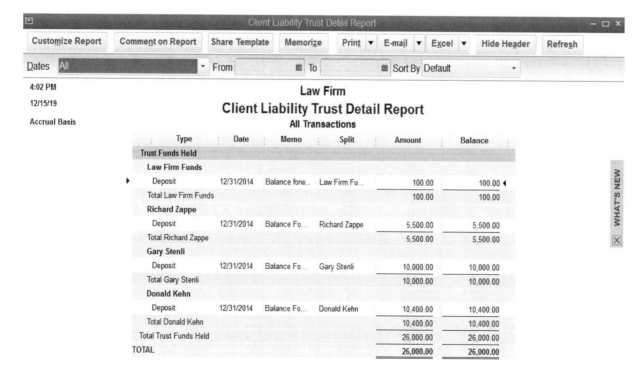

This is the best account to check the Trust Bank account vs Trust Liability Account. Once you know setup a folder for these reports and then you can run them in a matter of minutes. Each month you should perform a Bank Reconciliation, Trust Account Activity and the Client Trust Liability Reports to verify balances. These reports are the minimum you should probably run. Check with your State Bar Association to find out what reports they require on a monthly basis.

To run this report

1. Click Reports top Main Menu Bar, select Accountant & Taxes & Transaction Detail by Account.
2. Click Customize Report button, remove class from the Columns list
3. In the Filter Tab you will need to click on Account drop down list, choose multiple accounts and then click on you Trust Bank Account and your Trust Liability Account. By clicking on the main accounts the subaccounts were included on report.
4. Tab to Header/Footer and Change name to Trust Banking & Liability Detail by Account.
5. Click Ok. Then memorize.

Remove check mark by Class.

Select Multiple Accounts

Here's the report. I can't think of a better report to compare and verify your Trust Activity.

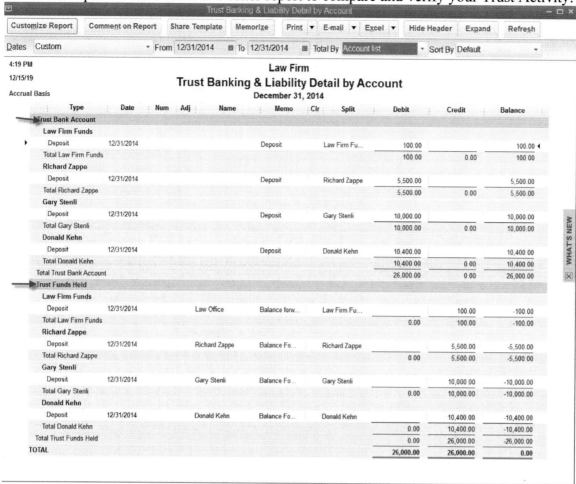

In the next chapter we will learn and go over you day to day Trust Account activities.

Chapter 13
Trust Account Activities

In this chapter we will go over daily activities such as paying client costs, writing checks, working with credit cards and creating closing statements with your Trust Account.

Trust Deposits

When you receive money from a client you will need to deposit in the trust account. If they are existing client you will go and make the deposit, but if they are new then you need to setup their subaccount in the Trust Bank and in the Trust Liability accounts.

1. Click on Banking from the top Main Menu Bar
2. Select Make Deposits
3. Make sure the Deposit To is the correct Trust Account
4. Make sure the Received from and from account are the correct Accounts from the correct client and last but not least the correct amount.
5. Click Save & New if you have more Deposits and when finished with last deposit click Save & Close.

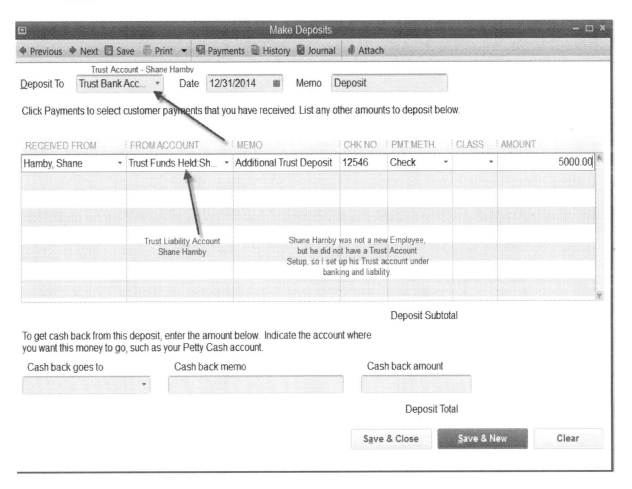

Credit Card Deposits - Trust Accounts

Credit Cards and Trust accounts can make things more difficult because the payment has to go directly into the Trust account. This means you either have to have two merchant accounts, one for the Trust and one for your operating account. The only other way a client can use their credit card for funds is to write you a check from a check that is a credit card check. If you are not completely clear as to what your State rules are then contact your State Bar Association to be sure.

The other problem by having a merchant account for the Trust Account is the credit card processing fees. The credit card fees cannot be transferred to the client. You will have to write a check out of the operating account and deposit it into the clients trust account to cover the exact fees deducted from their trust account for the credit card processing.

Steps to Receiving Credit Card Payments into the Trust Account.

1. Click on Banking from the top Main Menu Bar
2. Click on Make Deposits
3. From the Deposit to drop-down list, choose the correct client Trust Bank Account.
4. Received from is your Client name
5. From Account is your Client Trust Liability Account
6. Memo Colum give a good description.
7. Choose a payment method from the Pymt Method Column
8. Enter the amount of the deposit in the Amount Column. This increases your trust liability each time you deposit money; this increases what you owe clients.
9. The next line in the From Account Column, Select Law Firm Funds (This is the money you opened your Trust Account with, if you don't have enough money from this we will cover how to reimburse in the next section)
10. In the memo field type in the description of credit card fee.
11. In the amount field type in -5.00. Click Save & Close.

As you can see your deposit is 995.00 not 1,000.00, so your client is short 5.00 and will need to be taken from your firm funds in the trust account or write a check out of the operating account to cover this.

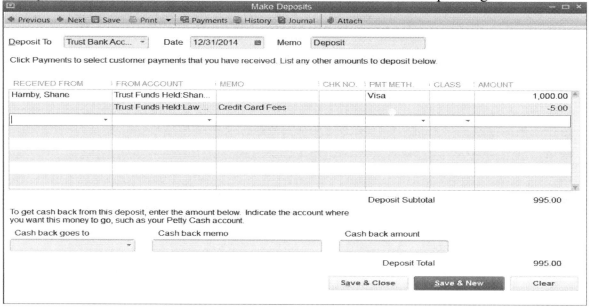

Credit Card Fees - Reimburse Trust Account

We want to reimburse the Trust Account for Credit Card Fees even if you have a small amount of firm funds, so that you don't ever have a chance of over drafting. We will write a check to the Trust Account from the Operating Account.

1. Click on Banking from the top Main Menu Bar and select Write Checks
2. Select Bank Account, Make sure this is the Operating Account
3. Make the check out to your Law Office in the name/Pay to the Order Field.
4. Type in the amount $5.00 in the $ field box.
5. Account field is Bank Service Charges, or Credit Card Fees, depending on your account.
6. In Memo type detailed description, Click Save & Close.

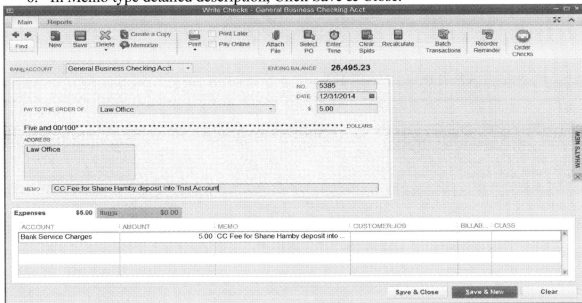

When you deposit the credit card reimbursement check into the Trust account be sure to choose Law Firm Funds. See Below.

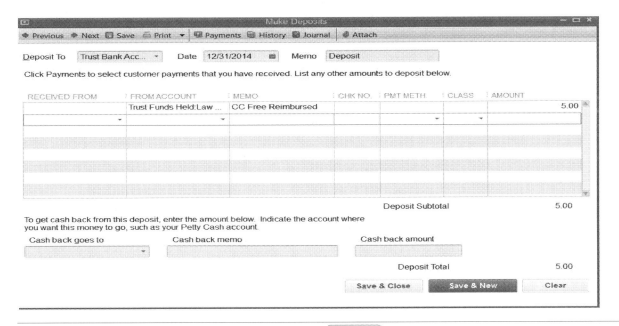

Replenishing funds in your Trust Account

When you need to deposit your own Law Practice funds into your Trust Account to maintain a minimum balance you will need to write a check from your operating account.

Steps to write check to Trust Account

1. Click Banking from the top Main Menu Bar, Select Write Checks
2. Choose Bank Account, make sure it's the operating account
3. Type in Pay to the Order of, Law Office, (the name of your firm)
4. Type in 100.00 or the amount you want in the Box $ then type in memo what it's for.
5. Set up account Due from Trust Account, type of account would be Other Current Asset Account.
6. Type in Memo for description as you did on check memo and click Save & Close

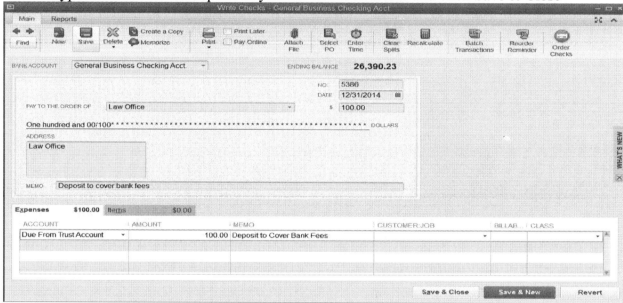

Now we will Deposit this check into the Trust Account.

1. Click Banking from the top Main Menu Bar and click Make Deposits
2. In the Deposit to box choose Trust Account - Law Firm Funds under the Trust Liability Account
3. Enter Check number, pmt method and the amount. Click Save & Close.

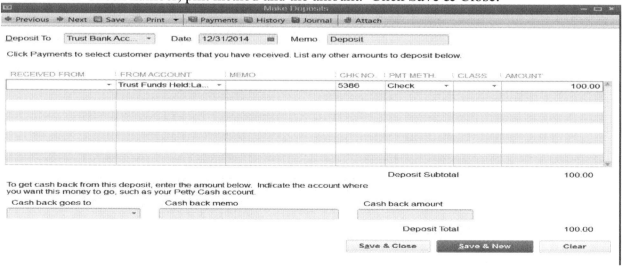

Sample of Trust Safe Deposit Receipt.

This does not have to be put into QuickBooks, although you can under attachments. If a client gives you property instead of money to hold in your Trust or really any reason, say keep guns to keep them from harming themselves or other's. You may need to fill out the following Trust Safe Deposit Receipt and follow your State Bar rules. It's a good idea to have a witness as to the items received and take pictures as well. To attach to Client save as PDF. See how to attach this or any document to Client File in QuickBooks on the next page.

Sample - Check with your State Bar Association

TRUST SAFE DEPOSIT RECEIPT

Received this _____ day of _____, 20___ by _____.

_____

_____

_____

(Description of item(s) being placed into safe deposit box -- if items are numbered such as stocks or bonds, specify numbers.) Description of larger items in other safe.

Item(s) being held in trust for: _____

Firm Name: _____

Client Case/Matter: _____

Item(s) being placed in the safe deposit box by: _____

_____ Partner _____ Associate (check one) or

Items that are large being held in Large Safe at:_____

Any questions about contents should be addressed to:

_____

_____

Safe Deposit Box ID Number: _____

(Applies if at Safe Deposit at Bank/Financial Institution)

Time Frame items will be held: From: _____ TO:_____

Client Signature:_____ Signature/Law Firm Representative_____

Date:_____ Date:_____

Witness Signature:_____

Date:_____

Attaching Documents to Clients QuickBooks Files.

You can attach any, or just about any, document, file, receipt to your Clients in QuickBooks. This is such a great feature. We are going to attach the Trust Safe Deposit Receipt to a Clients Account.

Steps to Attach Documents
1. Click on Customers in the top Main Menu Bar
2. Choose Customer Center
3. Highlight the Client you want to attach the document to and double click on the attach column. Notice the paperclip in the client's file under attach? That indicates he has a file attached.

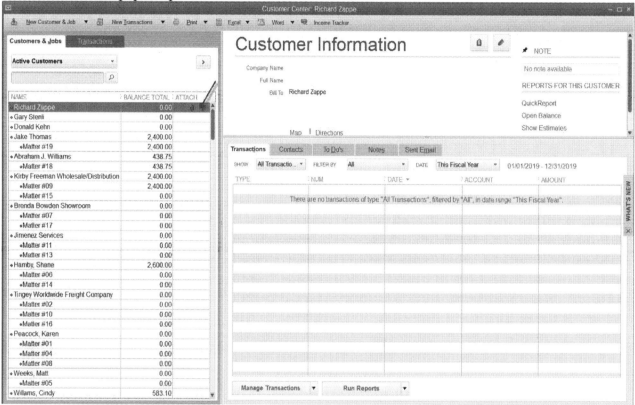

This is the screen that pops up when you double click on the attach column. To add the file click on computer, Scanner or Doc Center and click on the file to attach. The file is now attached. To view this or any file just double click on the paperclip icon in the clients attach column, then double click on the file to view. When finished click X to exit out of document and x out of this screen.

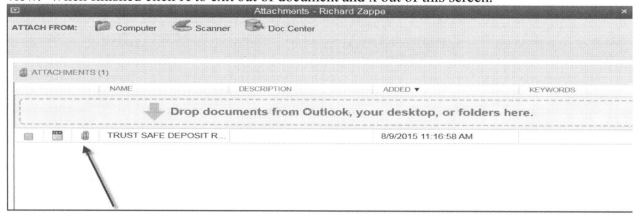

Paying Client Costs from their Trust Account

When you need to pay for client costs, you can write a check directly out of the Clients Trust Account.

1. Click Banking from the top Main Menu Bar
2. Click Write Checks
3. Choose the Clients Trust Account you are writing the check-out of
4. Pay to the order of box is who you are making payment to.
5. Type in the amount in the $ box.
6. The Account under the Expenses tab needs to be the Clients Liability Account
7. Enter the amount and Memo Description again.
8. Click Print, or Print later. If you don't use QuickBooks to print checks make sure none of the print buttons are checked and click Save & Close.

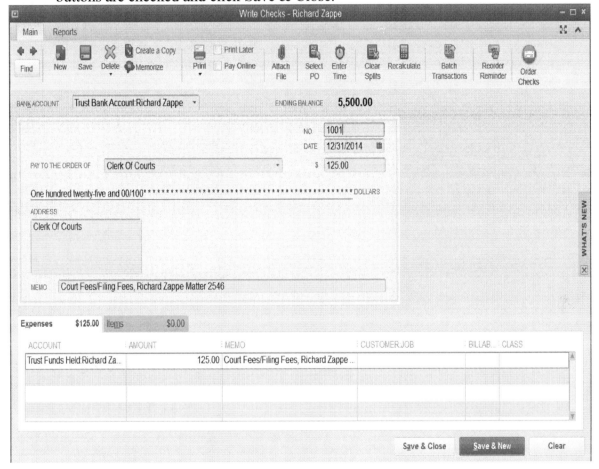

On the next page we will write checks for your legal services out of a Trust Account.

Writing Checks out of Clients Trust for your Legal Services

You need to invoice your client(s) to see how much they owe you and then you can write a check or checks. When you write a check for your legal services this will also reduce you liability to your clients. An Attorney has to obtain client approval before doing this. As always make sure you know the rules of your state, so check with your State Bar Association.

1. Click Reports from the top Main Menu Bar
2. Click on Customers & Receivables
3. Select Open Invoices Report. This report list what each Client owes you.
4. After invoice clients, this report shows they owe you $10,062.75.

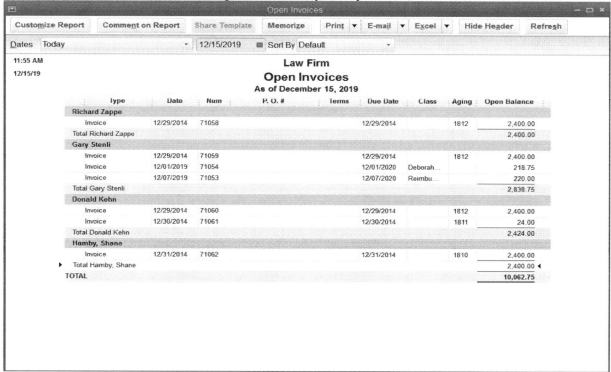

To write the checks click on the Write Checks on the home page under the Banking Section. Enter each check information and click save and new until all 4 checks have been written. Put the invoice number in the description/memo sections to have document to refer to.

Here's the checks ready to print from Trust Clients Invoiced amount. The total is $10,062.75 same as report.

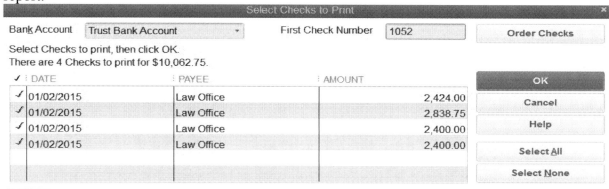

It's a good idea to run this report to verify accounts after writing checks out of the Client Trusts.

Law Firm
Trust Banking & Liability Detail by Account
December 28, 2014 through February 3, 2015

Type	Date	Num	Adj	Name	Memo	Clr	Split	Debit	Credit	Balance
Trust Bank Account										
Law Firm Funds										
Deposit	12/31/2014				Deposit		Law Firm Fu...	100.00		100.00
Deposit	12/31/2014				Deposit		Law Firm Fu...	100.00		200.00
Total Law Firm Funds								200.00	0.00	200.00
Richard Zappe										
Deposit	12/31/2014				Deposit		Richard Zappe	5,500.00		5,500.00
Check	12/31/2014	1001		Clerk Of Courts	Court Fees/...		Richard Zappe		125.00	5,375.00
Check	01/02/2015	1054		Law Office	Payment fo...		Richard Zappe		2,400.00	2,975.00
Total Richard Zappe								5,500.00	2,525.00	2,975.00
Gary Stenli										
Deposit	12/31/2014				Deposit		Gary Stenli	10,000.00		10,000.00
Check	01/02/2015	1053		Law Office	Payment fo...		Gary Stenli		2,838.75	7,161.25
Total Gary Stenli								10,000.00	2,838.75	7,161.25
Donald Kehn										
Deposit	12/31/2014				Deposit		Donald Kehn	10,400.00		10,400.00
Check	01/02/2015	1052		Law Office	Payment fo...		Donald Kehn		2,424.00	7,976.00
Total Donald Kehn								10,400.00	2,424.00	7,976.00
Total Trust Bank Account								26,100.00	7,787.75	18,312.25
Trust Funds Held										
Law Firm Funds										
Deposit	12/31/2014			Law Office	Balance forw...		Law Firm Fu...		100.00	-100.00
Deposit	12/31/2014				Credit Card ...		Shane Hamby	5.00		-95.00
Deposit	12/31/2014				CC Free Re...		Shane Hamby		5.00	-100.00
Deposit	12/31/2014	5386			Deposit		Law Firm Fu...		100.00	-200.00
Total Law Firm Funds								5.00	205.00	-200.00
Richard Zappe										
Deposit	12/31/2014			Richard Zappe	Balance Fo...		Richard Zappe		5,500.00	-5,500.00 ◄
Check	12/31/2014	1001		Clerk Of Courts	Court Fees/...		Richard Zappe	125.00		-5,375.00
Check	01/02/2015	1054		Law Office	Payment fo...		Richard Zappe	2,400.00		-2,975.00
Total Richard Zappe								2,525.00	5,500.00	-2,975.00
Gary Stenli										
Deposit	12/31/2014			Gary Stenli	Balance Fo...		Gary Stenli		10,000.00	-10,000.00
Check	01/02/2015	1053		Law Office	Payment fo...		Gary Stenli	2,838.75		-7,161.25
Total Gary Stenli								2,838.75	10,000.00	-7,161.25
Donald Kehn										
Deposit	12/31/2014			Donald Kehn	Balance Fo...		Donald Kehn		10,400.00	-10,400.00
Check	01/02/2015	1052		Law Office	Payment fo...		Donald Kehn	2,424.00		-7,976.00
Total Donald Kehn								2,424.00	10,400.00	-7,976.00
Total Trust Funds Held								7,792.75	26,105.00	-18,312.25
TOTAL								33,892.75	33,892.75	0.00

Note: By setting up Client subaccounts in the Trust Banking and The Trust Liability you have better and more information available and it's easier to prevent mistakes. The other way is one Trust Account and one Trust Liability account that is easier, but takes longer to reconcile and easier to make mistakes.

Client Detail Activity Statement

Closing a Client's Case you need to prepare a detailed Transaction Activity Statement for the client and issue a refund of unused Client Trust Funds, if any are left unearned.

Here's the report we went over and I memorized. To customize this report you need to bring up the memorized report, then go to Filters Tab, Click on Multiple Accounts and select the Clients Trust and The Clients Liability Trust account. I will show you another way to do this as well. You will write a refund check for $2975.00 to Mr. Richard Zappe.

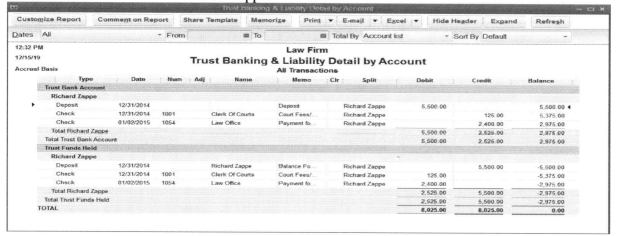

The Refund Check issued from Richard's Trust Bank Account and expense account issued against his Liability Account. Trust Refund in the Memo. Here's the report before and see below the report after.

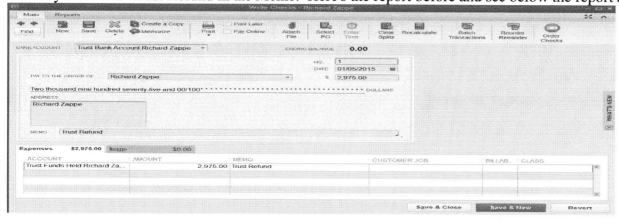

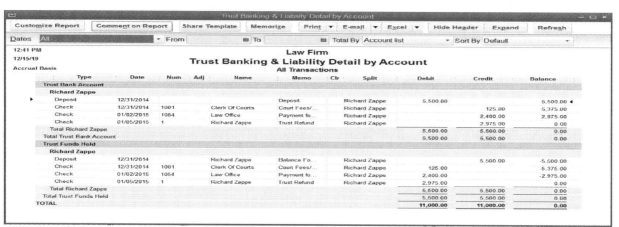

To run Client Transaction Report from your Standard Balance Sheet.

1. Click Reports at the top Main Menu Bar
2. Click Company & Financial
3. Select Balance Sheet Standard
4. Double Click on the Client you want to pull up and write a refund check to. I am writing the one with the red arrow. If you are using the method of one trust bank account and one trust liability account then you would click on Other Current Liabilities account just above the red arrow.
5. After you double click on your client and the transactions report comes up you need to click on the drop down dates list click on all. See Report below balance sheet report.

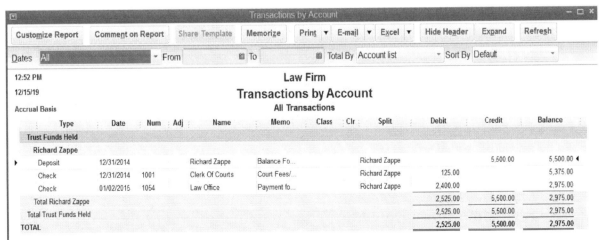

Here's the Standard Balance Sheet after issuing Refund Check. Richard Zappe is no longer owed any money, so his liability went away.

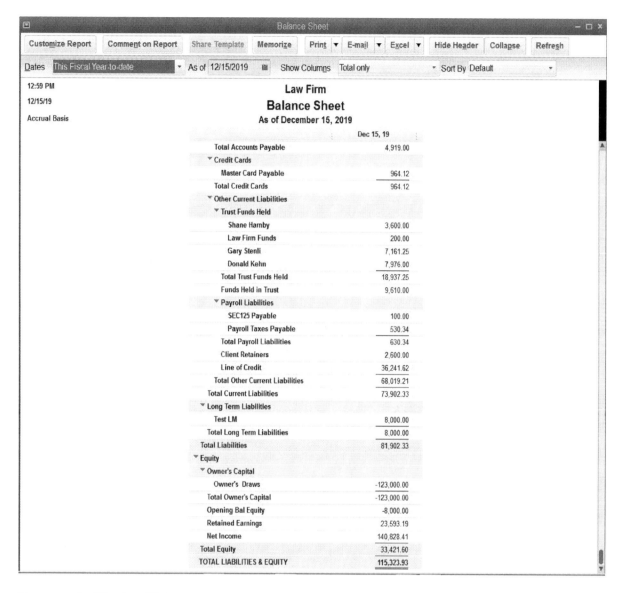

See sample Closing Statement on next page.

SAMPLE CLOSING STATEMENT

BE SURE TO CHECK TO MAKE SURE WHAT YOUR STATE REQUIRES THIS IS JUST AN EXAMPLE

Closing Statement

Client: _____

Matter/Case_____

Settlement Proceeds: $_____

    Less Attorneys' Fee (___%) $_____

    (Insert Firm Name of Co-Counsel, if Applicable) $_____

        Total Attorneys' Fees: $_____

    Less Costs Incurred During Suit $_____

    Less Future Costs $_____

        Total Costs $_____

    Less Outstanding Bills $_____

    (Any medical bills or other costs to be paid)

NET PROCEEDS: $_____

    (I) (WE) approve the disbursements shown above, and upon the receipt of
_____ dollars, (I) (WE) acknowledge that (I) (WE) have been paid in full from the recovery in (MY) (OUR) case and that (I) (WE) will holds the law firm(s) (<u>insert name of firms</u>) harmless from any additional bills incurred not mentioned above. (I) (WE) understand that the unused balance, if any, of future costs will be refunded to (ME) (US) in approximately two months.

    DATED this _____ day of _____, 20___.

Firm Name and Contact Information - Here

_____

Client's Signature
BY: _____

Chapter 14
Monthly Trust Account Activities

In this chapter we will go over preparing a Monthly Trust Account Certificate and other reports on Client Trust Accounts. Here again I stress with your State Bar Association for guidelines on Trusts. I have included a Sample Monthly Trust account certificate that you would fill out after you have reconciled your client's trust account.

Monthly Trust Accounting Certificate

Fill out the following Monthly Trust Accounting Certificate (or if you have a different one required by your state) and put with the reconciliation report. See the copy on next page. Print out bank reconciliation to review and make sure all checks have cleared and everything is correct. If you by chance have any old outstanding checks then you need to contact the party you wrote the check(s) to and ask them to cash them. They need to cash them or the money needs to be refunded to the client. I would say this is rare unless the check is lost. Since Trust accounts are so important to keep by law you should open your statements or a managing partner to be sure everything looks and is right.

SAMPLE - CHECK WITH YOUR STATE BAR ASSOCIATION TO BE SURE YOU HAVE WHAT IS REQUIRED.

MONTHLY TRUST ACCOUNT CERTIFICATE

For the period ___/___/___ to ___/___/___

Bank Account No.

_____

name and address of banking institution

1. During the fiscal period noted above to the best of my knowledge I maintained books, records and accounts to record all money and trust property received and disbursed in connection with the firm practice, and as a minimum maintained:

    a. A separate bank account or accounts located in (your State), in the name of the law firm clearly labeled and designated a "trust account".

    b. Original or duplicate deposit slips and, in the case of currency or coin, an additional cash receipts book, clearly identifying the date and source of all trust funds received, and specific identification of the client or matter for whom the funds were received.

    c. Original cancelled checks for all trust disbursements.

    d. Other documentary support for all disbursements and transfers from the trust account.

    e. A separate cash receipts and journal, including columns for receipts, disbursements, and the account balance, disclosing the client, check number, and the reason for which the funds were received, disbursed or transferred.

    f. A separate file or ledger, with an individual card, record or page for each client and matter, showing all individual receipts, disbursements and unexpended balance.

    g. All bank statements for all trust accounts.

    h. Complete records of all funds, securities and other properties of a client coming into my/our possession, and rendered appropriate accounts to the firms' clients regarding them.

2. During the same fiscal period identified above, to the best of my knowledge, I complied with the required trust accounting procedures, and as a minimum:

    a. Prepared monthly trust comparisons, including bank reconciliations and an annual detailed listing identifying the balance of the unexpended trust money held for each client or matter.

        Compared for the period of this report the total of trust liabilities, with the total of each trust bank reconciliation, and there were (check appropriate box):

        ___ no differences between the total, excepting those determined to be the result of bank error:

        ___ differences. Give full particulars below, identifying the amounts involved, and the reason for each item contributing to a difference. Attach additional pages if necessary.

    c. Inspected the listing for overdrawn accounts and there were:

        ___ no overdrawn accounts.

        ___ overdrawn accounts as set out below:

    To the best of my knowledge and belief the facts as reported herein are accurate.

    Signature _____

    Date _____

    Reviewed and signed by a partner this _____ date of _____, 20___.

    Partner Signature_____

Reconciling Checking Accounts

Reconciling is necessary to making sure that your checking accounts matches the banks records and to make sure something doesn't come through that could cause an overdraft.

Steps to Reconcile

1. Click Banking from the top Main Menu Bar
2. Click Reconcile
3. Enter Trust Bank Account for the Account, statement Date. This is first reconciliation is why it shows beginning balance 0.00 otherwise it would have the Beginning balance the same balance as last months ending balance.
4. Enter the Bank Statement's ending Balance that you are balancing to.
5. Click Continue

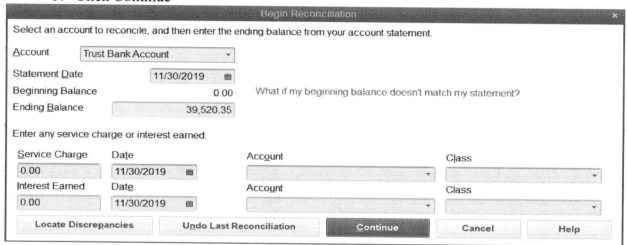

The Screen below pops up next after you click on continue. Go through and check cleared checks and deposits. Once you balance you will have 0.00 difference. Click Reconcile Now once you know you are balanced.

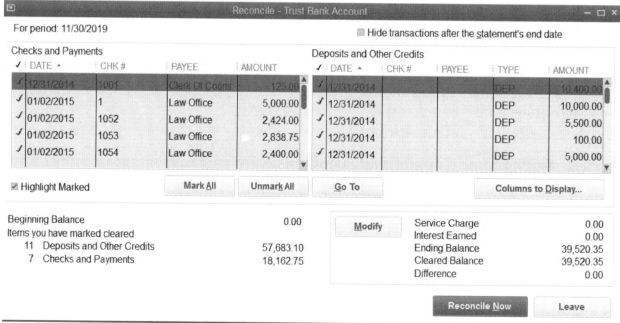

This is the following screen once you clicked Reconcile Now. You will want to print the reports, so Click Print. The report(s) will print and the open reconciliation and print screens will close.

Summary Reconciliation Report for Trust Account

1:43 PM	**Law Firm**	
12/15/19	**Reconciliation Summary**	
	Trust Bank Account, Period Ending 11/30/2019	

	Nov 30, 19	
Beginning Balance		0.00
Cleared Transactions		
Checks and Payments - 7 items	-18,162.75	
Deposits and Credits - 11 items	57,683.10	
Total Cleared Transactions	39,520.35	
Cleared Balance		39,520.35
Register Balance as of 11/30/2019		39,520.35
Ending Balance		39,520.35

Detail Reconciliation Report for Trust Account

1:43 PM	**Law Firm**	
12/15/19	**Reconciliation Detail**	
	Trust Bank Account, Period Ending 11/30/2019	

Type	Date	Num	Name	Clr	Amount	Balance
Beginning Balance						0.00
Cleared Transactions						
Checks and Payments - 7 items						
Check	12/31/2014	1001	Clerk Of Courts	X	-125.00	-125.00
Check	01/02/2015	1	Law Office	X	-5,000.00	-5,125.00
Check	01/02/2015	1053	Law Office	X	-2,838.75	-7,963.75
Check	01/02/2015	1052	Law Office	X	-2,424.00	-10,387.75
Check	01/02/2015	1055	Law Office	X	-2,400.00	-12,787.75
Check	01/02/2015	1054	Law Office	X	-2,400.00	-15,187.75
Check	01/05/2015		Richard Zappe	X	-2,975.00	-18,162.75
Total Checks and Payments					-18,162.75	-18,162.75
Deposits and Credits - 11 items						
Deposit	12/31/2014			X	5.00	5.00
Deposit	12/31/2014			X	100.00	105.00
Deposit	12/31/2014			X	100.00	205.00
Deposit	12/31/2014			X	995.00	1,200.00
Deposit	12/31/2014			X	5,000.00	6,200.00
Deposit	12/31/2014			X	5,000.00	11,200.00
Deposit	12/31/2014			X	5,500.00	16,700.00
Deposit	12/31/2014			X	10,000.00	26,700.00
Deposit	12/31/2014			X	10,400.00	37,100.00
Deposit	01/02/2015			X	5,000.00	42,100.00
Deposit	01/02/2015			X	15,583.10	57,683.10
Total Deposits and Credits					57,683.10	57,683.10
Total Cleared Transactions					39,520.35	39,520.35
Cleared Balance					39,520.35	39,520.35
Register Balance as of 11/30/2019					39,520.35	39,520.35
Ending Balance					39,520.35	39,520.35

There are many reports you can run as I have said in the Reports chapter. Below you will see the Check Detail report and the Deposit Detail Report. I kept and keep monthly files locked in a filing cabinet. In my files for the month were Bank Statement from the bank, QuickBooks Reconciliation reports, The Check Detail and the Deposit Detail. You will have to customize/modify each month dates with dates and specify under the filters tab for Trust Checking when you are doing just Trust Checking or otherwise the report defaults to all accounts. This is one I would memorize for Trust Account and memorize one for Operating Account.

Reporting on Client Trusts

The following Report accounts for detail transactions for your Trust Bank Account and your Trust Liability account along with all and any subaccounts to both accounts. We memorized it before and as all reports you will need to tweak the dates should be all you have to do. Notice the check marks in the Clr column, this tells you that you have reconciled your Trust Bank Account for the month that you are looking at. On this report you always want a 0.00 on the Total because that means your two accounts are in balance. Just make sure you have everything in the right accounts. The amount is balanced.

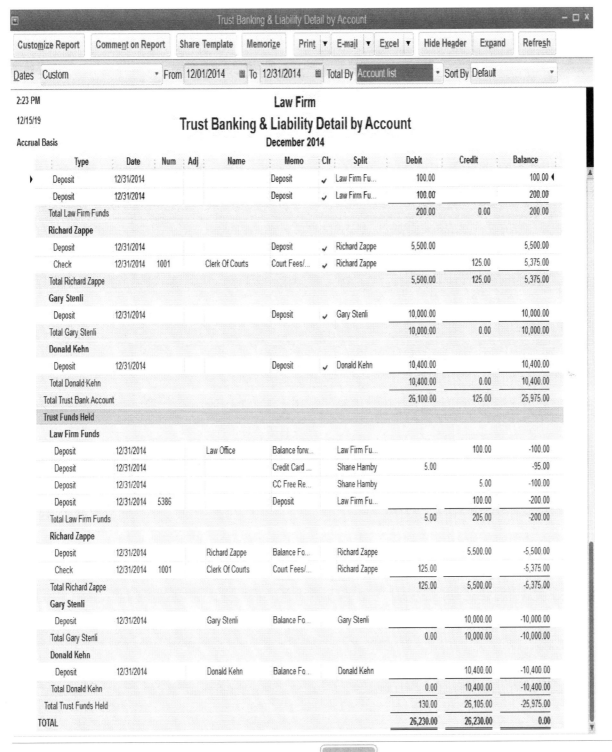

Correcting Trust Account Errors

When you are viewing any of your Trust documents and you find an error it is utmost important you take immediate action and correct any and all errors. As always keep track of any and all documentation on the error and correcting it.

As you know the Trust Accounting is very serious and that's why I continually mention if you don't know or aren't sure of your State's laws find out.

Trust Activities

Trust Deposits - This is all money that goes into the Trust Account that is going to be applied to a Client's trust liability account or a small amount of your firm's money to cover fees. The Client's Trust Liability Account is a subaccount under Client Trust Liability, other current liability.

Trust Withdrawals - This is all money being taken out of the Trust Account and is going to be applied to a client's Client Trust Liability account. The Client's Trust Liability Account is a subaccount under Client Trust Liability, other current liability.

Reconcile - Reconcile is reconciling your Trust Bank Account each month to the Bank Statement from your Bank or Financial Institution. Run your reports to check and verify Client balances.

Moving Trust Money - Write a check out of Trust out of the client's liability account. Receive the payment just like they came in the mail or came in and paid you. Deposit it into the Operating Account.

Chapter 15
Lists and More Lists

We went over and talked about some lists and some we haven't. I went over what most Attorney's use. I want to introduce you to what is available. Remember the more information you have the more and better reporting you can have at your fingertips. More information is another way to pull even more variations of reports as well. Plus you don't have to guess or go around looking if you fill in all the information you have and can.

Click on Lists at the top Main Menu Bar and you will find the following lists in the 2015 Premier Edition.

Chart of Accounts
Item List
Fixed Asset Item List
Price Level List
Billing Rate Level List
Payroll Item List
Payroll Schedule List
Class List
Other Names List
Customers & Vendor Profile List ➡ Sales Rep List
                                                         Customer Type List
                                                         Vendor Type List
                                                         Job Type List
                                                         Terms List
                                                         Customer Message List
                                                         Payment Method List
                                                         Ship Via List
                                                         Vehicle List

Templates
Memorize Transaction List
Add/Edit Multiple List Entries

Wow what a lot of lists. I will have a screen shot of each and explain them in summary form and ways you might use them in your Law Practice.

Another thing to keep in mind and that is always check your Preferences to see if you need to turn on a feature. You may add data to one of these lists and try to run reports and nothing shows and it could be something as simple as turning the feature on in your Preferences.

Last but not least if you are using Pro Version some of these lists may not be available.

List Available/Information in QuickBooks

1.   Chart of Accounts - This is the heart of your Practice basically. It tracks all money coming in and going out. These are the accounts you set up to enter everything into the appropriate category. You can use a preset chart of accounts, use your own set of chart of accounts or a combination of both.

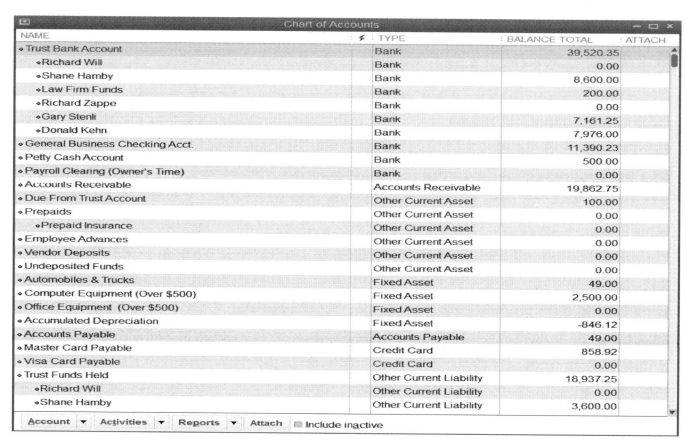

NAME	⚡	TYPE	BALANCE TOTAL	ATTACH
● Trust Bank Account		Bank	39,520.35	
●Richard Will		Bank	0.00	
●Shane Hamby		Bank	8,600.00	
●Law Firm Funds		Bank	200.00	
●Richard Zappe		Bank	0.00	
●Gary Stenli		Bank	7,161.25	
●Donald Kehn		Bank	7,976.00	
● General Business Checking Acct.		Bank	11,390.23	
● Petty Cash Account		Bank	500.00	
● Payroll Clearing (Owner's Time)		Bank	0.00	
● Accounts Receivable		Accounts Receivable	19,862.75	
● Due From Trust Account		Other Current Asset	100.00	
● Prepaids		Other Current Asset	0.00	
●Prepaid Insurance		Other Current Asset	0.00	
● Employee Advances		Other Current Asset	0.00	
● Vendor Deposits		Other Current Asset	0.00	
● Undeposited Funds		Other Current Asset	0.00	
● Automobiles & Trucks		Fixed Asset	49.00	
● Computer Equipment (Over $500)		Fixed Asset	2,500.00	
● Office Equipment (Over $500)		Fixed Asset	0.00	
● Accumulated Depreciation		Fixed Asset	-846.12	
● Accounts Payable		Accounts Payable	49.00	
● Master Card Payable		Credit Card	858.92	
● Visa Card Payable		Credit Card	0.00	
● Trust Funds Held		Other Current Liability	18,937.25	
●Richard Will		Other Current Liability	0.00	
●Shane Hamby		Other Current Liability	3,600.00	

Account ▼   Activities ▼   Reports ▼   Attach   ☐ Include inactive

Add New Account Screen for the Chart of Accounts. This is for Income, but change to any with the Account Type drop down list.

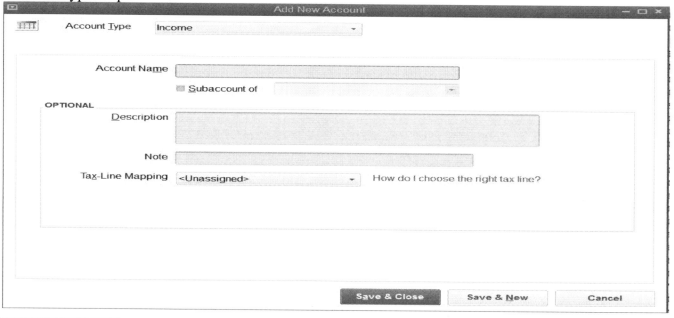

Account Type   Income

Account Name

☐ Subaccount of

OPTIONAL

Description

Note

Tax-Line Mapping   <Unassigned>   How do I choose the right tax line?

Save & Close   Save & New   Cancel

2.   Item List - The item list is what your Law Practice sells and resells in your business. Most of what you will list is your legal services, but some may sell products, so in this case you would have services and products. To invoice out any of your charges it should be set up on your item list.

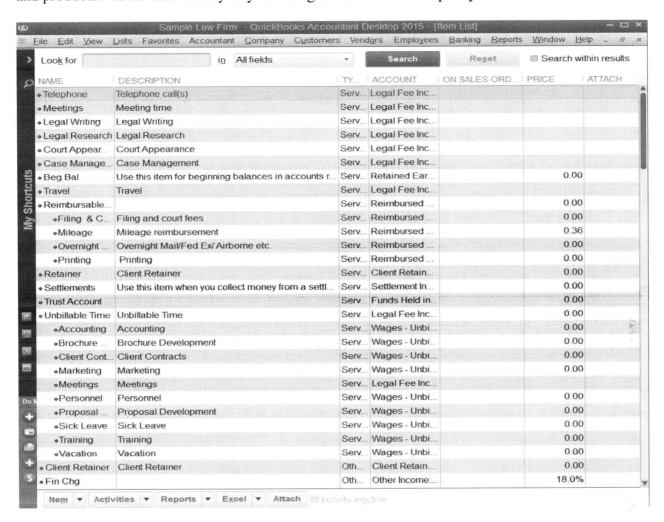

New Item entry screen for Service

3.   Fixed Asset Item List - Used for Property you purchase, Track and May eventually sell. Fixed assets are long-lived assets, such as land, buildings, furniture, equipment and vehicles.

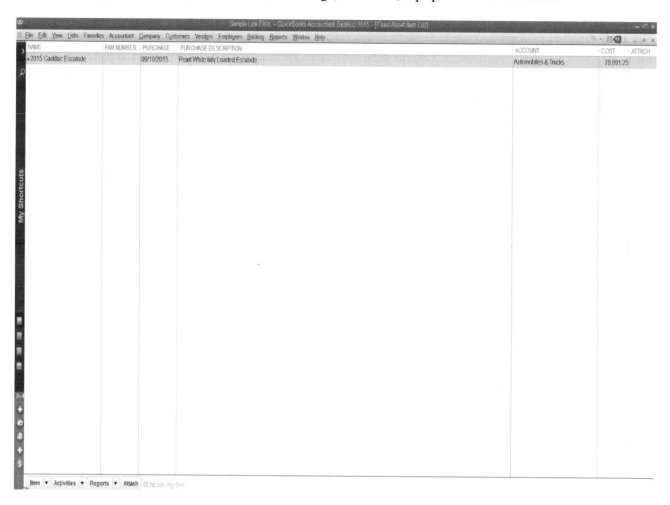

New Fixed Asset Item List entry screen

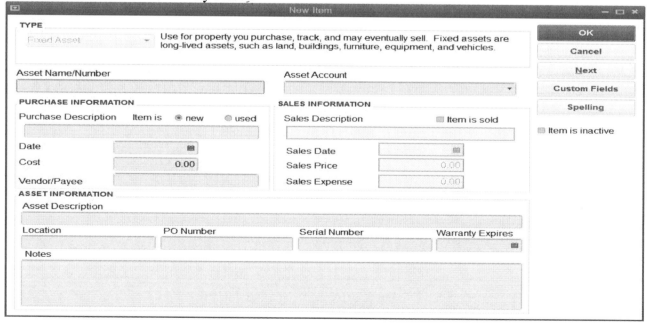

4.   Price Level List - Use this type of Price Level to set custom prices for individual items when setting up Prices for Different Customers or jobs.

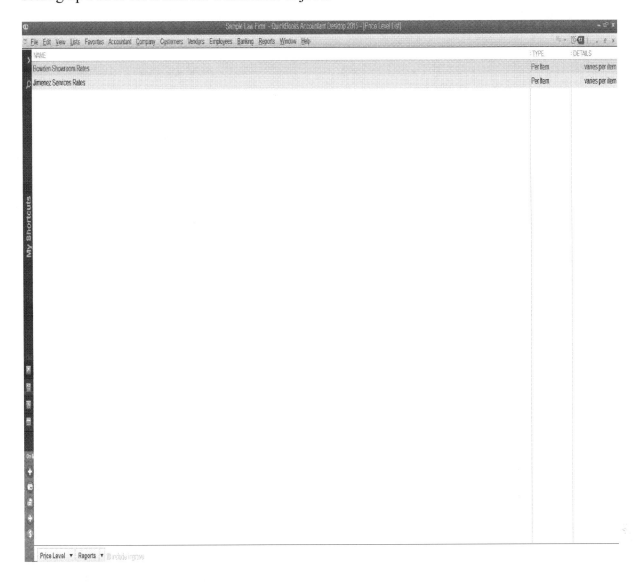

New Price Level Entry Screen

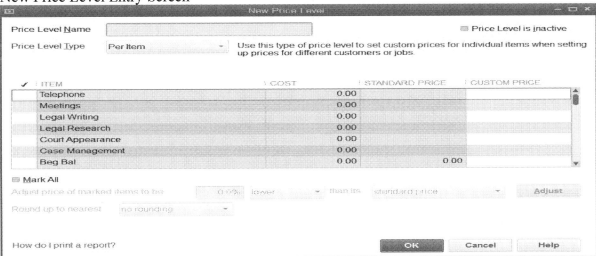

5. **Billing Rate Level List** - Billing rate levels let you set custom service item rates for different employees and vendors. You might want to use them if you find that one standard rate for a given service is not always sufficient. For example, different employees doing the same service might bill at different rates based on experience level or labor burden costs. Or you might charge different rates for an employee based on the difficulty of the task.

Once you create billing rate levels and associate them with employees and vendors, each time you create an invoice with billable time, QuickBooks automatically fills in the correct rate for each service item based on who did the work.

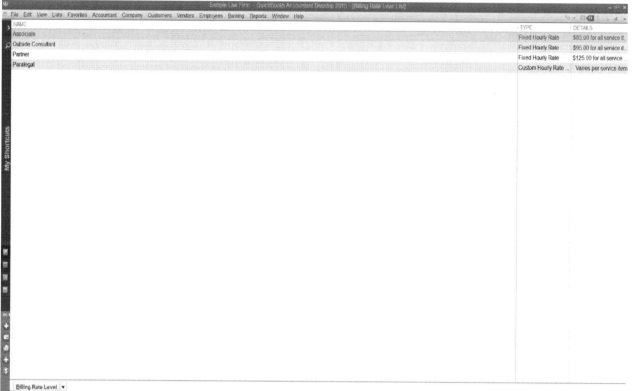

New Billng Rate Level Enter Screen

6.   Payroll Item List - QuickBooks uses payroll items to track individual amounts on a paycheck and accumulate year-to-date wage and tax amounts for each employee. There are payroll items for compensation, taxes, other additions and deductions, and company-paid expenses. You can assign these payroll items to different accounts as needed.

When the payroll feature is turned on, QuickBooks creates payroll items for federal taxes and advance EIC for you. To fully track your payroll, you may need to add more payroll items to the list. For example, you can add payroll items for state withholding, state disability, state unemployment, other state taxes, local taxes; employee deductions of any kind; additions (such as employee loans); commissions; and company-paid expenses (such as company-paid health insurance).

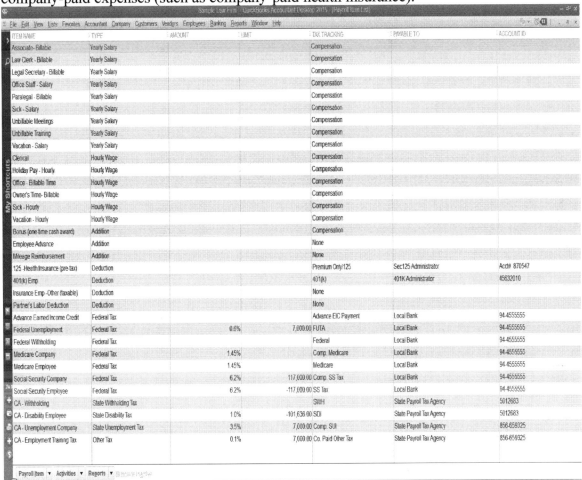

ITEM NAME	TYPE	AMOUNT	LIMIT	TAX TRACKING	PAYABLE TO	ACCOUNT ID
Associate - Billable	Yearly Salary			Compensation		
Law Clerk - Billable	Yearly Salary			Compensation		
Legal Secretary - Billable	Yearly Salary			Compensation		
Office Staff - Salary	Yearly Salary			Compensation		
Paralegal - Billable	Yearly Salary			Compensation		
Sick - Salary	Yearly Salary			Compensation		
Unbillable Meetings	Yearly Salary			Compensation		
Unbillable Training	Yearly Salary			Compensation		
Vacation - Salary	Yearly Salary			Compensation		
Clerical	Hourly Wage			Compensation		
Holiday Pay - Hourly	Hourly Wage			Compensation		
Office - Billable Time	Hourly Wage			Compensation		
Owner's Time - Billable	Hourly Wage			Compensation		
Sick - Hourly	Hourly Wage			Compensation		
Vacation - Hourly	Hourly Wage			Compensation		
Bonus (one-time cash award)	Addition			Compensation		
Employee Advance	Addition			None		
Mileage Reimbursement	Addition			None		
125 - Health Insurance (pre-tax)	Deduction			Premium Only/125	Sec125 Administrator	Acct# 870547
401(k) Emp	Deduction			401(k)	401K Administrator	45632010
Insurance Emp - Other (taxable)	Deduction			None		
Partner's Labor Deduction	Deduction			None		
Advance Earned Income Credit	Federal Tax			Advance EIC Payment	Local Bank	94-4555555
Federal Unemployment	Federal Tax	0.6%	7,000.00	FUTA	Local Bank	94-4555555
Federal Withholding	Federal Tax			Federal	Local Bank	94-4555555
Medicare Company	Federal Tax	1.45%		Comp. Medicare	Local Bank	94-4555555
Medicare Employee	Federal Tax	1.45%		Medicare	Local Bank	94-4555555
Social Security Company	Federal Tax	6.2%	117,000.00	Comp. SS Tax	Local Bank	94-4555555
Social Security Employee	Federal Tax	6.2%	-117,000.00	SS Tax	Local Bank	94-4555555
CA - Withholding	State Withholding Tax			SWH	State Payroll Tax Agency	5012683
CA - Disability Employee	State Disability Tax	1.0%	-101,636.00	SDI	State Payroll Tax Agency	5012683
CA - Unemployment Company	State Unemployment Tax	3.5%	7,000.00	Comp. SUI	State Payroll Tax Agency	856-659325
CA - Employment Training Tax	Other Tax	0.1%	7,000.00	Co. Paid Other Tax	State Payroll Tax Agency	856-659325

Add New Payroll Item Screen

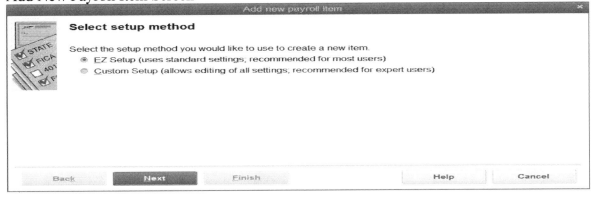

Add new payroll item

Select setup method

Select the setup method you would like to use to create a new item.

- ⊙ EZ Setup (uses standard settings; recommended for most users)
- ○ Custom Setup (allows editing of all settings; recommended for expert users)

Back   Next   Finish   Help   Cancel

7.   Payroll Schedule List - A payroll schedule defines when you should run your payroll so that you can pay employees on their payday. You can use payroll schedules to group together employees in whichever way makes the most sense for you to effectively run your payroll and your business. However, all employees grouped in the same payroll schedule **must** have the **same pay frequency** (for example, weekly, bi-weekly, semi-monthly, and so on).

You define how often you pay your employees (weekly, bi-weekly, semi-monthly, and so on), which date their paycheck is due, and which day you run payroll, and QuickBooks calculates your upcoming payroll schedule so that you can pay your employees on time.

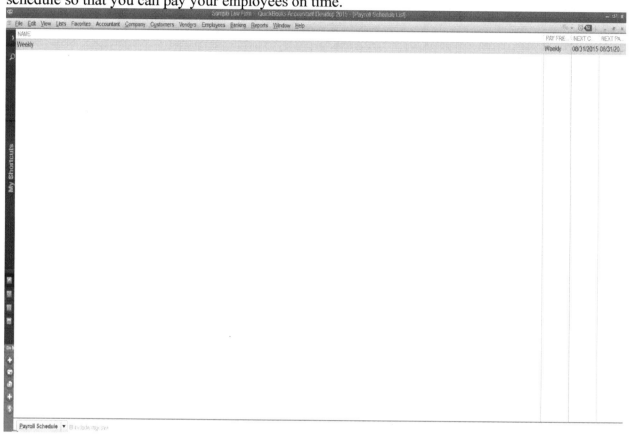

New Payroll Schedule Entry Screen

8.   Class List - This list contains the classes that you've set up. QuickBooks classes give you a way to track different segments of your business, and to break down your account balances for each segment. Classes can apply to all transactions, so they're not tied to a particular client or project.

As you create transactions such as invoices, purchase orders and bills, you assign the appropriate class for the transaction. At any time you can run reports to view account balances by class.

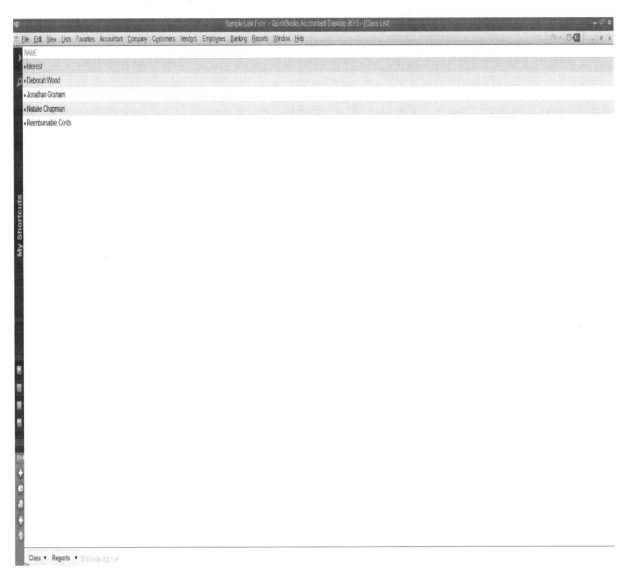

New Class Entry Screen

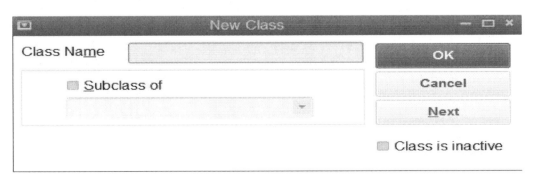

9.   Other Names List - The entries in the Other Names List show up in the drop-down menus for a few types of transactions, such as checks and credit card charges (page 202). But they don't appear for other types of transactions, like invoices, purchase orders, and sales receipts.

So what are Other Names good for? People who aren't customers, vendors, or employees--for example, *your* name as sole proprietor or the names of company partners. That way, when you write partners' distribution checks, you can choose their names from the Other Names List.

Entry screen for New Other Name

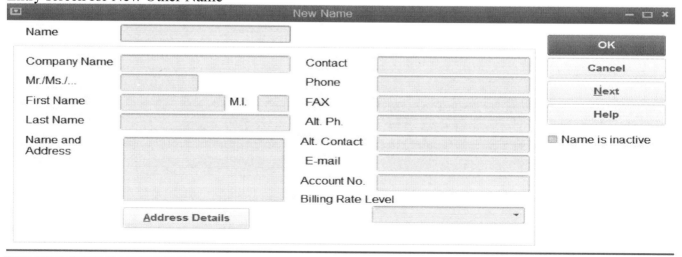

10.   Customer & Vendor Profile Lists - Sales Rep List - Your business may need to track the income that is associated with people who have a relationship with your business. These people may or may not be employees. For example, you might track income from a partner in a law firm or a 1099 vendor who is an independent contractor.

QuickBooks has a Sales Rep List that allows you to specify employees, vendors, or "other names" as sales reps. each sales rep is assigned initials. The names and initials appear on the Rep drop-down list on sales forms, allowing you to associate specific sales reps with specific sales so you can track their income.

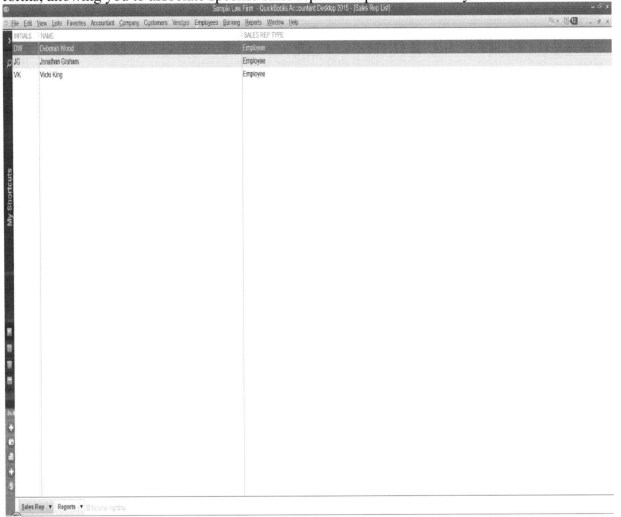

New Sales Rep Entry Screen

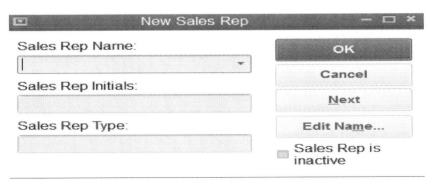

11.   Customer & Vendor Profile Lists - Customer Type List - This list shows the customer types you've set up. In QuickBooks, you use customer types to categorize customers and jobs in ways that are meaningful to your business.

Once you've assigned a customer type to each customer, you can create reports that provide useful information about the customers you serve. For example, if you've categorized your customers by market segment, you can create a separate sales report for each segment.

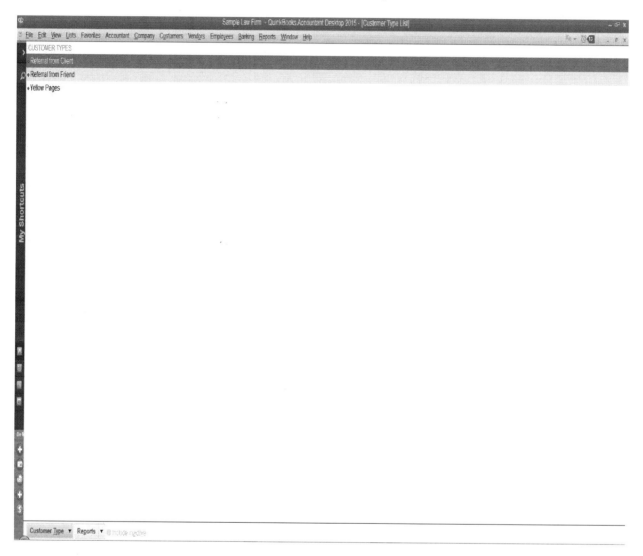

Enter Screen for New Customer Type

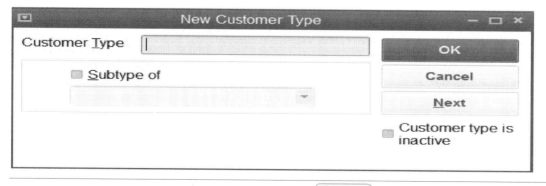

12.   Customer & Vendor Profile Lists - Vendor Type List - Use vendor types to categorize your vendors in ways that are meaningful to your business. For example, you could set up your vendor types so that they indicate a vendor's industry or geographic location. You can also place a vendor type as a subtype of another vendor type. For example, you might create the type Painters with the subtypes Exterior and Interior.

You can create reports and do special mailings that are based on your vendor types. For example, if you own a construction company and use subcontractors, you might want to use the ones closest to each job. You could then create a QuickBooks report that shows the subcontractors in each geographic area.

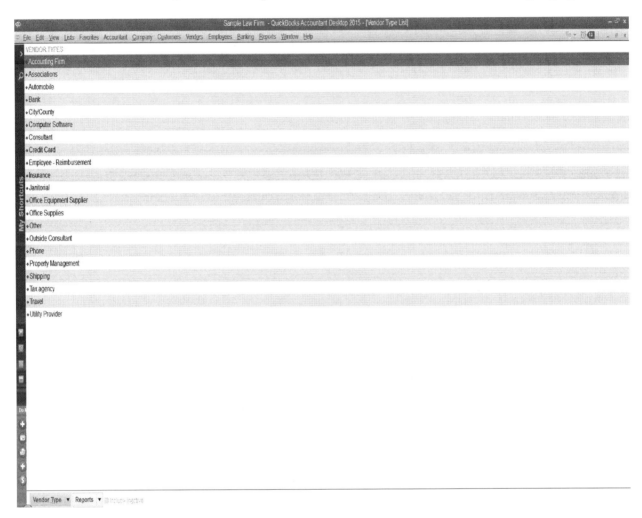

New Vendor Type Entry Screen

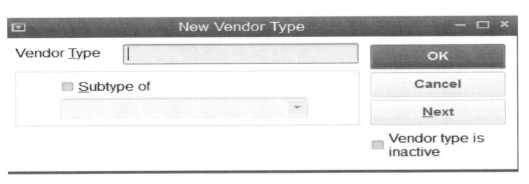

13.   Customer & Vendor Profile Lists - Job Type List - This list holds the job types you've set up for grouping and categorizing your jobs on reports. You can add new job types to this list whenever you need them.

The Job Type list is automatically available to you when you set up a job (in the New/Edit Job window) or enter job information about a customer (on the Job Info tab in the New/Edit Customer window). To add a job type, click the Job Info tab in the New/Edit Customer window and fill in the Job Type field.

New Job Type Entry Screen

14.   Customer & Vendor Profile Lists - Terms List - A shorthand way of expressing when you expect to receive payment from a customer, or when a vendor expects to receive payment from you. Terms show the number of days (or date) by which payment is due and can include a discount for early payment.

Example: 1% 10 Net 30 This means: payment due in 30 days, 1% discount if paid within 10 days.

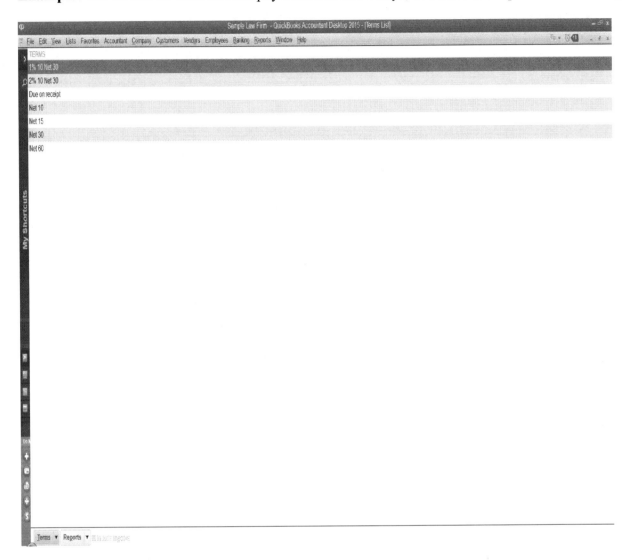

New Terms Entry Screen

15. Customer & Vendor Profile Lists - Customer Message List - The Customer Message list contains standard messages that you can include at the bottom of a printed sales form. For example, you might want to thank your customers for their business. Using the Customer Message list, you can create the "thank you" message once and include it on any invoice.

New Customer Message Entry Screen

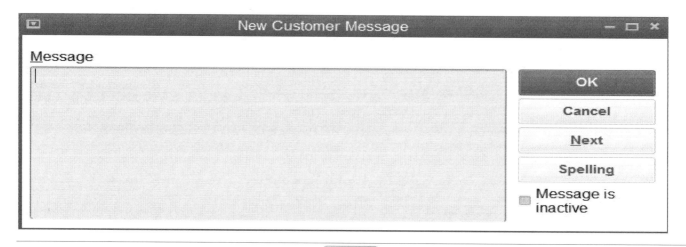

16.   Customer & Vendor Profile Lists - Payment Method List - Use this list to hold information about the different ways you receive payments from your customers (cash, check, Master Card, Visa, American Express, and so on). You can select a payment method from this list when you enter a customer payment. This lets you sort your deposits by payment method and create reports based on payment method.

If you don't separate deposits by payment method, you probably don't need to use payment methods.

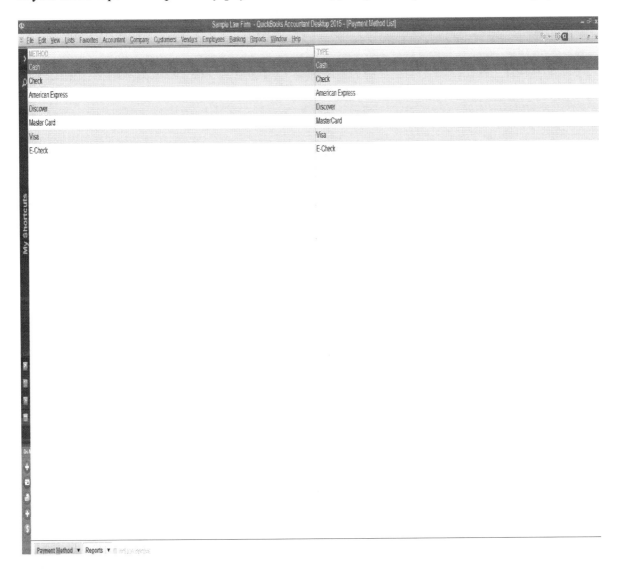

New Payment Method Entry Screen

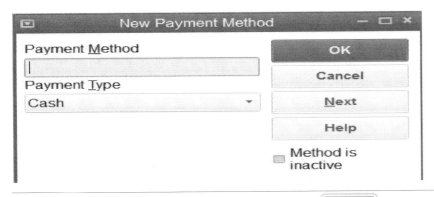

17.   Customer & Vendor Profile Lists - Ship Via List - Use this list to store the different shipping methods you use to send products to your customers. You can select a shipping method from this list when you write an invoice or a sales receipt.

Click the Shipping Method drop-down arrow to add, edit, or delete shipping methods. You can make a shipping method inactive, print the list, and more.

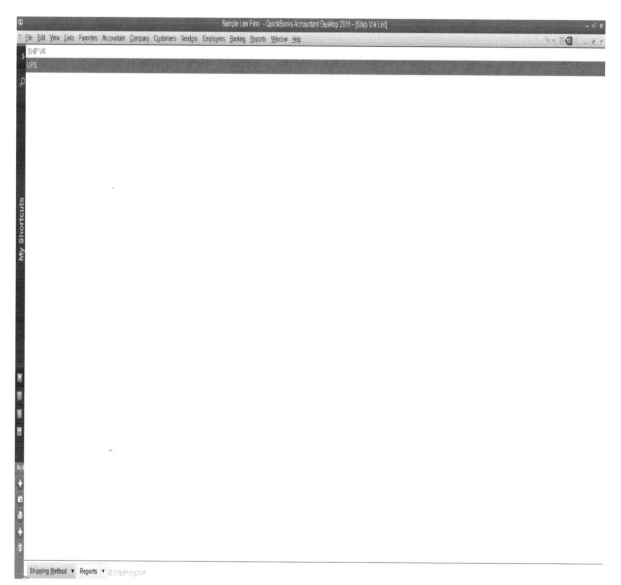

New Shipping Method Entry Screen

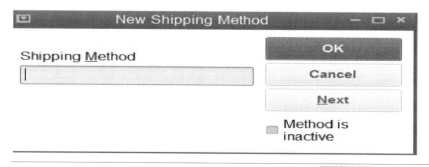

- 18. Customer & Vendor Profile Lists - Vehicle List - The Vehicle list stores the names and descriptions of your business vehicles. To track mileage for a vehicle, the vehicle must be entered on this list. You also may want to track your business vehicles in the fixed asset tracker.

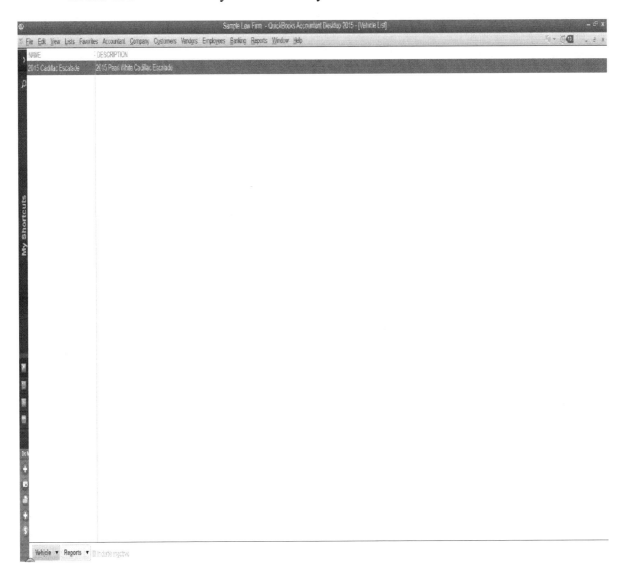

New Vehicle Entry Screen

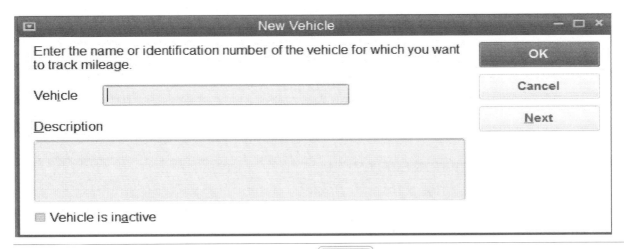

19. Templates - QuickBooks comes with a variety of templates for you to use for your invoices, estimates, credit memos, sales orders, purchase orders, sales receipts, statements, packing slips, and pick lists. A template determines the appearance of your forms such as which information is included, whether a logo appears, what color scheme is used, and where all elements are placed.

You can customize the templates that come with QuickBooks to control how they look and what information is included. You can also specify what you see when you fill out the form onscreen, and what shows on the form when you print it.

To decide which format is right for your company, consider the amount of detail you want your customers to see and the length of the usual line item description. The format you choose doesn't affect the information you see in reports.

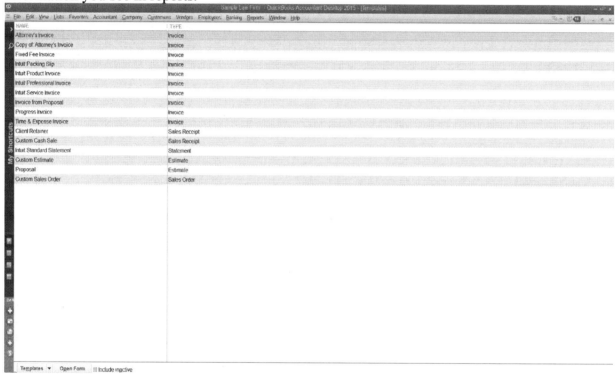

New Template Entry Form

20.   Memorize Transaction List - This list contains the transactions you have memorized and the memorized transaction groups you have created. Individual transactions appear in normal font. The names of groups appear in bold. Transactions within a group appear indented immediately below the group name.

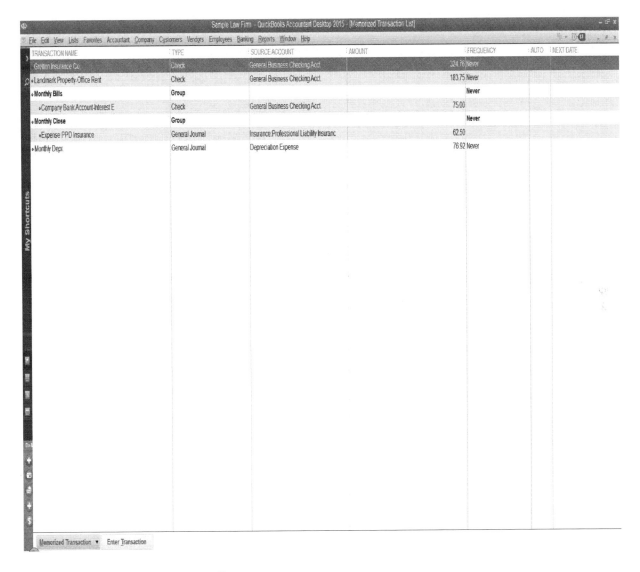

New Memorized Group Entry Screen

21.   Add/Edit Multiple List Entries - This is where you can add multiple entries at once like if you have say 10 customers you want to enter all at once instead of one at a time.

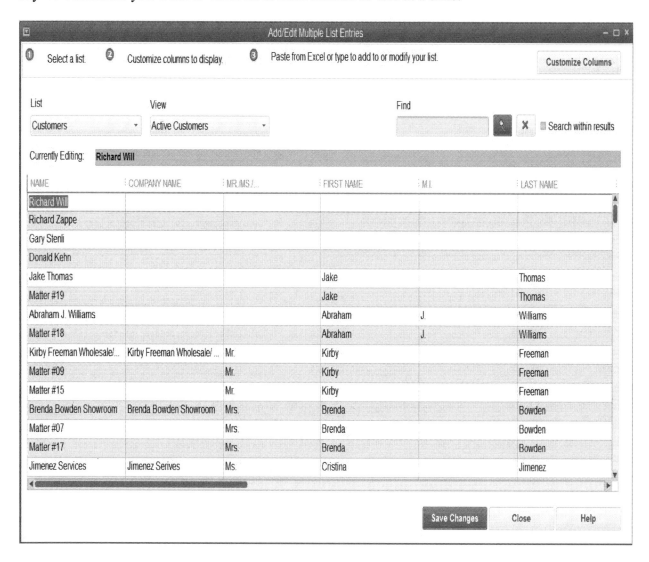

This is an over view of all your lists available. I hope this helps and take advantage of QuickBooks Powerful features.

Quick Tips

Now that you just finished setting up your new Company File back it up. This is number one always is to back up regularly. Depending on how many transactions/how big your company is you may want to back up daily. I would say at least back up once a week.

If you do not back up consistently and something happened to your QuickBooks file it could be very costly to have to reenter everything.

All these accounts can be edited and renamed. If there is an account you don't think you need or will ever use then delete it now. You can always delete an account as long as there are no transactions linked to that account.

If you have two accounts say that are similar and want to put them under just one account then you can merge them.

To merge most accounts whether it's a chart of accounts account, customer, or vendor this will work to merge.

Steps to merge accounts is to have one account the name you want it to be and then edit and change the name on the other account to the name of the account you want. A screen will pop up and say this account name is already in use would you like to merge them and you say yes then it combines them for you.

If you have any questions please email me at soswill@outlook.com.

Cristie

Handy Quick Reference Cheat Sheets
<u>Chart of Accounts</u>

Adding a New Account
1. Go to Menu Bar at the top of the screen, click on lists then click on Chart of Accounts
2. Click on the Account button at the bottom left of the screen and choose New.
3. Choose the Account type that you are wanting to set up and click continue.
4. Enter account information and when done click save and close.

Editing an Account
1. Go to Menu Bar at the top of the screen, click on lists then click on Chart of Accounts.
2. Click once on the account you want to edit to highlight the account.
3. Click on the Account button at the bottom left of the screen and choose Edit Account.
4. The account you had highlighted to edit opens up. Edit the information then click save and close.

Delete or Inactivate an Account
1. Go to Menu Bar at the top of the screen, click on lists then click on Chart of Accounts.
2. Click once on the account you want to delete or inactivate to highlight the account.
3. Click on the Account button at the bottom left of the screen and click on Delete Account or Make Account Inactive.
4. Click OK to confirm any deleted account. If you chose to make account Inactive it will just disappear from your list, but it's just inactive and can be made active again anytime.

Handy Quick Reference Cheat Sheets
Customers

Accessing Customer Center
- Go to Menu Bar at the top of the screen, click on Customers, then click on Customer Center

Adding a New Customer
1. Click the Customers & Jobs tab in the Customer Center once the Customer Center is opened.
2. Click on the tab just above the Customers & Jobs Tab that is named New Customer & Job.
3. Click on Add New Customer.
4. Enter all the necessary customer information on each tabbed section in the New Customer window then click OK when finished.

Adding a Job to a Customer
1. Click the Customers & Jobs tab in the Customer Center once the Customer Center is opened.
2. Highlight the existing customer that you want to add a job to.
3. Click on the tab just above the Customers & Jobs Tab that is named New Customer & Job then click on Add Job.
4. Give the job a name and go through the tabs entering the information about the job then click ok when finished.

Editing or Deleting a Customer
1. Click the Customers & Jobs in the Customer Center once the Customer Center is opened.
2. Highlight and double click on the Customer and/or Job you want to edit. Make necessary changes and click ok.
3. To delete a job, highlight the job and right click on the highlighted job then choose delete job.
4. To delete a Customer, highlight the Customer and right click on the highlighted Customer then choose Delete customer: job. (Note you cannot delete Customer or Job if linked to any transactions and if linked then Click on Inactivate.)

Handy Quick Reference Cheat Sheets
<u>Employees</u>

Accessing Employee Center
- Go to Menu Bar at the top of the screen, click on Employees, and then click on Customer Center.

Adding a New Employee
1. Click the New Employee tab in the Employee Center once the Employee Center is opened.
2. Fill in all the New Employee information and click OK.

Editing, Deleting or Inactivating an Employee

1. Once the Employee Center is open double click on the employee you want to edit.
2. Make the changes to the employee you are editing and click OK when done.
3. To delete an employee, highlight the employee you want to delete then right click on the employee and click on delete employee. (Note if employee is linked to any transactions you can only make them inactive).
4. To make employee inactive, highlight employee and right click on the employee and click on Make Employee Inactive.

<u>Creating Custom Fields</u>

Customers, Employees and Vendors
1. Click open the Customer, Employee or Vendor center to create the custom fields you want. Click open a customer or employee or Vendor and click on Additional Info Tab. Click Define Fields.
   1.
2. Start Entering Field Names and place check mark in field to whether it's a customer, employee or vender or a combination of the three. Click Ok when done.

Handy Quick Reference Cheat Sheets
<u>Vendors</u>

Accessing Vendor Center
- Go to Menu Bar at the top of the screen, click on Vendors, and then click on Customer Center.

Adding a New Vendor
1. Click the New Vendor Button just above the Vendors Tab after opening the vendor center.
2. Click on New Vendor
3. Enter in all the Vendor Information. Be sure to go through the Tabs and enter what is necessary then click ok when finished.

Editing, Deleting or Inactivating a Vendor
1. Once Vendor Center is open double click on Vendor to edit.
2. After edits are made to your Vendor then click OK.
3. To Delete a Vendor, highlight vendor and right click on the highlighted Vendor and click on Delete Vendor. Click ok to confirm delete.
4. If the vendor has transactions linked to that Vendor then you have to make them inactive.
5. To make Vendor inactive, highlight Vendor and right click on the Vendor and Click on Make Vendor Inactive.
   2.

Adding Fields to Vendors
1. Once Vendor Center is open double click on Vendor to edit.
2. Click on New Vendor just above Vendors Tab that is opened and then click on Add Multiple Vendors.
3. Click on Customize Columns.
4. The column that says available columns to the left can be added to your vendor information. You can add one or all or anything in-between. You customize to your business.

Handy Quick Reference Cheat Sheets
Managing List Items

Creating Item List Custom Fields
1. Go to the Menu Bar at the top of the screen and click on lists then click on Item List. Click on item list at bottom of screen, click New if adding new item or Click Edit if making changes to an item.
2. To customize fields to new items or edit items after opening item click on custom fields. If no fields are defined yet a screen will pop up saying no fields are defined yet and to define them click on the define fields, click ok then click define fields.
3. Enter Item Label name, click use & ok, enter values & ok.

Sorting Lists
1. Manual sort by click and drag the diamond next to the name.
2. Automatically sorting, click the column heading. You can sort by any column, so depending on your needs.
3. Remove the auto sort by clicking the new diamond to the left of the column heading.
4. Restore original sort order by selecting View from the top menu bar, then clicking on re-sort list then click ok.

Inactivating and Reactivating Items
1. Highlight Item and right click on the highlighted Item click Make Item Inactive.
2. To show all items including inactive items click on box, Include Inactive. Can also see all in lists by selecting all.
3. To reactivate show the inactive items within the list and click the X to change from inactive to active.

Renaming and Merging List Items
1. To rename open the item to rename it, type new name and click ok or save and close button to save changes.
2. To merge, change the name to the same as another item and choose yes when prompted to merge.

Handy Quick Reference Cheat Sheets
Sales Tax

Creating a Sales Tax Item or Group
1. First make sure in Preferences Sales Tax is turned on.
2. Select Lists then click on item lists.
3. Click on Item at the bottom of the screen and click on New.
4. Click on Sales Tax Item or Sales Tax Group from the list.
5. Enter tax item information and click ok.

Setting Default Sales Tax Preferences.
1. Go to edit on the Menu Bar at the top and click on Preferences then click on Sales Tax & Company Preferences.
2. Fill in all the necessary information and click ok.

Setting a Customer Taxable
1. Click Customers on top Menu, click on Customer Center.
2. Click the Customers & Jobs tab and the left side, double click name of the customer in the list, make changes, and click ok.

Sales Tax Settings for an Item
1. Click on Lists from the Menu Bar then click on Item List.
2. Highlight the item then click the item button and click edit.
3. Click Tax Code & choose appropriate selection & click ok.

Creating a Sales Tax Report
1. Click on Vendors on the Top Menu Bar, click Sales Tax, then Sales Tax Liability or Sales Tax Revenue Summary and change dates to the correct time period. Press Esc button to close report.
3.

Paying Sales Tax
1. Click Vendors from Top Menu Bar, Sales Tax then click pay sales Tax. Make selections for the Account and dates.
2. Click to select the Pay column for agencies to pay, click adjust button to make adjustments if necessary, click ok.
3. Click on Print Checks when ready to print the sales check you just created.

Handy Quick Reference Cheat Sheets
__Inventory__

Turning on Inventory in QuickBooks
1. Click on Edit then Preferences from the Top Menu Bar.
2. Click on Items & Inventory from the list.
3. Check the Inventory and purchase orders are active under the Company Preferences Tab, set rest of preferences & click ok.

Creating New Inventory Part Items
1. Click Lists then Item List from Top Menu Bar.
2. Click New from the Item Button on bottom of the screen.
3. Click Inventory part from the Type in the drop down menu.
4. Enter inventory part information and click ok.

Creating a Purchase Order
1. Click Vendors then click Create Purchase Orders from the Top Menu Bar.
2. Click the vendor from the vendor drop down list.
3. Enter Purchase Order information and click Save & Close or Save & New button, depending if creating more than one.

Creating Purchase Order Reports
1. Click lists then Chart of Accounts from the top Menu Bar.
2. Highlight purchase orders account, click reports button then click Quick Report: Purchase Orders from the menu.
3. You can access more detailed reports from the reports menu from the Top Menu Bar and click on Purchases.

Receiving Inventory with a Bill
1. Click Vendors, then Receive Items and Enter Bill from the top Menu Bar.
2. Click on the Vendor from the drop down list on the Bill entry.
3. Enter bill information and click the save & close button.

Handy Quick Reference Cheat Sheets
Inventory Continued

Creating an Item Receipt
1. Click Vendors then Receive Items from the top Menu Bar.
2. Choose the vendor from the Vendor drop down list.
3. Enter the receipt information and click the Save & Close button.

Matching a Bill to an Item Receipt
1. Click Vendors then Enter Bill for Received Items from the top Menu Bar.
2. Choose the vendor from the Vendor drop down list.
3. Choose the item receipt and click the ok button.
4. Enter the date when the bill was received in the Date field and click the Save & Close button.

Manually Adjusting Inventory
1. Click Vendors, then Inventory Activities then Adjust Quantity/Value on Hand from the top Menu Bar.
2. Choose the type of inventory adjustment to make from the Adjustment Type drop down list.
3. Make the necessary adjustments to the inventory.
4. Click the Save & Close button.

Handy Quick Reference Cheat Sheets
Other Items

Creating Other Items

Such as service, non-inventory parts, other charges, subtotals, groups, discounts and payments.

1. Click lists then Item List from the top Menu Bar.
2. Click New from the Item button from the bottom of the screen after opening the items list.
3. Choose the item type from the Type drop down list.
4. Enter the item information and click ok.

Changing Item Prices

1. Click Customers then Change Item Prices from the top Menu Bar.
2. Click the Item Type drop down to choose only items that match the item type you want.
3. Click the left column to check the item(s) you wish to change.
4. Adjust prices using the fields at the bottom.
5. Click the adjust button and then click ok.

Handy Quick Reference Cheat Sheets
Sales

Creating an Invoice or Sales Receipt

4. Click Customers then Create Invoices or click Customers then Enter Sales Receipts from the top Menu Bar.
5. Pick a template from the Template drop-down menu.
6. Choose the Customer: Job drop down list to select a customer.
7. Enter the invoice or receipt information and click save & close or save & new, depending on if you enter more than one invoice or receipt.

Finding Transactions

1. Open the form window for the type of transaction you need to find. For example, to find an invoice, open the Create Invoices window.
2. Click edit find, form type (such as invoices or bills), from the top Menu Bar.
3. Enter necessary information for values to find the transaction & click the Find button. Double click item to open it.

Previewing Invoices and Receipts

1. Click open the receipt or invoice for previewing.
2. Click the drop down arrow below the Print button in the Main tab of the Ribbon.
3. Choose the Preview from the drop down menu.

Printing Invoices and Receipts

1. Click open the sales form to print.
2. Click the Print button in the Main Tab of the Ribbon.
3. Set Preferred Printing Parameters.
4. Click the Print Button.

Handy Quick Reference Cheat Sheets
Price Levels

Creating New Price Levels
1. Click lists then Price Level List from the top Menu Bar.
2. Click the Price Level button and select New from the Pop up menu.
3. Type the name of the new price level into the Price Level Name field.
4. Enter the price level information
5. When finished entering information click ok.

Associating Defaults with a Customer
1. Click Customer the Customer Center from the top menu bar.
2. Double click on the customer on the Customers & Jobs tab of the customer center.
3. Choose the Payment Settings tab in the Edit Customer window.
4. Choose the appropriate price level from the Price Level drop-down menu.
5. When finished click ok.

Changing Line Item Rates
1. Choose the line item in the invoice or receipt.
2. Click into the Rate column.
3. Enter the Price Level.
4. Click Save & Close when done.

Handy Quick Reference Cheat Sheets
Billing Statements

Setting Finance Charge Preferences
1. Click edit then Preferences from the top Menu Bar.
2. Choose the Finance Charge icon to the left.
3. Enter your information on the Company Preferences tab and when finished click ok.

Entering State Charges
1. Click on the customer you want to highlight on the Customers & Jobs tab of the Customer Center.
2. Click on Customers then choose Statement Charges from the top Menu Bar.
3. Enter the charge & click Record Button then click the X or press Esc Button to exit out of screen.

Creating Statements
1. Click Customers then choose Create Statements from the top Menu Bar.
2. Choose statement options, customers and any other options you need.
3. Click Preview, Print, E-Mail or all three buttons to depending on your choice and the customer's preference as well.

Handy Quick Reference Cheat Sheets
__Payment Processing__

Recording a Payment in Full
1. Click Customers then choose Receive Payments from the top Menu Bar.
2. Choose the name of the customer from the Received From drop down list.
3. Enter the partial payment received information.
4. If you want to link the payment to any charge other than the oldest invoice, click the Un-apply Payment Button in the Main tab of the Ribbon.
5. Enter the amount received to apply to the correct invoice under the Payment column.
6. If an underpayment of the total amount due is entered, choose the Write off extra amount button to write off the remaining balance, of your choosing or Click on Leave this as an underpayment.
7. When finished click either the Save & Close or Save & New button, depending on if you have more than one payment to enter.

Applying One Payment to Multiple Invoices/Charges
1. Click Customers then choose Receive Payments from the top Menu Bar.
2. Select the name of the Customer from the Received from the Drop-Down List.
3. Enter the Payment Received Information.
4. Click the Un-apply Payment Button in the Main tab of the Ribbon, so you can apply the correct invoices directly to your payment received.
5. Enter the amount then start checking invoices to apply to the payment.
6. Click the Save & Close Button if you are done or if you have more payments to enter click Save & New Button.

Entering Overpayments
1. Click Customers then choose Receive Payments from the top Menu Bar.
2. Choose the name of the Customer from the Received from Drop down List.
3. Enter the Payment information received.
4. The Customers overpayment is shown as an overpayment at the bottom left corner. Select either the Leave the credit to be used later or the Refund the amount to the customer.
5. When finished Click Save & Close Button or if you have more payments to enter Click Save & New Button.

Entering Down Payments or Prepayments
1. Click Customers then choose Receive Payments from the top Menu Bar.
2. Choose the name of the Customer from the Received from drop down list.
3. Enter the payment amount received information.
4. The customer's down payment or prepayment amount is listed as an Overpayment in the bottom left corner. Select the Leave the Credit to apply to an invoice later.
5. Click Save & Close button if finished or if you have more payments to enter Click Save & New Button to continue.

Handy Quick Reference Cheat Sheets
Payment Processing Continued

Applying Customer Credits
1. Click Customers then choose Receive Payments from the top Menu Bar.
2. Choose the name of the customer from the Received from drop down list and choose the correct invoice to apply the customer's credit DO NOT mark it with a checkmark, but select it by Clicking on any other column available.
3. Click the Discounts & Credits button in the Main tab of the Ribbon.
4. On the Credits tab, click the checkmark column next to the credit in the Available Credits section.
5. To apply a partial credit you need to change the amount in the amount to use column.
6. Click the Done button and then either the Save & Close or the Save & New Button, depending on if you have more transactions to enter.

Making Deposits
1. Click banking then choose Make Deposits from the top Menu Bar.
2. Click to choose any payments to deposit in the Payments to Deposit Window then click ok.
3. In the make deposits screen select the bank account from the Deposit to Drop down list.
4. Enter the date of the deposit.
5. Click into the next row if you have any other payments going in this deposit.
6. Enter any Cash Back information if needed.
7. Click on the drop down arrow to the right of the toolbar's Print button and choose either Deposit Slip or Deposit Summary and then the Print button in the Print Box.
8. Click the Save & Close Button unless you have more separate deposits then Click Save & New.

Handling Bounced Checks
1. Click Customers, choose Receive Payments from the top Menu Bar.
2. Find the payment that contains the bounced check to display it in the Receive payments screen by using the Find button or the Previous and Next arrows.
3. Choose Record Bounced Check Button from Main tab in the Ribbon area. Enter Check Info then click next & finish.
4. Click the Save & Close button.

Refunding a Customers Purchases
1. Click Customers then choose Create Credit Memos/Refunds from the top Menu Bar.
2. Choose the customer from the Customer Job drop down list.
3. Enter the returned items in the line items area.
4. Choose Use Credit to Give Refund button in the Main tab of the Ribbon to issue a Refund check to the Customer.
5. Choose the correct account to issue funds for the refund check along with any other information necessary, click ok.
6. Click Save & Close button, Print check & credit memo.

Handy Quick Reference Cheat Sheets
Payment Processing Continued

Refunding Customer Payments
1. Click banking then choose Write Checks from the top Menu Bar.
2. Enter check Information then choose Accounts Receivable account on the Expenses Tab.
3. Click Save & Close button & print the check.
4. Click Customers then choose Receive Payments from the top Menu Bar then choose the customer from the Received from drop down list.
5. Click to choose the refund check you wrote and then click the Discounts & Credits button on the Main tab in the ribbon.
6. Choose the credit that matches the refund check amount on the Credits tab. Click Done, Save & Close Buttons.

Handy Quick Reference Cheat Sheets
__Enter & Pay Bills__

Entering Bills
1. Click Vendors, choose Enter Bills from the top Menu Bar.
2. Select a vendor from the Vendor drop down list.
3. Enter all the necessary bill information then Click the Save & Close button if you are done entering bills or Click Save & New Button if you have more bills to enter.

Paying a Bill
1. Click Vendors, choose Pay Bills from the top menu Bar.
2. Click the checkbox to the left of the bills to pay.
3. Change the amount to pay column if it's a partial payment.
4. When finished click the Pay Selected Bills button.

Apply Early Payment Discounts
1. Click Vendors, choose Pay Bills from top Menu Bar.
2. Click the checkbox to the left of the bill to pay then click Set Discount button.
3. Enter discount amount, click account then click done.
4. In the Pay Bills screen complete Bill Payment information and click the Pay Selected Bills Button.

Entering Vendor Credits
1. Click Vendors, choose Enter Bills from the top Menu Bar.
2. Choose the Credit option at the top of form.
3. Complete credit info and click the save and close button.

Applying Vendor Credits
1. Click Vendors, choose Pay Bills from the top Menu Bar.
2. Click the checkbox to the left of the bill to pay.
3. Click the Set Credits button.
4. If using only part of a credit, type the amount to apply in the Amount to use column then click the done button.
5. In the Pay Bills window, finish the bill payment information and click the Pay Selected Bills button.

Handy Quick Reference Cheat Sheets
<u>Bank Accounts</u>

Entering Transactions in the Register
1. Close out open screens you have open
2. Click Banking, choose Use Register from the top Menu Bar.
3. Choose the account from the drop down and click ok.
4. Record entry in the blank row and click the record button.

Write Checks Screen
1. Click Banking, choose Write Checks from the top Menu Bar.
2. Choose the correct checking account from the Bank Account drop down list.
3. Enter all the check information including the accounts/expenses to apply to check.
4. Click Save & Close button or if you have more checks to write click Save & New Button.

Writing Checks for Inventory Items
1. Click Banking, choose Write Checks from the top Menu Bar.
2. Enter the check information.
3. Choose the Items tab and select the inventory parts from the Item drop down and enter a quantity.
4. Click Save & close when finished.

Print a Single Check
1. Click Banking, choose Write Checks from the top Menu Bar.
2. Click on the arrows for previous or next or Find Button to display the check wanting to print.
3. Click the drop down arrow on the Print button in the Main tab of the Ribbon.
4. Choose Check from the drop down and then click ok.

Printing a Batch of Checks
1. Click Banking, choose Write Checks from the top Menu Bar.
2. Click the drop down arrow on the Print button in the Main tab of the Ribbon area and choose Batch.
3. Click to un-check any checks NOT to print.
4. Choose the correct bank account, enter a first check number and click ok.
5. Pick any other desired printing options in the Print Checks box and click the Print Button.

Transferring Funds
1. Click Banking, choose Transfer Funds from the top Menu Bar.
2. Enter the necessary transfer information.
3. Click Save & close unless you have more transfers then click save and new.

Voiding Checks
1. Click Banking, choose Write Checks from the top Menu Bar.
2. Use the Find Button or the Previous or Next arrows to locate the check to display.
3. Choose Edit, then Void Check from the top Menu Bar.
4. Click Save & Close then Yes to Confirm changes.

Handy Quick Reference Cheat Sheets
<u>Reports</u>

Creating a QuickReport
1. Click an item in any list, open a transaction form, or display the information.
2. Press the Control Button and Q Button at the same time for a QuickReport to Display.
3. Press Esc to close the report when finished.

Quick Zooming a Report
1. Place your mouse over the information in the report you are wanting to see until a magnifying glass with a Z appears and then double click.
2. The information you are looking to see will appear on screen.
3. Close the screen when finished by press the Esc button or clicking on the X in right hand of the report.

Modifying Reports
1. Modifying a preset report, open report you want to use for modification, choose Customize Report button on toolbar.
2. Creating a new transaction detail or summary report from scratch you would choose reports then click Custom Reports from the top Menu Bar and then select Transaction Detail or Summary from the menu.
3. In the Modify Report Box make the needed changes on the Display, Filters, Header/Footer and Fonts & Numbers tabs.
4. Click Ok to modify the report settings.

Customizing Report Columns
1. Rearrange report columns by placing the mouse over the name of the column in the heading until the pointer turns into a hand icon. Click, drag and release to the location you want.
2. Resizing columns in a report, place the mouse to the right of the name of the column to resize, where the three dots are at, until the mouse changes into a thin vertical by a cross arrow.
3. Click, drag left or right and release to resize.

Memorizing Modified Reports
1. Click the memorize button in the toolbar at the top of the modified reports window.
2. Enter the report name in the Name field.
3. Check and choose a Memorized Report Group if you want and then click ok.

Printing Reports
1. Click the Print button in the toolbar of the report you want and select Report from the drop down list.
2. Set print options in the Print Reports screen.
3. Set the options you need and click the Print button.

Batch Printing Forms
1. Click File, choose Print Forms from the top Menu Bar.
2. Click the type of form to print from the slide out menu to the right.
3. Set Printing options you need and click ok.

Handy Quick Reference Cheat Sheets
Estimating

Creating a New Job
1. Click Customers, choose Customer Center from the top menu bar.
2. Choose the customer in the Customers & Jobs list.
3. Click the New Customer & Job Button and select Add Job.
4. Enter your job name in the job name field.
5. Click on the Job Info tab and fill in all the necessary information.
6. When finished click ok.

Creating Estimates
1. Click Customers, choose Create Estimates from the top Menu Bar.
2. Choose the job from the Customer: Job drop down list.
3. Fill in the estimate information.
4. When done click Save & Close or Save & New if you have more estimates to enter.

Creating Invoices from Estimates
1. Click Customers, Create Invoices from the top Menu Bar.
2. Choose the job from the Customer: Job drop down list.
3. When the available estimates window appears choose the estimate you want to create an invoice from and click ok.
4. In the Create Progress Invoice Based on Estimate screen, choose an invoicing option and click ok.
5. When finished click save and close or save and new to continue invoicing from more estimates.

Making Estimate Inactive
1. Click Customers, Create Estimates from the top Menu Bar.
2. Use the Find button or the previous or next arrows to find the estimate you want to make inactive.
3. Click the Mark as Inactive button on the Main tab of the Ribbon, then click save & close button.

Purchases for a Job
1. Click Vendors, choose Click Purchase Orders from the top Menu Bar. You can also make a purchase using Enter bills, write checks or enter Credit Card Charges as well.
2. Enter the vendor information that you are making the purchases from.
3. Enter the first Item for the expense for the job in the line items area.
4. For each line item you need to use the drop down list to select the Customer: Job to be billed.
5. When finished Click the Save & Close unless you have more purchases then you Click Save & New button.

Handy Quick Reference Cheat Sheets
__Estimating Continued__

Invoicing Job Costs

1. Click Customers, choose Create Invoices from the top Menu Bar.
2. Choose the job from the Customer: Job drop down list.
3. In the Billable Time/Costs screen click the Select the outstanding billable time and costs to add to this invoice option button and then click ok.
4. Click the left column to select expense to bill out.
5. Enter all billable items and expenses then click ok.
6. When invoice finished select Save & New if need to do more invoicing or select Save & Close button if you are finished.

Creating Job Reports

1. Click Reports, then Jobs, Time & Mileage from the top Menu Bar.
2. Click the report name in the menu.
3. Select dates then hit the refresh Button.
4. You can of course customize to what you need.
5. Print if you need or save as a PDF.
6. When finished Press Esc button or click on the X in the top right hand corner of the report.

Handy Quick Reference Cheat Sheets
<u>Time Tracking</u>

Printing Blank Weekly Timesheets
1. Click Employees, choose Enter Time then select Use Weekly Timesheet from the top Menu Bar.
2. Click the drop down arrow to the right of the Print button and choose Print Blank Timesheet.
3. Click the Print Button enter the number of time sheets you want to print. Press Esc button or Click on X to exit.

Using Weekly Timesheets
1. Click Employees, choose Enter Time then Use Weekly Timesheet from the top Menu Bar.
2. Choose a name and date at the top of the screen.
3. Enter the timesheet information in the columns.
4. Click either Save & Close if you have finished entering timesheet information or Save & New if you need to enter more timesheets.

Entering Single/Time Activity
1. Click Employees, choose Enter Time then Enter Single Activity from the top Menu Bar.
2. Enter the employee activity information and click either Save & Close if finished entering time or Save & New if you need to enter more time.

Invoicing A Customer for Time/Services
1. Click Customers, create Invoices from the top Menu Bar.
2. Use the Customer: Job drop down list to choose the customer: Job to bill.
3. In the Billable Time/Costs screen click the Select the outstanding billable time and costs to add to this invoice option and click ok.
4. In the Choose Billable Time & Costs screen click the Time tab and choose hours to bill the customer by clicking the line items left column. Click ok, save & Close or Save & New.

Displaying Time Tracking Reports
1. Click Reports, choose Jobs, Time & Mileage from the top Menu Bar.
2. Click to choose the Report name in the menu in the slide out menu to your right.
3. Fill in dates needed and hit the refresh button and print if needed.
4. Press the Esc button when done.

Entering Vehicle Mileage
1. Click Company, choose Enter Vehicle Mileage from the top Menu Bar.
2. Enter all vehicle, job and mileage information necessary.
3. Entering mileage rates, click the Mileage Rates button at the top of the window, enter the rate then click the close button.
4. Click Save & Close if you are done or Save & New if you are entering more than one entry.

Handy Quick Reference Cheat Sheets
<u>Time Tracking Continued</u>

Invoicing Customers for Mileage

1. Click Customers, choose Create Invoices from the top Menu Bar.
2. Click on the Customer: Job drop down list to choose the name you have billable mileage to invoice out.
3. In the Billable Time/Costs screen click the Select outstanding billable time and costs to add to this invoice option and click ok.
4. Click the Mileage tab in the Choose Billable Time/Costs screen, then select the mileage to bill out by clicking the line item's left column.
5. Click ok
6. Click Save & Close if you are finished with invoicing for mileage or if you have more Click Save & New.

Handy Quick Reference Cheat Sheets
<u>Payroll</u>

Creating and Viewing Payroll Items
1. To look at your current set of payroll items you need to Click Lists, choose Payroll Item List from the top Menu Bar.
2. Click the Payroll Item button in the lower left corner of the payroll item list to add a new payroll item then select New.
3. In the Add new Payroll item screen answer the questions and click the next button on each screen until the new item is set up.
4. Click Finish.

Setting Employee Payroll Defaults
1. Click Employees, choose Employee Center from the top Menu Bar.
2. Click the Manage Employee Information button in the toolbar & select the Change New Employee default settings.
3. Enter employee default information and click ok.

Employee Payroll Information Set Up
1. Click Employees, choose Employee Center from the top Menu Bar.
2. Click the New Employee button to open the New Employee screen or double click an existing employee on the Employees tab to open the Edit Employee screen.
3. Click the Payroll Info tab and enter all the employee's payroll information and then click ok.

Payroll Schedules
1. Click Employees, choose Add or Edit Payroll Schedules from the top Menu Bar.
2. Create a New Schedule, click the Payroll Schedule button, and choose New. Enter the schedule info and click ok.
3. Editing schedules click to choose the schedule in the Payroll Schedule list screen. Click the Payroll Schedule button, Edit Payroll Schedule. Enter the Schedule info and click ok.

Creating Scheduled Paychecks
1. Click Employees, choose Pay Employees then select Scheduled Payroll from the top Menu Bar.
2. In the Pay Employees section, select the name of the payroll schedule and click the Start Scheduled Payroll button.
3. To make changes to a paycheck, click the linked employee name in the list to open the paycheck in the Preview Paycheck screen. Edit the employee information and click Save & Close button.
4. Click the continue button.
5. Review the summary and select check options.
6. Click the Create Paychecks button.
7. Click the Print Paychecks and print Paystubs buttons when needed.
8. Click the Close button when finished.

Handy Quick Reference Cheat Sheets
Payroll Continued

Creating Unscheduled Paychecks
1. Click Employees, choose Pay Employees then Unscheduled Payroll from the top Menu Bar.
2. Enter the payroll information, and click to place a checkmark next to the names of employees to pay.
3. Click the Continue button.
4. Review the Summary and choose Check Options.
5. Click on the linked name of any employee shown in the list if editing is needed and click Save & Close after editing.
6. Click the Create Paychecks button.
7. Click the Print Paychecks and print Paystubs buttons as needed and click Close when finished.

Creating Employee Termination Paychecks
1. Click Employees, choose Pay Employees then select Termination Check from the top Menu Bar.
2. Enter the payroll information and click to place a checkmark next to the names of employees to pay for termination.
3. In the Release Date column, enter the employee's release date and then click the Continue button.
4. Click either the Make Inactive or Keep as Active button to continue.
5. Review the Summary and select check options.
6. Click on the linked name of the employee in the list to edit the payroll information if necessary then click Save & Close.
7. Click the Create Paychecks button.
8. Click the Print Paychecks and Print Paystubs buttons when needed and then click when finished.

Handy Quick Reference Cheat Sheets
<u>Credit Cards</u>

Creating Credit Card Accounts
1. Click Lists, choose Chart of Accounts from the top Menu Bar.
2. Click the Account button & choose New.
3. Select the Credit Card option and click Continue.
4. Enter the account information and click Save & Close or Save & New if you need to enter other accounts.

Entering Credit Card Charges
1. Click Banking, choose Enter Credit Card Charges from the top Menu Bar.
2. Choose the card from the Credit Card drop down list.
3. Enter all credit card charge information and click Save & Close or Save & New.

Reconciling Credit Card Accounts
1. Click Banking, choose Reconcile from the top Menu Bar.
2. Select the account from the Account drop down list.
3. Enter the credit card statement date, ending balance, and any finance charges, then click the Continue button.
4. Click the checkmark column to mark cleared transactions.
5. Click the Reconcile Now button.
6. Select an option to either write a check or enter a bill to pay the credit card bill and click ok.
7. Select an option in the Select Reconciliation Report box. Click Display, Print or Close.
8. Select the Bank or credit card company to pay in the Write Checks or Enter Bills window and click Save & Close when finished.

Handy Quick Reference Cheat Sheets
__Loan Manager__

Working with the Loan Manager

1. Adding a Loan to the Loan Manager, click Banking, choose Loan Manager from the top Menu Bar.
2. Click the Add a Loan button.
3. Enter the loan information on each screen and click next until the wizard is completed.
4. Click the Finish button when done.

Editing a Loan in Loan Manager

1. Click Banking, choose Loan Manager from the top Menu Bar.
2. Click the loan name in the Loan List.
3. Click the Edit Loan Details button to return to the wizard to edit the loan or click the Remove Loan Button and Yes to remove if wanting to delete loan.

Handy Quick Reference Cheat Sheets
<u>Company Information</u>

Updating Company
1. Click Company, choose My Company from the top Menu Bar.
2. Click the Edit button.
3. Edit the company information and when finished click ok.

Reminders & Setting Preferences
1. Click Edit, choose Preferences from the top Menu Bar.
2. Click Reminders from the box at the left.
3. Click the My Preferences tab, and select Show Reminders List when opening a Company file.
4. When finished Click ok.

General Journal Entries
1. Click Company, choose make General Journal Entries from the top Menu Bar.
2. Click to select the accounts involved in the transaction and enter the credit and debit amounts.
3. When finished Click Save & Close to post the transaction.

QuickBooks Super Shortcuts

General

General action	Shortcut
To start QuickBooks without a company file	Ctrl (while opening)
To suppress the desktop windows (at Open Company window)	Alt (while opening)
Display product information about your QuickBooks version	F2
Close active window	Esc or Ctrl + F4
Save transaction	Alt + S
Save transaction and go to next transaction	Alt + N
Record (when black border is around OK, Save and Close, Save and New, or Record)	Enter
Record (always)	Ctrl + Enter

QuickBooks Super Shortcuts

Dates

In date fields, press the key for the symbol shown to quickly enter the date you want.

To change to	Shortcut key
Next day	+ (plus key)
Previous day	- (minus key)
Today	T
Same date in previous week	[(left bracket)
Same date in next week	] (right bracket)
Same date in last month	; (semicolon)
Same date in next month	' (apostrophe)
First day of the **W**eek	W
Last day of the wee**K**	K
First day of the **M**onth	M
Last day of the mont**H**	H
First day of the **Y**ear	Y
Last day of the yea**R**	R
Date calendar	Alt + down arrow

QuickBooks Super Shortcuts

Editing

Editing	Shortcut
Edit transaction selected in register	Ctrl + E
Delete character to right of insertion point	Del
Delete character to left of insertion point	Backspace
Delete line from detail area	Ctrl + Del
Insert line in detail area	Ctrl + Ins
Cut selected characters	Ctrl + X
Copy selected characters	Ctrl + C
Paste cut or copied characters	Ctrl + V
Increase check or other form number by one	+ (plus key)
Decrease check or other form number by one	- (minus key)
Undo changes made in field	Ctrl + Z

QuickBooks Super Shortcuts

Activities

Ctrl + O Copy check transaction in register	Ctrl + I Create invoice
Ctrl + D Delete check, invoice, transaction, or item from list	Ctrl + F Find transaction
Ctrl + G Go to register of transfer account	Ctrl + H History of A/R or A/P transaction
Ctrl + M Memorize transaction or report	Ctrl + N New invoice, bill, check or list item in context
Ctrl + A Open account list	Ctrl + J Open Customer Center (Customers & Jobs list)
F1 Open Help for active window	Ctrl + L Open list (for current drop-down menu)
Ctrl + T Open memorized transaction list	Ctrl + R Open split transaction window in register
Ctrl + Y Open transaction journal	Ctrl + V Paste copied transaction in register
Ctrl + P Print	Ctrl + Q QuickReport on transaction or list item
Enter = QuickZoom on report	Ctrl + S Show list
Ctrl + U Use list item	Ctrl + W Write new check

QuickBooks Super Shortcuts

Moving Around in a Window

Moving around a window	Shortcut
Next field	Tab
Previous field	Shift + Tab
Beginning of current field	Home
End of current field	End
Line below in detail area or on report	Down arrow
Line above in detail area or on report	Up arrow
Down one screen	Page Down
Up one screen	Page Up
Next word in field	Ctrl + Right arrow
Previous word in field	Ctrl + Left arrow
First item on list or previous month in register	Ctrl + Page Up
Last item on list or next month in register	Ctrl + Page Down
Close active window	Esc or Ctrl + F4

NOTES

NOTES

NOTES

NOTES

NOTES

Cristie Will, BBA, CHC, CIC, Author

Cristie was born and raised in Hobbs, New Mexico. She moved to Colorado 18 years ago and still living there loving all the beauty Colorado has to offer. She has a daughter Lauren and a son Josh along with beautiful grandchildren. She has been an accountant the last 30 years. Not only an accountant and Health Coach but a teacher as well, teaching QuickBooks, cooking, detoxing and weight loss classes too! She still has her accounting business and teaching QuickBooks.

In 2012, she lost her husband to lung cancer. After losing her husband to lung cancer she needed to make changes in her own health, so she did. Cristie went through a life transformation losing 200 pounds and went back to school to become a Nutritional Heath Coach adding Cleansing Intensive certification. She obtained her education from Institute of Integrative Nutrition for her Health Coaching. Her education for the Cleansing Intensive education was under Dr. Terry Willard CIH, PHD at the Wild Rose College. She is currently studying to add FDN, Functional Diagnostic Nutritionist to her skills to be able to help even more people.

Additional Resources & References

http://quickbooks.intuit.com/
QuickBooks Main Website

http://www.soswill.com/
My Accounting Website for additional Information, Books and Client Testimonials

www.cbwill.com
My Author Website for more information about me.

http://legalpediaonline.wikidot.com/state-courts
This is a great website that has all 50 State Bar and Court links

Made in the USA
San Bernardino, CA
22 December 2015